Democracy and Human Rights
in the Caribbean

Democracy and Human Rights in the Caribbean

edited by

Ivelaw L. Griffith
Florida International University

and

Betty N. Sedoc-Dahlberg
University of Florida

Routledge
Taylor & Francis Group
New York London

First published 1997 by Westview Press

Published 2018 by Routledge
605 Third Avenue, New York, NY 10017
2 Park Square, Milton Park, Abingdon, Oxon OX14 4RN

Routledge is an imprint of the Taylor & Francis Group, an informa business

A CIP catalog record for this book is available from the Library of Congress.

ISBN 13: 978-0-8133-2135-6 (pbk)
ISBN 13: 978-0-8133-2134-9 (hbk)

Contents

Tables

1

Introduction: Democracy and Human Rights in the Caribbean

Ivelaw L. Griffith and
Betty N. Sedoc-Dahlberg

In 1984 Samuel Huntington began to explore closely the question of whether more countries would soon become democratic.[1] The question was a significant one, for many societies around the world were breaking away from authoritarianism and seemed to be heading along a democratic path; the world appeared to be in the throes of democratic change. Huntington's question did not carry great import for the Caribbean since most countries there had functional, if not flourishing, democracies. Indeed, that same year—1984—the observation was made that "the Caribbean is the fourth most democratically ruled region in the world—after Anglo-America, Western Europe, and the Southwest Pacific."[2] The democratization question was not entirely irrelevant to the Caribbean, however, for there were countries outside the democratic fold, namely Cuba, Haiti, and Suriname, as well as countries with the structural features of democracy but in which functional democracy was either in jeopardy or in crisis, such as Guyana and the Dominican Republic.

The course of events around the world since 1984 has shown that the response to Huntington's question has been in the affirmative. Whereas 34 percent of the independent nations of the world were declared "free," and 31 percent "partly free" by Freedom House in 1984, by 1994 the proportions had grown to 40 percent and 32 percent, respectively.[3] The president of Freedom House also noted that "1994 saw a net increase in the number of democracies, from 108 [in 1993] to 114—the largest number in history and more than double the number of democracies since the early 1970s. Never before have there been as many countries attempting to play by democratic rules."[4] This democratic momentum has not bypassed the Caribbean. Guyana has been welcomed into the democratic comity since October 1992, Haiti is undergoing democratic (re)construction, and domestic and international forces have been combining to force the Dominican Republic and Suriname to resolve their democracy crises. Cuba, then, is the only Caribbean country squarely outside of the democratic camp.

Despite or perhaps because of the impressive record of democratic politics in the Caribbean, there has long been considerable interest in the subject of Caribbean democracy, from theoretical as well as empirical vantage points. The democratic explosion that the hemisphere and other parts of the world have witnessed since the late 1980s has further stimulated intellectual interest in the subject, and a large number of books, conferences, and journal articles devoted to democracy and allied subjects have appeared since the mid-1980s.[5] One of the allied subjects has been human rights.

Some Approaches to Democracy and Human Rights in the Caribbean

There is, of course, no single approach to the study of democracy, or of human rights, or of the democracy–human rights nexus. The most popular approach to democracy among contemporary Caribbean social scientists, though, is the Schumpeterian approach, which sees contestation and participation as the central denotative features of democracy.[6] According to Carl Stone, for example, "democracy can be defined as a process which seeks to distribute power from centers of power concentration to the majority of citizens in a political system."[7] Evelyne Huber is a little more explicit: "Democracy is defined by free and fair elections, at regular intervals, in the context of guaranteed civil and political rights, responsible government (i.e., accountability of the executive to elected representatives) and political inclusion (i.e., universal suffrage and nonproscription of parties)."[8] Other specialists view democracy as "a system of government in which there is meaningful and extensive political competition for positions of government power, at regular intervals, among individuals and organized groups, especially political parties."[9]

The Schumpeterian approach reflected in these definitions sees democracy essentially as electoral democracy, and we accept that elections are central to democracy. But because they are periodic contestations in which interest aggregation and representation are centered on political parties or individual contestants, it is important to extend the definition of democracy to account for participation and policy choice on a continual basis and beyond parties, to interest groups and other social movements.

Elections are a critical legitimizing mechanism for democracies, and hence they are a requirement of democracy, and they must be free and fair. Nevertheless, as Larman Wilson has noted, the crucial question about democracy is not the conduct of free elections—though this is nevertheless important—but acceptance of the election results by the former government, by the military, by major interest groups, and by the electorate. He notes: "Too often there is a preoccupation with elections and 'procedural democracy' and the assumption is that if they are free, that is tantamount to being democratic, or having a democracy."[10] Moreover, it is infeasible to use elections as the sole measure of the strength of a country's democratic robustness. As Douglas Payne observed, "to assume that elections alone are an accurate gauge of the health of democracies is naive at best."[11]

For us, a democracy requires not only free and fair elections with the results accepted by the various constituencies in the society but also the exercise generally of civil and political rights unencumbered by the instruments of state coercion. Hence a democratic environment should permit scope for political participation, access to decisionmakers and institutions of government, responsiveness by political rulers, and opportunity for economic development. Other attributes would include functional judiciaries and uncensored media. There would of course be conflict in such an environment, but conflict management mechanisms are required to prevent the resort to violence by individuals and groups for dispute resolution.

Irrespective of whether one embraces the Schumpeterian approach, the broader one we offer, or one based on economic determinism,[12] it is not difficult to appreciate the linkages between democracy and human rights. Indeed, the issue of human rights is central to some approaches to democracy, especially those that see democracy as primarily involving the use and distribution of power. In explaining the relationship between human rights and state power, Jack Donnelley, a foremost authority on human rights, notes that since man is a social animal, human potential and even personal individuality can be developed and expressed only in a social context. The performance of certain political functions becomes necessary in any society, and the state itself a necessity. "The state, however, also can present serious threats to human dignity and equal concern and respect if it seeks to enforce a particular version of the good life or to entrench privileged inequality."[13]

There are several philosophical approaches to this human-rights aspect of the relationship between individual, state, and society. Scholarship on the subject points to three basic philosophies: conservatism, liberalism, and communalism. Conservatism is essentially a philosophy of unequal rights. In the West, classical conservatism is associated with Edmund Burke, although its roots can be traced to Plato and *The Republic,* where the best system of rule was posited as that by a philosopher-king whose governance would be unchecked by the popular will or law. The central tenet of liberalism, in contrast, is a belief that the highest good or value is individual well-being and that personal well-being is founded on freedom and equality.

Two schools of thought are associated with the liberal philosophy. The first is the natural-law school, which holds that humankind is naturally free and equal, with certain inalienable rights. The second school, utilitarianism, posits that the pursuit of human happiness and welfare through freedom and equality is the highest good. Utilitarianism became group welfare through individualism, with the group determining what was good for the individual. But to counteract tyranny by the majority, individual freedom and equality became valued in and of themselves, even though they limited majority rule, the test for goodness being "the greatest good for the greatest number."

The third approach is communalism, or the solidarity school, which sees rights as stemming from membership in a community or group. Marxism is one strand of this philosophy, and it contends that individuals are defined by socioeconomic class. Societies are composed of various classes, and struggle in this context involves class conflict. In capitalist societies the working class is the engine of economic maintenance. Therefore, the argument goes, its rights should take precedence over those of other classes, especially the exploitative bourgeoisie.[14]

These philosophical propositions have influenced the evolution of human rights over time. So too have the rise of new political forces, technology, new methods of repression, and even human rights successes, by allowing attention to be shifted to threats that previously were insufficiently addressed or inadequately recognized. The emergence of social and economic rights is an example of this. The international community's concern with human rights has thus gone beyond civil and political rights, as is clear from scrutiny of the Universal Declaration of Human Rights and the International Human Rights Covenants, which specify a range of political, civil, economic, social, and cultural rights. And they are supplemented by several single-issue treaties on issues such as genocide, women's rights, racial discrimination, and torture. As the case studies in this volume show, human rights perspectives in the Caribbean, as reflected in domestic legal instruments, statements by political leaders, and charters of human rights nongovernmental groups, have been influenced by both the liberal and the communalist philosophies.

There is some variety among the types of political system in the Caribbean, and the differences among them may be traced to several factors, including the ideological orientation of colonizing powers, the duration of colonial domination, the amount of time that has passed since independence, political cultures, and the political economies of the countries generally and the nature of their export commodities specifically. Most of the contemporary state systems in the region are electoral democracies. There are also democratic pluralist regimes that look similar because of common institutional frameworks and bureaucratic rules.

Since the 1970s a number of Caribbean countries have undergone regime changes. There have been shifts from democratic-pluralist to authoritarian systems and back to democratic pluralism in Haiti, Suriname, Guyana, and Grenada. The Dominican Republic is slowly moving from its authoritarianism to democratic-pluralist rule. So far only Cuba has not substantially changed its Marxist-Leninist authoritarian orientation. Despite the collapse of its erstwhile ally, the USSR, Cuba's regime is still statist-populist.[15]

With the downfall of the USSR many traditional propositions about the development and transferability of political systems are being disputed. There is now both optimism and pessimism about (re)democratization among political scientists. The failure of any single democracy cannot simply be related to disputed elections or a weakly developed and malfunctioning infrastructure. The lack of satisfactory participation by major interest groups, often reflected in strikes and demonstrations, has contributed to the emergence of highly politicized nongovernmental organizations and social movements, and these formations are making increasing demands for a substantial input into policymaking in the areas of civil, political, economic, and social rights.

Unlike the classical liberalists, who focus on civil and political rights, most Caribbean leaders pay at least lip service to economic and social rights as well, such as in their ratification of the Universal Declaration of Human Rights.[16] Hence they profess to have accepted responsibility for maintaining for their citizens a certain quality of life consonant with the covenants on economic and social rights. In many Caribbean states (and as the chapter on Guyana in this volume shows) there are constitutional provisions relating to education, housing, health, and social welfare. But constraints on the execution of economic policies as well as poor management have contributed to gaps between legally adopted instruments that deal with economic and social rights and actual practice.

Evidence suggests that there was a correlation between a decline in socioeconomic performance and abuse of civil and political rights and shifts back and forth between democratic and authoritarian systems during the 1980s.[17] Hence political stability requires attention not only to civil and political rights but also to social and economic rights. As Zehra Arat has observed, "civil and political rights cannot prevail if socioeconomic rights are ignored, and the stability of political democracy (liberal democracy) depends on the extent of balance between the two groups of human rights."[18]

As mentioned earlier, democracy and human rights have generated considerable intellectual activity in the Caribbean. However, the scholarly analysis in English of links between the two subjects has tended to be either country-specific, issue-focused, or related to one subregion. This volume is a modest attempt to go beyond these circumscriptions by assessing the status of democracy and human rights and probing the nexus between them on a truly regionwide basis. Although we do not provide assessments for all countries in the Caribbean, our universe of analysis is the entire region. Moreover, we hold the view that linkages between civil and political rights on the one hand and economic and social rights on the other are such that any attempt to probe the dynamics of the democracy–human rights nexus requires attention to both sets of rights. Hence while contributors do not pay equal attention to both sets of rights, the thrust of this volume is an inclusive one that takes account of both.

The nature and outcome of the pursuit and maintenance of democracy and human rights in the region have been variable and multifaceted, and thus our undertaking requires us to adopt a multidimensional approach and to go beyond the boundaries of a single discipline, for there are political, historical, economic, cultural, and psychological factors involved. Further, our case studies cannot be limited to a single level of analysis because of the interplay among factors at the individual, group, national, and international levels.

Plan of the Book

As will become evident in this volume, initiatives to restore democracy and pursue human rights in many Caribbean countries have had external origins and stimuli, and so it is important to examine some of the regional and international dynamics involved. In addition, as the efforts of the United Nations (UN), the Organization of American States (OAS), and the Carter Center reveal, the actors at the regional and international levels as well as the domestic level come from both the governmental and the nongovernmental arenas. Hence Part One of this volume is devoted to issues and concerns that are common to the region and provides analyses of the impact of state and nonstate regional and international actors. In Part Two case studies on the status of democracy and human rights in various countries are presented.

In Chapter 2 Anselm Francis first looks at the development of international human rights, especially since World War II. He notes that though certain rights were long considered inalienable, rights were not originally meant to extend to the whole of mankind; slavery and the status of women until relatively recently are evidence of this. Human rights are no longer defined only in civil and political terms but now in economic, social, and cultural terms as well, and Francis explains the role of the United Nations in furthering both sets of rights. As for the Caribbean, Francis uses case law to show how Caribbean human rights practice has fit into the larger international context. This is important because although international law has paid considerable attention to human rights, it is under municipal law that enforcement is critical. Francis pays special attention to the human rights status of indigenous people in the region and calls for an end to the benign neglect of these rights.

In Chapter 3 David Padilla and Elizabeth Houppert review the history of the Organization of American States before presenting case studies of OAS action in Grenada, Suriname, and Haiti. In the case of Grenada the authors explain that before and directly after the Bishop regime the absence of effective nongovernmental human rights organizations and the unfamiliarity of Grenadians with the Inter-American Commission on Human Rights and its procedures resulted in only a very few formal complaints to the Commission. In the case of Suriname they show how the OAS played a crucial role in that country's shift from authoritarianism to democracy. In the case of Haiti, the Inter-American Commission began responding to complaints of human rights violations almost as soon as it became operational. Padilla and Houppert address the complex issue of the Haitian "boat people" and then go on to examine the requirements for implementation of democracy and improvement of human rights in Haiti.

The proposition is made by W. Marvin Will in Chapter 4 that monitoring activities by nongovernmental organizations (NGOs) and intergovernmental organizations (IGOs) not only contribute to legitimacy but also represent cost-effective means for promoting electoral democracy and addressing human rights issues. He examines electoral monitoring in Nicaragua and Guyana, two countries where he served as an elections monitor. Will goes beyond explaining the modalities of monitoring to examine the historical and political contexts of the countries' legitimacy crises and how monitoring helped crisis resolution by allowing their political elites to gain acceptability, both domestically and internationally. Yet because democracy hinges not only on political pillars but on economic ones, there is concern that the economic crises in Nicaragua and Guyana might serve to undermine some of the achievements in the political sphere.

Ivelaw Griffith and Trevor Munroe show in Chapter 5 that the drug phenomenon has implications for the nature and conduct of democracy in the region. The authors demonstrate that contrary to the public view of "a drug problem," the drug phenomenon is multidimensional, with production, consumption-abuse, trafficking, and money-laundering dimensions. These are not manifested with uniformity in the region but they are regionwide in scope and in impact, most notably in corruption and the infusion of drug money into local politics. Griffith and Munroe explain that the interface between drugs and democracy exists at several levels and arenas in the region: in law-enforcement institutions, constituency politics, community politics, and national politics. These arenas are all crucial to how political democracy works in the region. The authors believe that efforts to mitigate the impact of drugs should include greater attention to demand reduction by the United States, greater resource allocation to counternarcotics efforts by Caribbean governments, and serious attention to the decriminalization of marijuana.

In Chapter 6, the first of the case studies, Damian Fernandez argues that human rights groups in Cuba, albeit small and fragmented, have been a pivotal force in the political development of the island. According to Fernandez, the tradition of struggle for individual and collective rights in civil society in Cuba continued in a different fashion after 1959. Members of human rights groups in the 1970s sprang from the Left. In looking at communication channels with the external environment, he highlights the visit of the United Nations Commissioner for Refugees and the visit by former Soviet president Mikhail Gorbachev. Despite significant personal, ideological, and other differences within the human rights movement, it has been able to survive, challenge the state, and achieve legitimacy domestically and internationally. Fernandez takes the view that a future Cuban state will find it easier to meet the demand for civil and political rights than to satisfy an agenda of economic rights.

Larman Wilson in Chapter 7 examines the impact of domestic and international factors on the pursuit of democracy and human rights in the Dominican Republic. An important domestic factor has been the dictatorial and personalist system of absolute control, a legacy of Rafael Trujillo. Attention is also paid to racial and cultural dimensions of the Trujillo legacy, for these have affected human rights practices, especially in relation to black Dominicans, and to Haitians inside the Dominican Republic. Key external actors have been the United States and the OAS. Wilson's analysis of the status of both procedural and substantive democracy leads him to concur with the view that the situation there is "crisis-prone" despite the considerable progress made since Trujillo's death in 1961. The Dominican Republic is a party to several UN human rights treaties, including the Convention on the Elimination of All Forms of Racial Discrimination, but human rights problems remain, notably the mistreatment of Haitians.

In Chapter 8 Francis Alexis deals with the bills of rights of the eastern Caribbean countries, covering the legal philosophy of those rights. As an outgrowth of the "Westminster Constitution," the protection of the Bill of Rights is ensured by an independent judiciary. Several cases are presented to illustrate the functioning of the legal system, with particular attention to cases dealing with the deprivation of property without compensation. Alexis concludes that the best of the liberal democratic tradition is enshrined in the Westminster model constitutions of the countries in the Organization of Eastern Caribbean States (OECS).

In the Guyana case study in Chapter 9, Ivelaw Griffith looks at the relationship between regime change and democracy and human rights and explains that there has been both change and continuity in Guyana over the past decade: change in regime and regime policies and continuity in some policies from the regime of Desmond Hoyte to that of Cheddi Jagan. The author shows that civil society in Guyana has demonstrated an interest in civil and political rights as well as economic and social rights. He explains that though there have been considerable achievements in relation to civil and political rights, economic and social rights have not been advanced meaningfully given the state of the Guyana economy and the link between these rights and a society's economic health.

Robert Maguire argues in Chapter 10 that Aristide's return to Haiti is itself no guarantee that democracy will be restored, nor will human rights violations automatically end. More fundamental changes are required. The author explores the dynamics of the changing relations between the predatory Haitian state and the emerging, organized nation. Nongovernmental organizations and grassroots, community-based citizen groups, forming a bottom-up action for change, were able to survive violent oppression by the Haitian armed forces. Maguire reviews the history of the armed forces in Haiti and illustrates how the army's role—to fight and defeat citizens' resistance against oppression—is connected with the past. He indicates that consolidation of a democratic regime and implementation of human rights in Haiti require a change of approach by state actors.

In Chapter 11 Dorith Grant-Wisdom looks at how political and economic democracy in Jamaica are caught in the throes of globalization and structural adjustment. She indicates that efforts to attract foreign investment and promote private sector and market efficiency have forced the state to recast its policies toward the market, affecting relations between labor and capital and the general welfare of the national populace. The result is not only changes in the structure and orientation of the governmental machinery but also an intrusion by multinational institutions into domestic politics, raising questions about consent, participation, representation, and accountability, integral components of democracy. This serves to complicate the crisis of the state in its ability to mold social classes and build allegiance. Part of the crisis is reflected in decreasing voter participation in elections and in disaffection with political parties. In showing how "the sovereign capacity of consumers" has been undermined, the author demonstrates that the crisis extends beyond political democracy to economic democracy.

Betty Sedoc-Dahlberg indicates in Chapter 12 that appreciating the democracy and human rights experiences in Suriname requires coming to terms with the dynamic linkages involving political instability, economic stagnation, and regime security. These linkages have had both domestic and international dimensions. The Netherlands, France, the United States, Venezuela, and the OAS have been notable foreign shapers of the country's post-independence democracy and human rights pursuits. Like the authors of most of the volume's case studies, Sedoc-Dahlberg is concerned with both aspects of human rights. She shows that contemporary Suriname has made considerable strides in civil and political rights but that success in economic and social rights has been jeopardized by both the government's

preoccupation with the former and the structural adjustment program introduced to deal with the economic crisis. Sedoc-Dahlberg feels that communication with and participation of citizens on the conduct of the nation's political and economic affairs are vital for meaningful achievements in both the
civil and political and the economic areas.

In Chapter 13 Clifford Griffin examines the relationship between human
rights and state security in Trinidad and Tobago to determine whether the
Westminster-derived system of government guarantees political stability. He
suggests that three illegal attempts at governmental change indicate that a
democratic political culture, including civil and political rights, may not be
sufficient to guarantee stability and security when poor economic performance exists. He explains the various reasons for Trinidad's economic decline, indicating that these along with official corruption, police inefficiency,
and other factors combine to undermine the democratic system and the protection of human rights. Griffin argues that the failure of the state to fulfill
the economic expectations of citizens is the underlying reason for political
instability and human rights violations.

In the concluding chapter we argue that although the Caribbean faces several democracy and human rights challenges and has considerable room for
improvement in both areas, a fairly healthy situation exists in both overall.
Given present realities improvement efforts should focus on initiatives at the
national and international levels, by state and nonstate actors, and both
within and outside the realm of politics. Attention must be paid to at least
four areas of operations: regime politics, institutions, NGOs, and international regimes.

Notes

1. Samuel P. Huntington, "Will More Countries Become Democratic?" *Political
Science Quarterly*, vol. 99, no. 2 (Summer 1984):193–218.

2. Thomas D. Anderson, *Geopolitics of the Caribbean* (New York: Praeger, 1984),
p. 6.

3. See *Freedom at Issue*, no. 82 (January-February 1985):8–10; and *Freedom Review*, vol. 26, no. 1 (January-February 1995):21–22.

4. Adrian Karatnycky, "Democracies on the Rise, Democracies at Risk," *Freedom
Review*, vol. 26, no. 1 (January-February 1995):5.

5. See, for example, Paget Henry and Carl Stone, eds., *The Newer Caribbean: De-
centralization, Democracy, and Development* (Philadelphia: Institute for the Study of
Human Issues, 1983); Carl Stone, *Class, State, and Democracy in Jamaica* (New
York: Praeger, 1986); Donald C. Peters, *The Democratic System in the Eastern
Caribbean* (Westport, CT: Greenwood Press, 1992); Jorge I. Domínguez, Robert A.
Pastor, and R. Deslisle Worrell, eds., *Democracy in the Caribbean* (Baltimore: Johns
Hopkins University Press, 1993); Carollee Bengelsdorf, *The Problem of Democracy in*

Cuba (New York: Oxford University Press, 1994); and Carlene J. Edie, ed., *Democracy in the Caribbean: Myths and Realities* (New York: Praeger, 1994).

6. See Joseph A. Schumpeter, *Capitalism, Socialism, and Democracy* (New York: Harper and Bros., 1947). For Schumpeter, "the democratic method is that institutional arrangement for arriving at political decisions in which individuals acquire power to decide by means of competitive struggle for people's vote."

7. Carl Stone, "Democracy and Socialism in Jamaica: 1972–1979," in *The Newer Caribbean*, ed. Paget Henry and Carl Stone, p. 235.

8. Evelyne Huber, "The Future of Democracy in the Caribbean," in *Democracy in the Caribbean*, ed. Domínguez et al., p. 74.

9. Carlene J. Edie, "Introduction," in *Democracy in the Caribbean*, ed. Carlene J. Edie, p. 2.

10. Larman C. Wilson, "The OAS and the Transition to Democracy in Haiti: The Effort to Restore President Aristide" (paper delivered at the eighteenth annual conference of the Caribbean Studies Association, Jamaica, May 1993, p. 11).

11. Douglas W. Payne, "Ballots, Neo-strongmen, Narcos, and Impunity," *Freedom Review*, vol. 26, no. 1 (January-February 1995):27.

12. For a discussion of different approaches to democracy, see Giovanni Sartori, *The Theory of Democracy Revisited* (Chatham, NJ: Chatham House Publishers, 1987); Larry Diamond and Marc F. Plattner, eds., *The Global Resurgence of Democracy* (Baltimore: Johns Hopkins University Press, 1993); and Georg Sorensen, *Democracy and Democratization* (Boulder: Westview Press, 1993).

13. Jack Donnelley, *Universal Human Rights in Theory and Practice* (Ithaca: Cornell University Press, 1989), p. 69.

14. See David P. Forsythe, *Human Rights and World Politics* (Lincoln: University of Nebraska Press, 1983), pp. 158–175.

15. The regime typology used here is that of Carl Stone. See his *Power in the Caribbean Basin: A Comparative Study of Political Economy* (Philadelphia: Institute for the Study of Human Issues, 1984), chapter 1 and p. 37. See also Pranab Bardhan, *Dominant Proprietary Classes and India's Democracy* (Princeton: Princeton University Press, 1988).

16. With the Additional Protocol in the Area of Economic, Social, and Cultural Rights—the Protocol of San Salvador—the Organization of American States (OAS) has covered the full range of human rights. However, the OAS's Inter-American Commission on Human Rights focuses basically on civil and political rights. Unlike the United Nations, which has the International Labor Organization, the OAS does not have a specific body to deal with economic and social rights.

17. See Stone, *Power in the Caribbean Basin*, pp. 75–115. For an empirical study of the relationship between improvement of a country's economy and level of basic needs, see Norman Hicks, "Growth vs. Basic Needs: Is There a Trade-off?" *World Development*, vol. 7 (1979):985–994. For a discussion of the consequences and fulfillment of human rights in developing countries, see Leonard Binder et al., eds., *Crises and Sequences in Political Development* (Princeton: Princeton University Press, 1971).

18. Zehra Arat, *Democracy and Human Rights in Developing Countries* (Boulder: Lynne Rienner, 1991), p. 4.

PART A

International Dimensions and Common Problems

2

International Law and Human Rights: A Caribbean Context

Anselm A. Francis

Fundamental changes have taken place in international law in the postwar era, but the elevation of human rights to the international plane must be considered one of the most salutary developments in international law and international relations.[1] The Charter of the United Nations (UN) represents a very important landmark in the development of international human rights. The individual is vested with certain basic rights and fundamental freedoms, and every state is under an obligation to respect them. Obviously the Charter could only treat human rights in a general way, but the UN has worked assiduously for the growth and development of human rights. Initially, discussion on human rights focused on civil and political rights.[2] This is hardly surprising because the great philosophers to whose works the genesis of human rights may be traced concentrated on man as a political animal. However, as a result of "the change in the geography of international law, new dimensions have been added to the traditional civil and political rights. Economic, social, and cultural rights are now regarded as an integral part of human rights."[3] More recently, many developing countries have been clamoring for the recognition of the right to development as a human right.[4]

Such developments merit close attention. The impression may be conveyed that it is possible to place the different categories of human rights into neat, tight compartments. Yet any critical examination of human rights will show the interrelatedness of the different categories[5] and show that they mutually reinforce each other. Moreover, human rights should not only be considered in the abstract; attention should be paid to the declaration and exercise of rights. Hence governments must develop the programs necessary to have rights attained. It is also necessary to recognize that in some cases individuals face problems not because basic freedoms are unprotected but because of their membership in a particular group that may have been disadvantaged over a long period of time. Thus although it is important to understand constitutional guarantees in order to assess a country's human rights situation generally, it is vital to know the dynamics of the entire society to appreciate why an entire group of people may be comparatively worse off than the rest of the population.

The characterization of human rights as international must be understood in a particular political, social, or cultural context. It is this context that has helped to shape Caribbean jurisprudence and that explains the decisions reached by Caribbean courts in cases arising out of the interpretation or application of international human rights standards. Precisely because human rights standards have universal application, as both scholars and statesmen are obliged to acknowledge, the line between things internal and international is becoming blurred.[6]

This chapter discusses the nature of human rights and the measures that have been taken at the international level to protect those rights. Although the most effective steps to human rights protection must be taken at the national level,[7] the role of the UN and other international-level organizations is crucial. Moving beyond the international level, the discussion uses case law to show how Caribbean human rights practices fit into the larger international context. Special attention is also paid to the human rights status of indigenous people in the region.

The Nature of Human Rights

Most scholars and statesmen accept that human rights are inalienable—that human beings are born with those rights and that such rights are not merely conferred by legislative bodies.[8] Hence they cannot be taken away. Indeed, this was the main explanation of Western philosophers, and since their writings have been highly influential in the promulgation of those rights at the national level, this concept of human rights cannot be dismissed. For example, toward the end of the eighteenth century when the Americans were establishing their new national order, they relied heavily on John Locke's *Two Treaties of Government* and *Commentaries* by William Blackstone.

An observation worthy of note is that the rights claimed were not meant to be applicable to the whole of mankind. If they were, how could the proclamation of those rights be reconciled with the practice of slavery? It appears that a particular elite was seeking justification for certain revolutionary acts. In spite of this, it should not be denied that the efforts of the elite groups helped to advance the cause of human rights as we know them today. In human affairs the demonstrative effect of developments that could lead to the liberation of human beings should not be underestimated.

Although it is useful to refer to the works of the great philosophers in try- ing to understand the nature of human rights, we cannot afford to allow them the last word on the subject. When some philosophers referred to the "rights of man," that term was not used to include women. This explains why the term had to be changed to human rights. The change in status was secured by legislation and in many cases after a long and hard struggle. What pertains to gender is also applicable to race. It is well known that non- Europeans suffered discrimination in almost every area of national life simply because of their race. They did not have the right to a decent education and even found it difficult to obtain justice before courts of law. It took changes in the law to make the non-European the equal of the European in a formal sense. It is appreciated that in spite of the legal changes, some of the earlier disabilities still persist because ingrained attitudes die hard.

In dealing with human rights, philosophers generally emphasized civil and political rights and little attention was paid to economic, social, and cultural rights. When national legislatures first took action to have human rights en- shrined in their constitutions, the situation was similar. This may be ex- plained by the fact that the nature of economic, social, and cultural rights renders them nonjusticiable in most cases. When it is said that the individual has the right to a fair trial—a civil right—it is understood that the state has the duty to protect that right. If the state neglects its duty, the aggrieved in- dividual may seek redress.

However, in the case of many economic, social, and cultural rights, it is not always possible to determine on whom the duty is imposed. For exam- ple, the right to work exists in human rights instruments,[9] but it is not al- ways clear who has the duty to provide employment. In the free enterprise system, it cannot be said that the government has the duty to provide every- one with a job. Private corporations are involved in employment, and indi- viduals may be self-employed. This means that the unemployed person has no recourse before the courts simply because he is unemployed. He may only be able to bring action if he is unfairly dismissed or is denied unemploy- ment benefits to which he is entitled.

Even though economic rights were not guaranteed under national consti- tutions, many governments intervened—to the extent that their resources allowed—to ensure that individuals and families were not left destitute. The philosophy that inspired such intervention has now been replaced by one that says that the state can ill afford to be eternally beneficent. Policies based on this new philosophy put at risk even the traditional civil and political rights. However, the fact that economic rights are not generally written into constitutions does not make them any less important. Whereas civil and po- litical rights are often "rules of abstention," meaning that the state must re- frain from acting in a particular way toward the individual, economic rights suggest that the state must help create the conditions for individuals to live in dignity. The contention here is not that the individual should not assume responsibility for his well-being, but it must be recognized that there are those who would be unable to cope with the rigors of modern-day living and would be reduced to lives of misery and destitution. In such circumstances elementary considerations of humanity dictate that the state must take action to alleviate the plight of these people.

Even if one accepts in principle the need for state intervention in circumstances in which the lives of people are seriously threatened, the resources needed to make the intervention effective may be inadequate or even lacking. It is in such a context that the call for development as a human right must be seen. This would necessitate a transfer of resources[10] from rich countries to poor ones. Rich countries do not readily accept this principle, but in many developing countries such transfers are essential for the provision of basic human needs. The problem is that development means different things to different people. For some it is nothing more than changing the urban landscape by, among other things, the wholesale felling of trees and replacing them with buildings and factories. The damage done to the environment may be incalculable, but this is considered a necessary cost of development. If the concept of development instead placed people at the center of development, the availability of resources would begin to make a difference in the protection of human rights.

The introduction of development as a human right must be understood in the context of the fundamental changes that have taken place in the international community since World War II. International law has changed considerably, from comprising mainly rules of abstention, to seeking to provide the framework for active cooperation among states as well as for the promotion of human welfare. For this reason, matters that were essentially within the domestic jurisdiction of states have become the legitimate concern of the international community.[11]

Although the human rights focus of the Universal Declaration of Human Rights was mainly on civil and political rights, the document recognized the importance of the economic, social, and cultural rights for the dignity and free development of the personality of the individual.[12] With the conclusion of the International Covenant on Civil and Political Rights and the International Covenant on Economic, Social, and Cultural Rights—both in 1966— the organic link between both groups of rights was established. In addition to these two human rights instruments, human rights conventions have been concluded at the regional level,[13] and they provide the individual with the means of vindication in the event of human rights violation.[14] This marks a radical departure from the traditional approach, which regarded individuals as mere objects of international law. Now individuals enjoy international personality and have *locus standi* before international tribunals in order to assert their rights. Thus attention is devoted not only to setting standards and promoting rights but also to protecting and enforcing those rights. One international-level agency that has played a crucial role in this respect is the UN.

Role of the United Nations

One of the stated purposes of the UN is the promotion of human rights[15] and fundamental freedoms for all people without distinction as to race, sex, language, or religion. No doubt the founding personalities of the UN held the view that respect for human rights could help to preserve international peace and security. The international community, like any other community, is made up of individuals, and if those individuals are treated with respect and dignity the likelihood of armed conflict would be considerably less.

Article 56 of the Charter goes beyond stating that it is one of the purposes of the UN to promote respect for human rights and actually commits the members to take joint action for their realization. In its *Advisory Opinion on Legal Consequences for States of the Continued Presence of South Africa in Namibia (South-West Africa), Notwithstanding Security Council Resolution 276 (1970)*, the International Court of Justice (ICJ) stated: "Under the Charter of the United Nations the former Mandatory had pledged itself to observe and respect, in a territory having an international status, human rights and fundamental freedoms for all without distinction as to race. To establish instead, and enforce, distinctions, exclusion, restrictions and limitations exclusively based on grounds of race, color, descent or national or ethnic origin which constitute a denial to fundamental human rights is a flagrant violation of the purposes and principles of the Charter."[16] The court reiterated this position in the case involving the United States and Iran[17] with respect to the latter's taking of hostages, noting that wrongful denial to human beings of their freedom is incompatible with the principles of the Charter of the UN as well as with the fundamental principles enunciated in the Universal Declaration of Human Rights. It is therefore reasonable to conclude that it is now settled law that the UN Charter imposes obligations on states to respect human rights.

The UN has consistently investigated concrete human rights situations.[18] In 1953, for example, the General Assembly found that the racial policies of the Government of South Africa were contrary to the Charter.[19] In 1962 the General Assembly established the Special Committee on the Policies of Apartheid of the Government of South Africa, authorizing it to keep the racial policies of South Africa under review when the assembly is not in session.

Discussion of the role of the UN in the promotion and protection of human rights would be incomplete without mention of the Human Rights Commission, however briefly. It was established by the UN Economic and Social Council (ECOSOC) under Article 68 of the UN Charter. It comprises forty-three member states, and membership is distributed among the various UN political blocs.[20] The commission is authorized to investigate allegations of gross violations of human rights. At the end of the conduct of the investigations, a report is prepared for discussion at public Human Rights Commission meetings. This public procedure is complemented by a confidential procedure established under ECOSOC Resolution 1503 of 1970 in which communications from individuals or nongovernmental organizations are considered in private, provided that the express consent of the state concerned has been obtained.[21] Although the commission has made a positive contribution to the development of human rights, it is sometimes handicapped by political considerations and a lack of mandatory powers to hear cases or to enter a territory to conduct investigations.

Although the machinery to protect human rights under regional human rights instruments is more effective than that under the aegis of the UN,[22] it should be noted that the Universal Declaration of Human Rights has served as the inspiration for these regional conventions.[23] Moreover, it is this document that is mainly responsible for human rights standards being regarded as having universal application. The legal significance of the Universal Declaration of Human Rights was once a controversial matter. It was contended that it was a General Assembly resolution and that resolutions are not an independent source of law.[24] There is no specific mention of resolutions under Article 38(1) of the Statute of the ICJ. Nor does the UN Charter vest the General Assembly with legislative authority. There is considerable merit in this argument, but the proliferation of human rights conventions since the adoption of the Universal Declaration of Human Rights would seem to provide cogent evidence of state practice, and consequently it has passed into the corpus of customary international law.

Admittedly, practice, however widespread, is not sufficient to constitute customary law. The ICJ has consistently stated that the element of *opinio juris* is an essential prerequisite for the existence of customary law.[25] However, one could argue that *opinio juris* may be gleaned from the numerous human rights conventions concluded subsequent to the adoption of the Universal Declaration of Human Rights. More important, the ICJ has stressed the legal significance of the declaration and has cited it as enunciating fundamental principles of international law.[26]

In very recent times the Security Council has been intervening in countries on general humanitarian grounds, for example, in Somalia and Bosnia. In such instances it often invokes its powers under Chapter VII of the Charter to maintain or restore international peace and security. Such action may be placed under the rubric of peacekeeping in its new and evolving form, but the link with the protection of human rights should be obvious. For example, as Chapter 10 of this volume shows, the condition of human rights in Haiti has been dire for some time, and the UN has made several attempts to place the human rights situation there on a more secure basis.[27]

Formerly, the situation in Haiti would have been characterized as an internal matter, since no foreign interference had been reported. However, such a characterization cannot be justified because of the flagrant violation of human rights in Haiti. Judge Nagendra Singh of the ICJ has referred to the right of a state to concern itself, on humanitarian grounds, with atrocities affecting human rights in another country.[28] It is true that Judge Singh was speaking of intervention by a state, but if a state has such a right, *a fortiori,* then the UN must also have that right because it has primary responsibility for the maintenance of peace and security, and one of the purposes of the Charter is to promote respect for human rights. In other words, whenever the question of the protection of human rights arises, the matter ceases to be one pertaining to domestic jurisdiction. An examination of the situation in the Caribbean will afford a better appreciation of this proposition.

Human Rights in the Caribbean

The major focus of this section is on the Commonwealth Caribbean, comprising mainly island-states, some of them with populations below 100,000. However, reference is made to other Caribbean countries for purposes of comparison, with the assessment done mainly through a discussion of relevant cases in order to show the crucial role of the domestic judicial machinery in the protection of rights.

Article 3 of the Universal Declaration of Human Rights proclaims that everyone has the right to life, liberty, and security of person. Any critical examination of human rights would show that this terse provision is the foundation of all human rights because these rights are essential to the enjoyment of all others. Undoubtedly, the passing of human rights into the corpus of international law is a welcome development, but it must be appreciated that implementation of human rights is achieved best through the medium of national law, with local courts playing a vital role. The question therefore arises of whether Caribbean states have provided sufficient constitutional guarantees for the enforcement of human rights. The various constitutions contain bills of rights that entrench human rights and fundamental freedoms. They also provide for judicial independence, without which it would be difficult for human rights to be enforced, because when allegations of violations of human rights are made it is usually state agencies that are challenged.

Right to Fair Hearing
Within a Reasonable Time

In the Caribbean, as elsewhere, the freedom of the individual and the right to a fair trial have gained considerable attention. This is hardly surprising, since deprivation of liberty and the provision of justice lie at the heart of basic rights and fundamental freedoms. The crucial issue to be addressed here is the public interest in keeping an individual who has violated the law behind bars, as against his right to liberty. If the public interest is to be served by detaining the individual, the court will then have to consider whether there has been any avoidable delay on the part of state authorities.

In *Bell v D.P.P. and Another* (1986),[29] the appellant claimed that his right to a fair hearing within a reasonable time under S.20 of the Constitution of Jamaica had been infringed. He had been convicted by the Gun Court on October 20, 1977, of several offenses involving firearms and was sentenced to life imprisonment. The convictions were quashed by the Court of Appeal on March 7, 1979, and a retrial was ordered. However, notice of this order did not reach the Gun Court until December 19, 1979. On March 21, 1980, the appellant was released on bail; on November 10, 1981, the Crown offered no evidence against him and he was discharged. On February 12, 1982, he was arrested again and his retrial was ordered to commence on May 11, 1982. Both the Supreme Court and the Court of Appeal of Jamaica dismissed his application that his right to a fair trial within a reasonable time had been infringed.

However, when the appeal came before the Privy Council, the declaration was granted that S.20(1) of the Jamaican Constitution had been infringed. The Privy Council weighed two fundamental principles against each other: the fundamental right to a fair hearing within a reasonable time and the public interest in the attainment of justice. It is interesting to note that the Privy Council did not merely consider the principles in the abstract but in the context of the local legal system and the prevailing economic, social, and cultural conditions.

Relevant factors cited for consideration in a particular case where unreasonable delay is alleged include: the length of the delay; the reasons given by the prosecution to justify the delay; the responsibility of the accused for asserting his rights; the likelihood of prejudice to the accused resulting from the delay.[30] What is clear here is that delay is a relative matter. A period of time that may be considered reasonable in one case may be viewed as unreasonable in another. Obviously if the case is very complex, the prosecution would need additional time to prepare its case. The number of accused persons and the number of witnesses to be called would have a bearing on the length of time required by the prosecution. Likewise, the need for translation services to be provided would necessitate additional time.

If the delay is attributed to the accused's exhausting all his rights, then he must be precluded from invoking that very delay as a violation of his constitutional right. It would be a travesty as far as the public interest is concerned if the constitutional provisions guaranteeing basic rights and fundamental freedoms are invoked simultaneously as shield and sword. Unfortunately, delays in the administration of justice are inevitable. The increasing crime rate spawned by deteriorating social conditions puts considerable pressure on the judicial system, increasing the disparity between the demand for and the supply of legal services.

In *Re Applications by Thomas and Paul* (1986),[31] the two applicants had been convicted of murder, alleged to have occurred on August 27, 1973, and had been sentenced on May 20, 1975, to death by hanging. The Court of Appeal in Trinidad and Tobago dismissed their appeal on November 12, 1976. Their appeal to the Privy Council was dismissed on June 22, 1981. The present motions were filed on July 6, 1981, but were not heard until October 17 and 22, 1984. The applicants argued that the lapse of time—four and a half years—between the Court of Appeal decisions and the Privy Council decision constituted an infringement of S.4(a) of the Constitution of the Republic of Trinidad and Tobago, namely, their right not to be deprived of their liberty except by "due process of law." In dismissing the motions, the Privy Council ruled that for the state to be held to have failed to ensure the "due process of law," there must be so protracted and unreasonable a period of delay as to lead to the conclusion that the "due process of law" had virtually broken down and the incarcerated person had been left to languish without any proper determination of his appeal. When that test was applied the state was exonerated because the delay was attributable to the invocation by the applicants of the appeal procedures and the bringing of motions.

Freedom of Expression

In *Hector v Attorney-General of Antigua and Barbuda and Others* (1991),[32] the issue was not undue delay in the trial or wrongful detention but the freedom of expression. However, in a general discussion of liberty of the individual, it should be appropriate to consider the freedom of expression. Freedom should not be confined to physical liberty but should include the freedom to think freely, to hold and disseminate opinions.

The appellant, editor of a newspaper in Antigua, was charged with printing a false statement in the newspaper that was likely "to undermine public confidence in the conduct of public affairs" contrary to S.33B of the Public Order Act 1972. The appellant challenged the prosecution on the ground that S.33B violated his rights under the Constitution of Antigua and Barbuda not to be "hindered in the enjoyment of his freedom of expression" and was not "reasonably required in the interests of public order." Justice Matthew granted the appellant declarations that his constitutional rights had been infringed by the criminal proceedings and that the law was not reasonably required for any of the purposes specified in S.12(4)(a) and, accordingly, that S.33B was unconstitutional to the extent that it contained the words "or to undermine public confidence in the conduct of public affairs."

The decision was reversed by the Court of Appeal of the Eastern Caribbean Supreme Court and appeal was made to the Privy Council. The Order of Justice Matthew was restored. The Privy Council reasoned that it would have been a grave impediment to the freedom of the press if those printing or distributing matter reflecting critically on the conduct of public authorities could only do so with impunity if they had first verified the accuracy of all statements of fact on which the criticism was based. Moreover, the Privy Council argued that any attempt to stifle or fetter criticism of government by criminalizing such statements was political censorship of the most insidious kind, to be viewed with the utmost suspicion.

Death Penalty and Other Deprivation of Life

Although nongovernmental organizations clamor for the abolition of the death penalty, the human rights instruments do not prohibit the death penalty, and in the Commonwealth Caribbean the death penalty is mandatory for murder. But until two years ago—and this was because citizens clamored for a harsh response to increasing crime—the death penalty was not administered in the majority of Caribbean states, which left many condemned prisoners languishing on death row. For many years in Trinidad and Tobago, for example, death warrants were read to prisoners who had been sentenced to death, but the convicts succeeded in cheating the hangman. They filed constitutional motions for stay of execution on the ground that it would be cruel and unusual punishment for the death penalty to be carried out after it had been held in abeyance for many years.

In *Robinson v Jamaica*,[33] the accused was without legal representation on a murder charge because counsel refused to appear on the ground that he did not receive payment and the trial judge did not entertain any request for an adjournment of proceedings. The matter came before the Human Rights Committee, and it was held to be axiomatic that legal assistance be available in capital cases.

Traditionally, the right to life has been interpreted to mean that no one should be deprived of his life in the absence of due process of law. In *Baboeran v Suriname*,[34] the Human Rights Committee reiterated this position in holding that the Surinamese authorities acted in contravention of Article 6(1) of the International Covenant on Civil and Political Rights by summarily executing fifteen prominent Surinamese citizens associated with attempts to introduce democracy into Suriname.

In *Camarzo v Colombia*,[35] police officers shot suspected kidnappers without warning, and Decree No. 0070 was invoked as justification for the police action. The decree provided the police with a defense to any criminal charge arising out of acts committed "in the course of operations planned with the object of preventing and curbing kidnapping" as long as Colombia was in a state of siege. The Human Rights Committee ruled that Decree No. 0070 did not provide adequate protection to the right to life and as such was inconsistent with Article 6(1) of the International Covenant on Civil and Political Rights.

Security of the Person

In human rights instruments the terms *liberty* and *security of the person* almost invariably appear together. The question is whether we are looking at a single idea or at autonomous concepts.[36] The Inter-American Commission of Human Rights prefers the latter approach. For example, torture is considered a violation of "security of the person." The important issue here is that even if persons are lawfully detained, they must be treated with humanity and with respect for the inherent dignity of the human person. This is also applicable to persons in educational and medical institutions.

In *Pratt and Morgan v Jamaica*,[37] the Human Rights Committee of the UN declared that notification of a stay of execution only forty-five minutes before the scheduled time of the execution constituted cruel and inhuman treatment within the meaning of Article 7 of the International Covenant on Civil and Political Rights. Consistent with Article 7 methodology, it is submitted that the cruel treatment suffered by the accused amounted to a violation of the right of security of the person.

Right to Property

The right to property is enshrined in the constitutions of Commonwealth Caribbean countries, but the precise scope of the right has been left for development by the courts. In the St. Kitts case, *Attorney-General v Lawrence* (1985),[38] it was held that property should be given a wide and liberal construction to include not only concrete rights of property, but also abstract rights such as rights of management of a company. In *Trinidad Island-Wide Cane Farmers' Association v Prakash Seereeram* (1975),[39] the issue was whether the statutory authority vested in manufacturers to deduct certain amounts of money by way of cess—a form of taxation—from the price they paid to cane farmers for cane was a violation of the applicant's constitutional right to the enjoyment of property. It was argued that the applicant consented to participate in an industry that he knew was regulated. The Court rejected this argument on the ground that there was no consent to the deduction of the cess; the deduction was made only because the statute required it.

In *Re Application by Bahadur* (1986),[40] the applicant sought a declaration to the effect that a notice from the Transport Commissioner suspending his driving permit, pursuant to Section 3.61 of the Motor Vehicle and Road

Traffic Ordinance, infringed his rights under S.4 (a), (b), and (d) of the Constitution of Trinidad and Tobago. Even though "property" is normally construed very widely, the Court did not find it possible to declare that a driving permit was "property" within the meaning of S.4(a) of the Constitution.

Although brief, the foregoing discussion suggests that a fairly impressive body of jurisprudence has been developed and that the scope of the rights outlined in the various constitutions is now more precise. Consequently, lawyers find it easier to advise their clients on their rights and represent them in court. Of course a constitution is a living document and it should be expected to adapt to changing social conditions. The Privy Council is the court of final appellate jurisdiction for Commonwealth Caribbean countries, Guyana being the only exception. Hence a Privy Council decision for one Caribbean country has implications for judicial interpretation and action in other countries in the region.

The discussion also indicates that human rights protection in the Caribbean goes beyond civil and political rights to economic and social rights, although there is comparatively more attention to the former. Undoubtedly, parties to the cases are not always happy with the verdicts rendered by the courts, even of the highest tribunals involved. Yet there is a broad acceptance that the constitutional guarantees both for rights and for judicial independence are honored fairly well. Generally, even if justice is not done, it appears to be done, because the process is transparent and the judicial machinery works, albeit too slowly in some cases and inefficiently in many. Yet there is a fairly common agreement among both scholars and statesmen in the Caribbean that much remains to be done when it comes to the protection of the human rights of the region's indigenous people.

Protection of Indigenous Peoples

As a result of the genocide that took place in the colonial era, only a few Caribbean countries have significant communities of indigenous peoples. In Dominica there are the Caribs who have title to 3,700 acres of territory.[41] In Guyana, there are the Arawak-speaking Wapisiana and the Carib-speaking Akawaio, Patamona, Arekuna, Makusi, and Waiwai. In addition, there are Amerindians who live on the Guyanese coast, but they are largely acculturated. Belize, like the other countries on the Central American Isthmus, also has an Amerindian population.

The UN General Assembly designated 1993 as the International Year for the World's Indigenous Peoples.[42] This designation has served to highlight one reality facing the indigenous peoples of the Caribbean: that their human rights problems are inadequately addressed in the constitutional provisions

regarding basic rights and fundamental freedoms. Some effort should therefore be made to understand the nature of human rights in relation to indigenous peoples, a situation in which we should see not only individuals but individuals living in a community; if we are predisposed to treat indigenous
peoples only on an individual basis, then there is a real risk that we may deny
them their identity. In order to preserve this identity within the existing
state, indigenous peoples should be granted the right to self-determination,
allowing them some degree of autonomy, as has been done in at least one
country in neighboring Central America. In 1987 Nicaragua enacted legislation granting its indigenous population control over the promotion of cultures and languages, land, water, and forests—a laudable act.

The advocacy here is not for dismemberment of the state, but for the development of a new attitude toward the problems of indigenous peoples. It
is conceivable that there could be conflict between the cultural traditions of
the indigenous peoples and national law, and so the question of resolution
must be considered. One view may be that national law should prevail, but
this could lead to alienation among the members of the indigenous community. With a view to avoiding such an unsatisfactory outcome, a better approach might be that indigenous peoples be treated as a special case so that
they would be free to observe their customs within their communities, provided, of course, that such customs are not incompatible with an informed
and enlightened public policy.

One place in the region that lacks such a policy is Dominica. In Dominica
certain Carib customs are outlawed on the ground that their practice would
prevent future "integration" of the Caribs with other Dominicans. Such a
policy is based on the assumption that acculturation is a desirable goal, and it
ignores the fact that it threatens the cultural identity of the Caribs. Harmonious relations between Caribs and other Dominicans are necessary, but they
should not be at the expense of Carib social and cultural development. What
one scholar said in relation to the Caribs of Suriname is certainly true of
those in Dominica and elsewhere in the Caribbean: There is a widespread
feeling among them of a "moral right to aid, resources, territory, recognition, and anything else that the state has to offer."[43] Certainly human rights
protection is one of those things that the state has to offer.

The circumstances of the indigenous people of the Caribbean are identical
to those of indigenous people elsewhere in at least one respect: When indigenous peoples are not faced with unwarranted interference in their traditional
way of life, they find themselves subjected to a policy of benign neglect. Invariably, they are the most marginalized section of the population. Their rate
of illiteracy is highest, and poor housing and malnutrition condemn them to
a miserable existence. Positive action is required to remedy this malady, but
care must be taken to preserve their traditional way of life in the process.

Former UN Secretary-General Boutros Boutros-Ghali put it succinctly when he said that the promotion and protection of the human rights of indigenous people require a special sensitivity to particular situations.[44]

Conclusion

The emergence of human rights on the international plane represents one of the most significant developments in international law and international relations. The individual is clothed with some degree of personality on the international plane, and this enables him to be an actor in the defense and protection of his basic rights and fundamental freedoms. Various treaties have established machinery providing the individual with *locus standi* before international tribunals.

Unlike the situation under classical international law, the individual is no longer totally dependent on the state of which he is a national to provide him with protection in cases in which his human rights are infringed. Fundamental changes have also taken place in the content of human rights. According to Rousseau's concept of human rights, they comprised a set of rules that were negative in nature. The state was simply required to refrain from doing anything that would infringe the individual's basic rights. It was not called upon to do anything that would enhance the dignity and worth of the human person. Socialist philosophy devoted a great deal of attention to the social condition of the individual and was highly influential in the development of economic, social, and cultural rights.

For the purposes of analysis, it may be useful to speak of civil and political rights, and of economic, social, and cultural rights, but the effective exercise and enjoyment of those rights necessitate a holistic view of both groups of rights. Man is not only a political animal, he is also a social animal. Furthermore, in the exercise of his cultural rights, he sees himself first and foremost as part of a group, and not as an individual. In light of the rising tide of nationalism, it is important that we begin to address the issue of minority rights in a serious manner. In the period between the two world wars, the League of Nations was instrumental in developing several treaties on minorities that sought to preserve their culture, language, religion, and social customs.

The UN paid less attention to minorities and concentrated on the rights of the individual. One would hazard a guess that in the coming years the UN will be much more active in attending to the rights of minorities. In fact the process has already begun. The UN Subcommission on Prevention of Discrimination and Protection of Minorities has been formed, and it has highlighted the plight of indigenous peoples. Although international law has busied itself with the protection of human rights, it is still under municipal law that enforcement would be most effective. This ought not to be a problem, but it requires the mobilization of public opinion at the national level to ensure that there is respect for human rights. As part of this mobilization, there is a need for the continued involvement of nongovernmental organizations. This is true of the Caribbean as it is for other regions where the protection of human rights is seen as not merely legislated entitlements but inalienable rights.

Notes

1. David Harris, *Cases and Material on International Law* (London: Sweet & Maxwell, 1991), p. 600.

2. Harris, *Cases and Materials on International Law*, p. 601.

3. Referred to as "second generation" rights.

4. The so-called "third generation" rights; Declaration on the Right to Development 1986, UN General Assembly Resolution 41/128, 41st Sess., Supp. 53, p. 186.

5. Article 6(2) of UN General Assembly Resolution 41/128.

6. Article 2(7) of the Charter forbids the UN to interfere in the international affairs of a state.

7. Nagendra Singh, *Enforcement of Human Rights in Peace and War and the Future of Humanity* (Dordrecht, Neth.: Martinus Nijhoff, 1986), p. 81.

8. In the preamble to the major human rights instruments the rights are referred to as the inalienable rights of all members of the human family.

9. For example, Article 23(1) of the Universal Declaration of Human Rights; Article 6(1) of the International Covenant on Economic, Social, and Cultural Rights.

10. See Article 3(3) of the Declaration on the Right to Development.

11. Philip Alston, "Conjuring Up New Human Rights: A Proposal for Quality Control," *American Journal of International Law,* vol. 78 (July 1984):607.

12. Article 22.

13. The European Convention for the Protection of Human Rights and Fundamental Freedoms; the Inter-American Convention on Human Rights, 1969; the African Charter on Human and People's Rights.

14. For example, see Articles 44 and 45 of the Inter-American Convention on Human Rights. Barbados, Colombia, Costa Rica, Dominican Republic, El Salvador, Grenada, Guatemala, Haiti, Honduras, Jamaica, Mexico, Nicaragua, Panama, Suriname, Trinidad and Tobago, and Venezuela are parties. Of these only Colombia, Costa Rica, Guatemala, Honduras, Nicaragua, Panama, Suriname, Trinidad and Tobago, and Venezuela accept the jurisdiction of the Court pursuant to Article 62 of the Convention. (Source: Christina M. Cerna, "The Structure and Functioning of the Inter-American Court of Human Rights, 1979–1992," *British Yearbook of International Law,* vol. 63 (1992):135).

15. Article 1(3) of the Charter.

16. *I.C.J. Reports*, 1970, para 134.

17. *I.C.J. Reports*, 1980, p. 42.

18. Egon Schwelb, "The International Court of Justice and the Human Rights Clauses of the Charter," *American Journal of International Law,* vol. 66 (1972): 337, 341–346.

19. Singh, *Enforcement of Human Rights*, p. 24.

20. Membership is distributed as follows: 12 African states; 7 Asian states; 8 Latin American states; 5 East European states; and 11 West European and other states.

21. Harris, *Cases and Materials on International Law*, p. 603.

22. See Article 28, International Covenant on Civil and Political Rights.

23. Ian Brownlie, *Basic Documents on Human Rights* (Oxford: Clarendon Press, 1981), p. 21.

24. Meyers McDougal et al., "Human Rights in the United Nations," *American Journal of International Law,* vol. 58 (1964):603.

25. Lotus Case, *P.C.I.J. Reports*, series A, no. 10; Anglo-Norwegian Fisheries Case, *I.C.J. Reports*, 1951, p. 116; Asylum Case, *I.C.J. Reports* 1950, p. 266; North Sea Continental Shelf Cases, *I.C.J. Reports*, 1969, p. 3.

26. See Article 56.

27. Report of the Secretary-General, "The Situation of Democracy and Human Rights in Haiti," (A/47/908). Cited in *UN Chronicle*, vol. 30, no. 2 (June 1993):29.

28. Singh, *Enforcement of Human Rights*, p. 34.

29. *Law Reports of the Commonwealth* (Const.), 1986, p. 392.

30. See also the Bahamian Case, *Commissioner of Police v Triana and Others* (1990), *Law Reports of the Commonwealth* (Const.), p. 431.

31. *Law Reports of the Commonwealth* (Const.), 1986, p. 285.

32. *Law Reports of the Commonwealth* (Const.), 1991, p. 237.

33. *Human Rights Committee Report*, General Assembly, 44th Sess., Supp. 40, p. 241.

34. *Selected Decisions of the Human Rights Committee,* vol. 172 (1985).

35. *Selected Decisions of the Human Rights Committee,* vol. 112 (1982).

36. J. Murdoch, "Safeguarding the Liberty of the Person: Recent Strasbourg Jurisprudence," *D.C.L.Q.,* vol. 42, no. 3 (1993):494.

37. *Human Rights Committee Report*, General Assembly, 44th Sess., Supp. 40, p. 22 at p. 230 (1989).

38. *Law Reports of the Commonwealth* (Const.), 1985, p. 921.

39. *West Indian Law Reports*, vol. 27 (1975):329.

40. *Law Reports of the Commonwealth* (Const.), 1986, p. 297.

41. *World Directory of Minorities* (Harlow, Essex: Longman, 1989), p. 52.

42. *UN Chronicle*, vol. 30, no. 2 (June 1993):40.

43. Gary Brana-Shute, "An Inside-Out Insurgency: The Tukuyana Amazones of Suriname," in *Size and Survival: The Politics of Security in the Caribbean and the Pacific*, ed. Paul Sutton and Anthony Payne (London: Frank Cass, 1993), p. 64.

44. *UN Chronicle*, vol. 30, no. 2 (June 1993):43.

3

The OAS and Human Rights in the Caribbean

David J. Padilla and Elizabeth A. Houppert

The Inter-American system, which dates back to the First International Conference of American States in 1890, was consolidated, strengthened, and recreated as the Organization of American States (OAS) in 1948. There were twenty-one original member states of the OAS: the Spanish-speaking American states, Brazil, Haiti, and the United States. The decolonization of the Caribbean has led to the inclusion of almost all of the English-speaking islands, as well as Belize, Guyana, and Suriname. With the addition of Canada in 1990, there are now thirty-five member states of the OAS.[1] Cuba is a member of unique standing, deemed to have "suspended itself" from the organization in 1962 for embracing principles contrary to the Charter.[2]

The purposes of the OAS are articulated in its Charter: to strengthen the peace and security of the continent; to promote and consolidate representative democracy; to ensure the pacific settlement of disputes; to provide for common action in the event of aggression; to seek solutions to political, juridical, and economic problems; to promote economic, social, and cultural development; and to limit conventional weapons in order to devote "the largest amount of resources" to economic and social development.[3]

During World War II, the American states had convened an Inter-American Conference on Problems of War and Peace to examine the conflict and its consequences and to prepare for peace. The Inter-American Treaty of Reciprocal Assistance, a mutual defense pact, was subsequently adopted in 1947. Until very recently the priorities of the OAS, and its activities in the hemisphere in general and in the Caribbean specifically, were viewed within the context of the Cold War. Nascent guerrilla movements were spawned in the early 1960s following Fidel Castro's revolution in Cuba, and insurgent movements challenged the ruling elites in many areas of Latin America. The OAS both observed and participated in the struggle between the super-powers.

This chapter reviews the role of the OAS with respect to human rights in the Caribbean. The first section provides an introduction to the Inter-American human rights system, its mandate, functions, and activities. The second section covers three specific cases that illustrate the various types and levels of OAS involvement in the Caribbean: Grenada, Suriname, and Haiti. A third section offers some concluding observations.

The Inter-American Human Rights System

The Inter-American system for the protection of human rights was initiated concurrently with the adoption of the Charter of the OAS in 1948 by the Ninth International Conference of American States. Elaborating upon the Charter-based duty of member states to respect, without discrimination, the fundamental rights of the individual, the 1948 Conference adopted the American Declaration of the Rights and Duties of Man.[4] The American Declaration, like the Universal Declaration on Human Rights adopted seven months later, recognizes a broad range of civil and political rights and freedoms. Significantly, the declaration acknowledges that the state does not confer rights upon individuals; rather, "the essential rights of man . . . are based upon attributes of his human personality." In 1959 the ministers of foreign affairs of the member states established the Inter-American Commission on Human Rights (IACHR), the initial inter-American mechanism to promote respect for the human rights as set forth in the American Declaration while the member states considered how a treaty-based system could be elaborated.[5] This development was not realized until the 1969 adoption of the American Convention on Human Rights.[6]

The commission is composed of seven members who are elected to four-year terms by the OAS General Assembly from the panels of candidates proposed by member states. Whereas the European and African Human Rights Commissions were established as convention institutions, the Inter-American Commission was created by resolution and evolved into its present functions and competence. The commission's initial statute, adopted in 1960, was tentative, enabling the commission to receive and study information concerning human rights and to make recommendations to the member states. In 1965 the statute was strengthened, and an individual petition system was articulated to institutionalize the commission's receipt of and response to complaints concerning human rights violations. This enhancement of the commission's competence was critical, as the individual petition procedure remains a key component of the commission's oversight process. The evolution of the commission continued with its elevation to the status of a principal organ of the OAS through the adoption of amendments to the Charter in 1967. The amended Charter designated the IACHR "to promote the observance and protection of human rights and to serve as a consultative organ of the Organization." The Charter amendments also anticipated the adoption of an Inter-American convention on human rights, which upon entry into force would determine the structure, competence, and procedure of the commission. The American Convention on Human Rights was adopted in 1969 and entered into force in 1978 when Grenada became the eleventh member state to ratify it.[7] This ratification played an important role in the inter-American human rights system, as the entry into force of the American Convention transformed the legal and institutional nature of the system. The commission now acts as a convention institution in relation to member states that have ratified the convention and as a Charter organ in relation to nonratifying member states.

The American Convention also established the Inter-American Court of Human Rights as the systemic institution capable of exercising binding juridical authority. The court is composed of seven judges, nominated and elected by convention parties to six-year terms. It is empowered to exercise its binding jurisdiction only at the request of the commission or a state party where all states concerned have ratified the convention and expressly accepted the court's compulsory jurisdiction. It may exercise its advisory jurisdiction at the request of a member state, the commission, or other qualified organs of the OAS. Additional instruments promulgated to complement the American Declaration and the American Convention are: the Inter-American Convention to Prevent and Punish Torture (1985); the Additional Protocol in the Area of Economic, Social, and Cultural Rights—"Protocol of San Salvador" (1988); the Protocol to Abolish the Death Penalty (1990); the Inter-American Convention on Forced Disappearance of Persons (1994); and the Inter-American Convention to Prevent, Punish, and Eradicate Violence Against Women (1994).

The commission has three primary functions among its many activities: processing individual cases; conducting on-site visits; and preparing and publishing special studies and reports. Any person or group may lodge a complaint alleging that a member state has violated a protected right. The rights protected are those of the convention in the case of ratifying states or those of the American Declaration in the case of nonratifying states. Interstate petitions may be lodged only where all the states concerned have accepted the commission's competence to consider such cases.

The processing of complaints by the commission only varies slightly depending on whether it is exercising its convention-based or declaration-based jurisdiction. According to the most basic requirements the claimant must: (1) provide basic facts that allege a violation by a member state of a protected right; (2) indicate that scope for legal redress in the state concerned has been exhausted, although this requirement is subject to important exceptions; (3) present the petition in a timely manner; and (4) not have previously brought the complaint before another international body. Once an appropriately founded petition has been reviewed, the commission informs the government of the complaint and requests a response. Any reply is transmitted to the petitioner, who may in turn submit observations thereon. Should the government fail to respond, the commission may decide to presume the facts of the denunciation to be true.[8] The commission may also conduct its own inquiry into the complaint by holding hearings or conducting an on-site investigation. If a petition indicates that a person's life or physical integrity is in danger, the commission may adopt special measures to respond to the urgency of the situation.

The commission approaches human rights issues in member states by attempting to work with the member state involved in seeking a resolution. Public censure or other measures perceived to be more "adversarial" are resorted to only when cooperation has been unsuccessful. Whenever possible the commission will offer to facilitate a friendly settlement between the parties to a case.[9] If that is not possible, the commission will issue its conclusions and recommendations on the case and forward them to the government for action. Where a violation is found, the commission will generally recommend that the government investigate and determine responsibility for the breach and that it repair the breach, compensate the victim, and desist from further violations. Should the government fail to comply with the recommendations within the specified period of time, the commission will either publish the report, or, in the case of member states that have ratified the American Convention and accepted the compulsory jurisdiction of the Inter-American Court, it may decide to bring the case before the court.

In cases in which the court determines that a violation of a protected right has occurred, the ruling will generally direct that the victim be ensured of the future enjoyment of the right concerned and that the consequences of the breach be remedied and the victim compensated. As of December 1994 the Court had issued thirteen advisory opinions, with one pending before it, and seven opinions in binding cases, with four then under consideration.

The commission is empowered to conduct on-site investigations of specific cases, or, with the consent of the government concerned, it may carry out an on-site visit to assess the overall situation of human rights or a specific problem in a member state. The activities of a visit generally include meetings with government authorities, usually with key representatives of the branches of government and of the ministries with special responsibility relating to human rights. The delegation meets with representatives of various social sectors, community leaders, and representatives of nongovernmental organizations. The delegation often splits into working groups to travel to different sites. The commission delegation also receives individual complaints during on-site visits. The commission's first on-site visit was undertaken in 1961 in the Dominican Republic. The commission's visit initiated an intensive involvement that resulted in additional visits in 1963, and again in 1965 and 1966. The visits varied in scope. The first was to investigate complaints of widespread violations; the second was initiated to investigate a particular case but was expanded to assess the overall situation; the third was a wide-ranging protective action taken at the request of rival factions during a period of civil strife.[10]

As noted earlier, the commission also pursues its mandate through the preparation and publication of reports and special studies. It publishes an annual report that includes: a summary of its activities; individual case reports; updates on the situation of human rights in selected member states; thematic studies, including discussion of areas in which further action is required to advance respect for human rights in the hemisphere; and the commission's observations and recommendations in that respect. Thematic studies allow the commission to gather information, to explore new issues, or to comprehend the dimensions of a problem of regional or hemispheric scope and address it comprehensively.

The commission also publishes special country reports on a regular basis, most often in conjunction with an on-site visit to the member state. This type of report includes: a review of recent activities of the commission in relation to the country; a contextual overview of the domestic legal framework; a detailed analysis of the situation of human rights in the member state in terms of compliance with the American Declaration or Convention; and observations and recommendations aimed at resolving specific issues and enhancing respect for human rights. The special country report has proven to be a valuable tool because it contains a comprehensive examination of the human rights situation and provides a means to approach large-scale violations of human rights not easily or adequately addressed by the individual case process.

Case Studies

Grenada

Grenada became a member state of the OAS in 1975 when it ratified the Charter. Three years later it hosted the annual General Assembly of the OAS in its capital, St. George's. Despite its record in the area of human rights abuses, it was under the Eric M. Gairy regime that Grenada became the eleventh OAS member state to ratify the American Convention on Human Rights, thereby bringing the treaty into force. It was speculated by some that this action was intended to placate the administration of U.S. President Jimmy Carter and to make Grenada a more palatable site for the General

Assembly. During the Assembly, Gairy's opposition mounted a political demonstration protesting the prime minister's heavy-handed political tactics, which included police brutality, laws aimed at controlling public demonstrations and meetings, confiscatory property laws, and political gerrymandering. Riot police were summoned, and they opened fire on the crowd, killing one person and wounding several others.[11]

Against the backdrop of the growing strength of the combined opposition to the Gairy regime (which had won six seats to the Grenada United Labor Party's [GULP] nine in the 1976 elections), the radical New Jewel Movement (NJM) led by Maurice Bishop ousted Gairy in a predawn coup d'état on March 13, 1979, while Gairy was out of the country.[12] The OAS adopted a wait-and-see attitude. No special meeting of foreign ministers was convened and no condemnation was issued.

Bishop's takeover permitted the installation of the People's Revolutionary Government (PRG) and its own brand of repression. This included the confiscation of the *Torchlight* newspaper and the *Catholic Focus*, a church bulletin. The first occurred on October 13, 1979, when army chief Hudson Austin, implementing orders of the PRG, closed the newspaper "in the interest of peace, order and national security." The *Torchlight*, which was owned by the *Trinidad Express*, brought its case before the IACHR. With respect to both publications, in its 1982/83 annual report the commission stated: "[I]n accordance with the American Convention on Human Rights, [it] has been acting as agent for peaceful solution in order to reach a solution [*sic*] to this case based on respect for human rights, taking into account that the parties in dispute have accepted its participation."[13] In another case, referred to in the same annual report, the commission noted: "In Grenada, Leslie Pierre, editor of the 'Voice,' has been under arrest without charges since 1981 because of the government's opposition."[14]

During the rule of the PRG, numerous persons were detained without due process of law, but very few formal complaints were brought to the attention of the commission. This may perhaps be explained in terms of Grenada's relatively new membership in the OAS, the absence of an organized, effective, nongovernmental human rights organization on the island, and the unfamiliarity of the Grenadian people with the commission and its procedures. While in power the PRG abolished habeas corpus for political prisoners, suspended the country's constitution, and refused to call elections.[15] Another issue that faced the OAS while the PRG was in power was the exclusion of Grenada from the multilateral assistance provided by the United States through its Caribbean Basin Initiative. Grenada's ambassador to the OAS complained bitterly about this discrimination in the spring of 1983, and the point was underscored by Prime Minister Bishop himself in a subsequent protocolary speech to the Permanent Council.[16] While the legal issue of differential treatment of potential beneficiaries of multilateral aid was still being debated in the OAS, events overtook the controversy.

Frictions within the NJM leadership led to the murder-massacre of Maurice Bishop and some of his supporters on October 19, 1983, prompting the invasion by U.S. armed forces on October 25, in concert with forces by the governments of the Organization of Eastern Caribbean States (OECS).[17] The OAS played no role in the invasion. In contrast to the United Nations (UN) Security Council, which condemned the U.S. invasion as a violation of international law by an 11–1 vote, the OAS Permanent Council split largely along regional lines. The member states of the OECS spoke strongly of their need to take preemptive defensive action and their request for U.S. military assistance. The majority of Latin American spokesmen, on the other hand, criticized the intervention in varying degrees. The debate ended without the adoption of a resolution.[18]

After the invasion, several additional individual petitions were presented to the commission alleging human rights violations by U.S. military forces and the new provisional government of Prime Minister Nicholas Brathwaite. The first petition alleged U.S. responsibility for mistakenly bombing a mental asylum and thereby killing more than twenty patients. The petition by Disabled Peoples International was apparently deemed by the commission to have been resolved when the U.S. government rebuilt the mental health facility and compensated the relatives of the victims.[19]

The second case brought against the United States was presented on behalf of Bernard and Phyllis Coard and fifteen other NJM leaders charged in Bishop's death. Here the petitioners alleged violations of the defendants' due process rights, particularly their having been held incommunicado on U.S. naval vessels and interrogated without the presence of counsel. This case was declared admissible as a procedural matter in February 1994, and the IACHR will proceed to consider the matter on its merits.[20] It may be noted that Bernard Coard and his codefendants were originally condemned to be hanged, but pursuant to a request from the IACHR, the death sentences were commuted to life imprisonment. This was done in line with the commission's long-established policy of objecting on humanitarian grounds to the imposition of capital punishment.[21]

The final case, which was still pending before the commission as of December 1994, was brought against the new government of Grenada. The petition alleges that the Coards and the others charged with responsibility for the October 19 killings were subjected to physical mistreatment during incarceration and were detained in inhumane conditions.

Suriname

Suriname, a crown colony of the Kingdom of the Netherlands for two centuries, gained its independence in 1975 and became a member of the OAS on June 8, 1977.[22] By 1980 the people of Suriname were sufficiently weary of the real or perceived corruption in the government that they largely welcomed the coup d'état led by Sergeant Desi Bouterse and a group of fellow noncommissioned officers who were angry about their low salaries. Within two years, however, the "revolution" turned ugly. For example, on the night of December 7, 1982, fifteen of Suriname's most prominent leaders were arrested at their homes, taken to army headquarters at Fort Zeelandia, and executed.

For peaceful Suriname, the event was traumatic. Internationally, indignation was translated into sanctions from which Suriname is still trying to recover. First, the Netherlands ended development assistance of some $100 million, part of the separation agreement from the mother country.[23] The United States also suspended its $1 million of annual development aid. Multilateral lenders such as the World Bank and the Inter-American Development Bank also ceased assistance.

In June 1983 the IACHR conducted the first of several on-site human rights observations in Suriname. During that visit Lieutenant Colonel Bouterse (he had promoted himself) defended the deaths of the fifteen as necessary to protect the revolution. In its report issued in October of that year the commission cited the military government for violations of the right to life, physical integrity (specifically including torture), and personal liberty. The commission found the government responsible for the denial of due process and for restrictions on the freedoms of press and assembly as well as for the dictatorship's violation of the political rights of the citizens of Suriname to elect their own government.[24] The investigation also involved the taking of testimony from some of the widows and relatives of the executed men, from their location in exile in Amsterdam and Leiden, Holland.

The commission made another on-site visit in 1984, during which it, inter alia, visited political prisoners and insisted that the murderers of 1982 be brought to account. Lieutenant Colonel Bouterse reiterated his insistence that the murders were the result of "revolutionary necessity." The commission's more comprehensive second report, published in 1985, further documented large-scale human rights violations as the dictatorship sought to consolidate its hold on power.[25]

By 1986 Suriname's political and human rights situation had become even more complicated. On the one hand, a slow process had been set into motion to adopt a new constitution, an undertaking that would lead to elections and the restoration of formal democracy in 1987. In an effort to improve its human rights image, Suriname ratified the American Convention on Human Rights and accepted the compulsory jurisdiction of the Inter-American Court of Human Rights in late 1986.[26] On the other hand, some of Suriname's Maroon population began rebelling against the military authorities in mid-1986. Faced with increasingly harsh conditions in the interior and violations of their treaty rights, a small number of Maroons under the leadership of Ronnie Brunswijk, a former Bouterse bodyguard, formed a guerrilla organization called the Jungle Commando.[27]

Forays by the Jungle Commando were met by broad and merciless repression against the Maroon population in general, culminating in a massacre at a Djuka village called Moiwana in the fall of that year. The IACHR (among other governmental and nongovernmental human rights organizations) reported that over 200 persons, including women and children, had been slain in cold blood.[28] One result of the slaughter was the formation of Suriname's first nongovernmental human rights organization, under the leadership of educator and Djuka tribesman Stanley Rensch. Rensch's organization, among other things, presented denunciations to the IACHR in connection with numerous wrongful deaths. One was the murder of seven Maroon boatmen in Atjoni, in south-central Suriname, a case that became known as *Aloeboetoe et al. v Suriname*.[29] The second was the death of a returning Surinamese immigrant, who had allegedly hanged himself while being held in incommunicado detention by the military police in 1987. This case became known as *Gangaram Panday v Suriname*.[30]

Both cases were processed by the commission, which in due course found the government of Suriname responsible for the violation of the right to life of the various victims. Both cases were then taken by the commission to the Inter-American Court for litigation. In the matter of *Aloeboetoe*, the government eventually accepted responsibility and was ordered to pay an indemnity of $453,000 to the boatmen's next of kin.[31] In *Panday*, the court held that there had been an illegal detention but that there was insufficient proof to conclude that the victim had been tortured or murdered. Suriname was ordered to pay $10,000 to the victim's widow.

The commission conducted further visits to the country in 1987 and 1988, and Suriname continued to be subject to commission reporting into the early 1990s.[32] Progress toward true democracy stumbled in December 1990 when Bouterse's allies in the armed forces staged another coup d'état. However, prompt and intense international pressure forced the holding of elections several months later. OAS actions included the observation of national elections by expert observers in 1991, the negotiation of the peaceful return from French Guyana of thousands of Maroons and Amerindian refugees who had fled Suriname during the civil war of 1986–1987, and the eventual disarmament and demobilization of the Jungle Commando and several Maroon and Amerindian surrogate forces that had been sponsored by the army. The secretary-general's representatives also cooperated with the Surinamese government in the defusing and removal of mines. In addition, they provided technical assistance in civil education and worked on projects to strengthen democratic institutions.[33] The OAS continues to maintain a reduced presence in Suriname to monitor compliance with the peace accords.

This account is at best a thumbnail sketch of the events of the 1980s in Suriname and of the constructive role played by the OAS through three of its organs—the Inter-American Commission on Human Rights, the Inter-American Court of Human Rights, and the General Secretariat. Each of these OAS bodies made crucial contributions in the factual reporting of developments in Suriname to the political organs of the OAS—the Permanent Council, the Meeting of Consultation of Foreign Ministers, and the General Assembly. They also served to pressure the parties to reduce human rights violations, to free political prisoners, to negotiate truces, and to reach and implement peace and disarmament accords. In some exemplary cases, the commission was able, through the Inter-American Court, to obtain money damages for human rights victims. Similarly, the OAS played a critical role in inducing the various actors in Suriname to adopt a constitution (and later to effect key amendments) and to hold free and fair elections. Though Suriname faces many difficulties, civil processes have been set into motion, democracy has been restored, and the country has an opportunity to address the social and economic challenges that confront it.

Haiti

The case of Haiti illustrates dramatically the essential linkage between a functioning system of representative democratic governance and the maintenance of the conditions necessary to guarantee respect for human rights. The tragic history of Haiti, with its cycles of escalating violence and repression and deteriorating human rights, has warranted numerous crisis interventions by the IACHR and the political organs of the OAS. Haiti holds the dubious distinction of being the subject of nine special reports (with two follow-up reports) by the commission—the most on a single member state.

The successive regimes of François Duvalier and his son Jean-Claude were characterized by the practice of severe, widespread human rights violations coupled with the extension of impunity to the perpetrators. It was hoped that the triumphant inauguration of Father Jean-Bertrand Aristide, Haiti's first democratically elected president, on February 7, 1991, would mark the end of abusive authoritarian rule. Instead, the September 30, 1991, overthrow of the Aristide government threw Haiti back into a regime of political repression and persecution and into a new cycle of grave human rights abuses.

The IACHR began responding to complaints of human rights violations in Haiti almost as soon as it became operational. Prompted by the gravity of the complaints, in the fall of 1962 and again in the spring of 1963, the commission requested the consent of the Haitian government to conduct an on-site visit to assess the situation. The government ignored the first request and adamantly refused the second, arguing that such requests constituted interference in the internal affairs of the republic.

The political organs of the OAS followed with particular concern the tensions between Haiti and the Dominican Republic after the inauguration of Dominican President Juan Bosch in 1963. The Duvalierists were then carrying out a particularly vicious spasm of terror in Haiti. A few months after Bosch's inauguration, Duvalierist police took over the Dominican embassy in Port-au-Prince and also invaded the grounds of the Dominican ambassador's residence. Bosch appealed to the OAS, which approved the dispatch of a delegation to Haiti to investigate. The delegation returned almost immediately, however, having been clearly rebuffed.[34] Duvalier was not swayed by OAS pressure; his assumption of the presidency for life was itself in violation of the OAS Charter provisions concerning representative democracy.

In 1967 the commission published a report on the situation of Haitian citizens repatriated by Dominican authorities during the spring of 1966.[35] Denunciations received by the commission reported that some of these citizens had been executed in the Haitian border area of Tilori. In 1968 the commission published the report, "Haiti and the Right of Political Asylum," which set forth the commission's findings and analyzed the likely consequences of the government's denunciation of international conventions on the right of asylum.[36]

Despite the government's continued refusal to consent to an on-site visit, the commission issued a comprehensive special report on the situation of human rights in Haiti in 1969. The report notes the 1963 suspension by decree of a number of constitutional guarantees, which enabled the government to deprive specified citizens of their Haitian nationality and to confiscate their goods and property.[37] The report contains the pertinent parts of complaints received throughout the mid-1960s concerning arbitrary and incommunicado detention, torture, and the massacres of scores of people at a time, including entire families, committed by the military, by the Tonton Macoutes, and by others under government order.

In 1977, under the regime of Jean-Claude Duvalier, Haiti ratified the American Convention on Human Rights. In response to a government invitation, the commission conducted an on-site visit to Haiti the following year and reported its findings.[38] Though the commission noted some improvement in the human rights situation during the initial years of the regime, the government was found to be responsible for numerous violations of the right to life and physical integrity. The almost permanent "state of siege" had eliminated any separation of powers and had restricted legal guarantees. Many people were subject to detention without procedural guarantees and without access to counsel. The right of political participation and the enjoyment of economic, social, and cultural rights were determined to be virtually nonexistent. The commission recommended specific measures, such as the repeal of several laws to bring domestic legislation into line with the American Convention, and other actions to remedy the violations identified. The commission also called upon international organizations to provide aid to improve socioeconomic conditions.

In early 1986, just weeks before he went into exile, Jean-Claude Duvalier had invited the commission to conduct another on-site visit. That visit was aborted, but in July of that year Haiti's National Governing Council issued a new invitation, and the on-site visit was held from January 20 through 23, 1987. The commission perceived advances in the freedoms of expression and association, but it criticized the status of the right to personal liberty and of due process and noted that detainees were held in deplorable conditions.

Prompted by the tragic outcome of election day, November 29, 1987, in March 1988 the commission requested, and was granted, consent to conduct another on-site visit. General Henri Namphy's assumption of power on June 20, 1988, prompted the Permanent Council of the OAS to meet on June 29. The Permanent Council reaffirmed the Charter principles of respect for representative democracy and human rights and requested the commission to examine and report to the next General Assembly on the situation of human rights in Haiti. The commission delegation carried out the on-site visit in Haiti from August 29 through September 2, 1988, and issued a special report later that year.[39] The commission's report particularly emphasized the urgent need to establish a timetable for free and fair elections to be held to establish a democratic civilian government. In light of the tragic disruption of the 1987 elections and the population's doubt that the military would turn over power to a popularly elected civilian government, the commission recommended that international election observers be utilized to supervise the electoral process.

After General Prosper Avril's assumption of power in September 1988, the Permanent Council of the OAS requested that the commission conduct another on-site visit to Haiti and continue "giving priority attention to the human rights situation in Haiti." It also recommended that the OAS secretary-general dispatch a mission of election observers (if so requested) to the upcoming election.[40] While the commission was attempting to set the terms for the visit, General Avril was replaced as the head of government by President Ertha Pascal-Trouillot, who consented to an on-site visit that took place from April 17 through 20, 1990. As a result of the visit, the commission submitted a special report to the 1990 OAS General Assembly meeting in Paraguay that emphasized as critical the establishment of the security necessary for the people to express their political will in the forthcoming election. As an initial step, this would require the establishment of respect for basic human rights—personal freedom, free expression, assembly, and association. It would also require that those accused of committing grave human rights violations be brought to trial. Citizens had reported a complete lack of effort to investigate or punish those responsible for violations—sustaining a climate of fear that would be likely to disrupt the next election.

The commission emphasized the critical importance of professionalizing the police and army, of separating the two forces, and of subordinating both to civilian control. The delegation also recommended that the disarming and disbanding of paramilitary groups and armed militias be made a priority. Further, the commission noted that the system of Section Chiefs (persons appointed by the armed forces to maintain security in rural areas) was a major cause of the climate of fear. The commission emphasized that only under the appropriate conditions of respect for human rights could Haiti secure democratization. In light of the commission's report, and with particular concern that the next election be held in conditions of security for the voters, the General Assembly approved a resolution entitled "Support for the Democratic Process in the Republic of Haiti."[41]

While election preparations proceeded, the commission received information that the human rights situation was deteriorating further. The commission dispatched a small delegation to investigate from September 10 through 14, 1990, and the full commission visited Haiti from November 14 through 16, 1990. In its 1990/91 annual report, the commission published an update on the situation in Haiti and noted with encouragement that the election had been conducted successfully and peacefully, as validated by OAS and UN electoral observers.[42]

The ouster of constitutionally elected President Jean-Bertrand Aristide by the military both challenged and frustrated the OAS, initiating a period of intensive action on the part of the political organs of the OAS and the commission. The Permanent Council of the OAS met in emergency session immediately after the coup. It condemned the violent interruption of the constitutional exercise of power in Haiti and demanded the restoration of the democratically elected president.[43] On October 1, 1991, the commission issued a press release expressing grave concern over the events comprising the coup, which constituted violations of political rights and other fundamental rights and freedoms. In an emergency meeting the following day the ministers of foreign affairs of the OAS drafted and adopted a resolution designed to embargo and diplomatically isolate the illegal regime.[44] The ministers called upon the IACHR "to take all measures within its competence to protect and defend human rights in Haiti." During the suspension of the constitutional government, the commission conducted three on-site visits to Haiti and issued three special reports to the General Assembly of the OAS.

During its October 1991 period of sessions the commission consulted with President Aristide, the secretary-general of the OAS, and the representative of the Haitian mission to the OAS and subsequently dispatched a special delegation to Haiti in December 1991 to gather information, identify specific problems, and assess prospects for the commission to continue its work there. The delegation reported to the Permanent Council that the grave institutional crisis, extreme poverty, political polarization, widespread violence, and the lack of a democratic tradition had created a highly volatile and dangerous situation.

In February 1992 the OAS sponsored the meetings that led to the Washington Accords, which were later abandoned as impossible to implement. The subsequently adopted Florida Declaration requested the assistance of the international community in finding a political solution and specifically requested that the OAS send a civilian mission to Haiti. The OAS dispatched a delegation to Haiti from August 18 through 20, 1992, as a means of reopening negotiations and as the first step toward initiating an OAS civilian mission. This led to negotiations in Washington between the envoys of President Aristide and Marc Bazin, which resulted in the authorization of an eighteen-member civilian mission to be sent to Haiti to contribute to a reduction of the violence, encourage respect for human rights, help to assess progress toward a political settlement, and assist in the distribution of humanitarian aid. The OAS civilian mission began its work in September 1992. After only three months, the Ministry of Foreign Affairs informed the mission that there was no legal basis for their presence and that it could not guarantee their safety. The OAS and the UN nevertheless continued efforts to strengthen and expand the civilian mission. In February 1993 an enhanced joint mission was established with the principal mandate of ensuring respect for human rights in order to cultivate conditions for the restoration of democracy.[45]

After the ouster of President Aristide, the commission repeatedly requested the consent of the de facto government to carry out an on-site visit. The de facto government responded that as it had already consented to the presence of an OAS civilian mission, which was assessing the human rights situation, a commission visit was not necessary. In spite of this lack of cooperation, the commission nevertheless prepared a special report on the human rights situation in Haiti in 1992, by relying on complaints received from victims of violations and information from human rights groups operating inside and outside of Haiti.

The commission again met with President Aristide during its March 1993 regular period of sessions and at his behest requested consent to conduct another on-site visit. After a period of nonresponsiveness from the de facto regime, the visit was permitted and carried out from August 23 through 27, 1993. The commission delegation met with political leaders and officials from the Ministry of Foreign Affairs, with members of the OAS/UN civilian mission, and with representatives of various nongovernmental organizations and social sectors. Commission working groups traveled from Port-au-Prince to the Central Plateau and Arbonite regions. In the course of the visit, the commission received many complaints of violations of the rights to life, liberty, and security, and of the rights to freedom of expression and assembly. The commission verified that the extant climate of fear and repression was prompting the large-scale internal displacement of persons fleeing their homes and living in hiding. Many persons seeking to provide information to the commission insisted on clandestine meetings, fearing reprisals by the military authorities.

The commission issued press releases on September 24 and October 15, 1993,[46] expressing deep concern over killings and other violent acts perpetrated by neo–Tonton Macoutes paramilitary groups against Aristide supporters. The releases specifically noted the assassinations of well-known Aristide supporters Antoine Izméry and Minister of Justice Guy Malary. Also cited were reports of violent demonstrations organized by the Haitian Front for Advancement and Progress (FRAPH) and other paramilitary groups, carried out with the support of police, in which citizens were threatened and terrorized and diplomatic personnel and journalists were threatened and harassed.

In the face of the worsening situation of human rights in Haiti, the commission made another on-site visit to the country from May 16 through 20, 1994. The delegation confirmed a marked deterioration in the human rights situation since its August 1993 visit and pointed to "an increase in the number and brutality of human rights violations by the Army, FRAPH, and other paramilitary groups working in tandem with the military (attachés) in the country's interior."[47] The commission reported on numerous extrajudicial executions, disappearances, kidnappings, and torture and described the practice of mutilating bodies for the purpose of terrorizing the population. The commission also drew special attention to the use of rape as an instrument of terror against the wives and female relatives of supporters of the democratic regime. The overall human rights picture in Haiti was "one of very serious deterioration in the most elementary human rights . . . all part of a plan to intimidate and terrorize a defenseless people."[48]

The commission has also taken special action to meet human rights consequences outside of Haiti generated by the crisis, most critically with respect to the plight of Haitian refugees. A case has been opened against the United States, based on the claim that the forcible return by authorities of "Haitian boat people" intercepted on the high seas, without any screening of asylum claims, is a violation of the American Declaration. On March 12, 1993, the commission issued precautionary measures in the case, calling upon the United States to halt its practice of repatriation without asylum screening and to ensure that Haitians in the United States are not returned without such screening.

Large numbers of Haitians fled to the Bahamas as well, creating a potential flash point: The Bahamian government lacked sufficient resources to deal with the influx, and the situation generated considerable social tension. The commission received information that there were between 40,000 and 50,000 undocumented Haitian immigrants in the Bahamas—equivalent to almost 20 percent of the Bahamian population.[49] The commission carried out an on-site observation in the Bahamas in May 1994 to assess the situation more fully. On the one hand, the delegation expressed concern as to whether Haitians were being accorded adequate due process in the determination of their refugee status in the Bahamas and whether those being detained were held in adequate conditions. On the other hand, it recognized the contribution of the Bahamas in hosting a large proportion of Haitians fleeing violence and repression in their home country and in extending to them access to basic social services. The commission noted with dismay that while the international community had vociferously condemned the situation in Haiti, virtually no state had been willing to accept fleeing Haitians, and it called upon the international community to provide support to the government of the Bahamas in its efforts. The commission reiterated that the solution to the situation of Haitian refugees was linked to the restoration of democracy in Haiti, a task in which "all the states of the hemisphere must share responsibility."[50]

The commission visited Haiti again from October 24 through 27, 1994. The delegation met with President Aristide and expressed its "profound satisfaction with the restoration of the democratic regime" as well as its interest in collaborating with his administration in addressing the human rights challenges that lie ahead. Among the issues identified by the commission as pressing are: the disarming of the paramilitary groups; the establishment of a legitimate police force and an effective judiciary; a review of prison conditions and the status of those incarcerated; and "an accounting of exactly what happened during the military dictatorship and, in particular, a detailed review of the human rights violations suffered by the Haitian people."[51] These are just some of the prerequisites for establishing a civil society based on respect for the rule of law.

Conclusion

Decolonization in the Caribbean region occurred largely in the context of declared acceptance of parliamentary democracy and respect for democratic institutions and ideals—with respect for civil and political rights expressed as the counterpart of this political-institutional framework. The reality of the relationship between the governors and the governed in the region has historically been far more complex, and the commitment to democratic practice and respect for the individual has been subject to notable exceptions. The cases presented here, for example, arose in the context of a breakdown in constitutional protections and a concomitant rise in human rights abuses.

In Haiti as well as in Grenada, Suriname, and the rest of the Caribbean, respect for human rights has been and continues to be inextricably linked with the pursuit of participatory representative government. In the post–Cold War era, the regional consensus on the validity of democratic political systems and the common interest in free market economic reform provide a new basis for hemispheric cooperation.[52] "The Santiago Commitment to Democracy and the Renewal of the Inter-American System," adopted by the OAS General Assembly in 1991, explicitly recognizes that the current political and economic climate presents a new opportunity for cooperative regional action to advance the basic purposes of the OAS.[53] The Inter-American Commission on Human Rights, as the OAS's principal human rights mechanism, has played and will continue to play an important role in confronting the failings in democratic practice and in strengthening democratic institutions in order to enhance the respect for and observance of human rights in the hemisphere.

The case studies demonstrate some of the lesser-known but very important work of the commission and the OAS. For example, in the case of Suriname, the commission played a significant role in chronicling and drawing international attention to very grave human rights violations. The Inter-American Court of Human Rights adjudicated two contentious cases against Suriname. The political organs played a critical role in observing and providing technical assistance to the 1991 electoral process. The OAS maintained an observer presence throughout the pacification process, and it continues to carry out projects in Suriname through its Unit for the Promotion of Democracy. Other components of the OAS have played an important role throughout the Caribbean. For example, the Inter-American Economic and Social Council and the Pan American Health Organization have sponsored initiatives in the areas of development, education, and health.

Most Caribbean member states have been very supportive of action by the OAS and the commission in the field of human rights. Barbados, Dominica, Dominican Republic, Grenada, Haiti, and Jamaica are party to the American Convention; Antigua and Barbuda is currently pursuing ratification. Suriname and Trinidad and Tobago are party to the Convention and have accepted the compulsory jurisdiction of the Inter-American Court. This represents important progress in the process of consolidating the Inter-American system for the protection of human rights. The Caribbean member states could play an even more significant role in the Inter-American human rights system if they all would ratify the Convention and accept the compulsory jurisdiction of the Inter-American Court.

Notes

The opinions presented in this chapter are those of the authors and do not necessarily reflect those of the Inter-American Commission on Human Rights or the Organization of American States.

1. The OAS member states are: Antigua and Barbuda, Argentina, the Bahamas, Barbados, Belize, Bolivia, Brazil, Canada, Chile, Colombia, Costa Rica, Cuba, Dominica, Dominican Republic, Ecuador, El Salvador, Grenada, Guatemala, Guyana, Haiti, Honduras, Jamaica, Mexico, Nicaragua, Panama, Paraguay, Peru, St. Kitts and Nevis, Saint Lucia, Saint Vincent and the Grenadines, Suriname, Trinidad and Tobago, United States, Uruguay, and Venezuela.

2. See Resolution VI entitled "Exclusion of the present Government of Cuba from participation in the Inter-American system," adopted by the Eighth Meeting of Consultation of Ministers of Foreign Affairs in January 1962. OEA Ser. F/III.8 (Span.), p. 298.

3. Charter of the Organization of American States, adopted April 30, 1948, T.S. No. 1-E, OEA/Ser.A/2 (Eng.), rev. 3, Article 2.

4. American Declaration of the Rights and Duties of Man, adopted by the Ninth International Conference of American States, Bogota, Colombia, 1948. The text of the Declaration is reprinted in *Basic Documents Pertaining to Human Rights in the Inter-American System*, OEA/Ser.L.V./II.82, doc. 6, rev. 1, July 1, 1992, p. 17.

5. The resolution of the Fifth Meeting of Consultation (Santiago, Chile, August 12–18, 1959), entitled "Human Rights," is recorded in Final Act, OAS Off. Recs., OEA/Ser.C/II.5, pp. 10–11.

6. American Convention on Human Rights, November 22, 1969, OAS T.S. No. 36 in 1, OAS Off. Rec. OEA/Ser. L/VII.23, doc. 21, rev. 6 (1979), reprinted in *Basic Documents*, p. 25.

7. Ibid.; signatures and current status of ratifications (through July 1992) are at p. 53.

8. Regulations of the Inter-American Commission, Article 42. The regulations are reprinted in *Basic Documents*, p. 103.

9. American Convention, Article 48.1.f; Regulations, Article 45.

10. See R. Norris, "Observations in Loco: Practice and Procedure of the Inter-American Commission on Human Rights," *Texas International Law Journal*, vol. 15 (1980):46 (reviewing the commission's early practice with respect to on-site visits).

11. Donald Trotman and Keith Friday, *Human Rights in Grenada* (Bustamante Institute of Public and International Affairs, 1984), p. 3.

12. See Gregory W. Sandford, *The New Jewel Movement: Grenada's Revolution, 1979–1983*, edited by Diane B. Bendahmane (Washington, DC: U.S. Department of State, 1985), p. 37.

13. *Annual Report of the Inter-American Commission on Human Rights, 1982–83*, OEA/Ser.L/V/II.61, doc. 22, rev. 1, October 7, 1983, p. 23.

14. Ibid.

15. Trotman and Friday, *Human Rights in Grenada*, p. 37.

16. The speech is recorded in OEA/Ser. G CP/ACTA 528/83.

17. See Sandford, *The New Jewel Movement*, pp. 176 ff.

18. OEA/Ser. G CP/Acta 543, October 26, 1983.

19. *Annual Report of the Inter-American Commission on Human Rights, 1986–87*, OEA/Ser. L/V/II.71, doc. 9, rev. 1, September 24, 1987, p. 198.

20. Case No. 10.951, Decision on Admissibility, scheduled to be published in the annual report of the IACHR for 1994.

21. Though capital punishment is lawful under the American Convention on Human Rights, expansion of the death penalty by state parties subsequent to ratification is limited. See American Convention, Article 4. This reflects the ambivalence of the Convention's framers on an issue considered very controversial.

22. See *Charter, Status of Signatures, Ratifications, Declarations and Reservations to the Charter and Its Protocols*, annexes 1–3.

23. See Betty N. Sedoc-Dahlberg, "Suriname: 1975–1989," in *The Dutch Caribbean: Prospects for Democracy*, ed. Betty N. Sedoc-Dahlberg (New York: Gordon and Breach, 1990), pp. 29–30.

24. *Report on the Situation of Human Rights in Suriname*, OAS/Ser.L/V/II.61, doc. 6, rev. 1, October 6, 1983, p. 1.

25. *Second Report on the Situation of Human Rights in Suriname*, OAS/Ser.L/V/II.66, doc. 21, rev. 1, October 2, 1985.

26. See *Basic Documents*, p. 53.

27. *Annual Report of the Inter-American Commission on Human Rights, 1987–88*, OEA/Ser.L/V/II.74, doc. 10, rev. 1, September 16, 1988, p. 327.

28. *Annual Report of the Inter-American Commission on Human Rights, 1989–1990*, OEA/Ser.L/V/II.77, doc. 7, rev. 1, May 17, 1990, p. 178.

29. *Annual Report of the Inter-American Commission on Human Rights, 1990–91*, OEA/Ser.L/V/II.79, doc. 12, rev. 1, February 22, 1991, pp. 496–497.

30. Ibid.

31. See David J. Padilla, "Reparations in *Aloeboetoe v. Suriname*," *Human Rights Quarterly*, vol. 17, no. 3 (1995):541–555.

32. *Annual Report of the Inter-American Commission on Human Rights, 1991*, OEA/Ser.L/V/II.81, doc. 6, rev. 1, February 14, 1992, pp. 250–253.

33. See generally the *Report of the Secretary General on the Observation of the Electoral Process in Suriname*, OEA/Ser. G/CP/INF. 3192/91, November 13, 1991. For an overview of OAS election observation missions in the Dominican Republic, El Salvador, Haiti, Nicaragua, Paraguay, and Suriname, see D. Padilla and E. Houppert, "International Election Observing: Enhancing the Principle of Free and Fair Elections," *Emory International Law Review*, vol. 7 (Spring 1993):73–132.

34. For a review of the varying accounts of the meeting between Duvalier and the OAS delegation, see Robert Heinl and Nancy Heinl, *Written in Blood* (Boston: Houghton Mifflin, 1978), pp. 632–633.

35. *Requests for Information Transmitted to the Government of Haiti on the Case of the Haitian Citizens Returned to Their Country from the Dominican Republic and the Case of the Beauvoir-Florez Family*, OEA/Ser.L/V/II.16, doc. 2, rev., February 16, 1967.

36. OEA/Ser.L/V/II.19, doc. 6, rev., April 18, 1968.

37. OEA/Ser.L/V/II.21, doc. 6, rev., May 21, 1969.

38. OEA/Ser.L/V/II.46, doc. 66, rev. 1, December 13, 1979.

39. OEA/Ser.L/V/II.74, doc. 9, rev. 1, September 7, 1988.

40. Resolution 537, adopted February 23, 1990, reprinted in the 1990 special report, OEA/Ser.L/V/II.77, doc. 18, rev. 1, May 8, 1990.

41. Doc. AG/RES. 1048 (XIX-0/90) of June 8, 1990.

42. Doc. OEA/Ser.L/V/II.79, doc. 12, rev. 1, February 22, 1991.

43. See "Support to the Democratic Government of Haiti," CP/RES. 567 (870/91), September 30, 1991, and AG/Res. 1080 (XXI-0/91). The Permanent Council denounced the loss of life resulting from the coup and called for the punishment of those responsible in accordance with international law.

44. See "Support to the Democratic Government of Haiti," MRE/RES. 1/91, doc. OEA/Ser.F/V.1, October 3, 1991. The General Assembly of the United Nations voted its unanimous support for the OAS embargo on October 11, 1991. On October 4, 1991, an OAS mission composed of the secretary-general and six ministers of foreign affairs of member states arrived in Port-au-Prince to open negotiations with the de facto regime, but immediately returned to Washington due to the refusal of the de facto authorities to negotiate. The OAS secretary-general later designated a special representative to participate in negotiations aimed at the restoration of democracy held in November and December. For a comprehensive review of OAS action in response to the Haitian crisis, including an analysis of why an initially strong reaction was less than effective, see Domingo Acevedo, "The Haitian Crisis and the OAS Response: A Test of Effectiveness in Protecting Democracy," in *Enforcing Restraint: Collective Intervention in Internal Conflicts*, ed. Lori F. Damrosch (New York: Council on Foreign Relations Press, 1993), pp. 119–155.

45. Dante Caputo was serving as the UN Special Envoy of the UN and OAS secretaries-general and was conducting negotiations between the parties. Negotiations during the first half of 1993 proved unfruitful due to the lack of cooperation from the de facto authorities. As a result, UN Security Council Resolution 841 entered into effect on June 23, 1993, imposing a ban on the shipment of oil and weapons to Haiti and calling for the freezing of the foreign assets of the de facto leaders and their supporters.

46. The texts of these releases are annexed to *Report on the Situation of Human Rights in Haiti*, OEA/Ser.L/V/II.85, doc. 9, rev., February 11, 1994.

47. IACHR Press Release (11/94), issued at Port-au-Prince, May 20, 1994.

48. Ibid. See also IACHR Press Release (19/94), issued at Washington, DC, August 31, 1994.

49. See D. Payne, "Caribbean Democracy," *Freedom Review*, June 1993, pp. 19, 22.

50. See IACHR Press Release (13/94), issued at Nassau, the Bahamas, May 27, 1994.

51. IACHR Press Release (22/94), issued at Port-au-Prince, October 27, 1994.

52. See Viron Vaky and Heraldo Muñoz, *The Future of the Organization of American States* (New York: Twentieth Century Fund Press, 1993), p. 3 (positing that these common concerns have engendered a revival of interest in the OAS on the part of member states).

53. The intertwined objectives of achieving effective representative democracy and realizing respect for human rights reiterated and reinforced in the 1991 Santiago Commitment to Democracy and the Renewal of the Inter-American System are restatements of the long-standing goals of the OAS, as set forth in the OAS Charter, in the American Convention on Human Rights, in the Declaration of Caracas of 1954, and in the Santiago Commitments of 1959 and 1991.

4

NGOs and IGOs as Promoters of Liberal Democracy in the Caribbean: Cases from Nicaragua and Guyana

W. Marvin Will

The major hypothesis of this chapter is that electoral monitoring activities by appropriate nongovernmental organizations (NGOs) and intergovernmental organizations (IGOs) achieve three things: They contribute to the international legitimacy of governments; they represent a cost-effective means of promoting electoral democracy; and they promote human rights in authoritarian or semiauthoritarian countries. This appears especially true in the post–Cold War era for countries where there has been a pattern of U.S. or allied intervention and where there are severe economic downturns accompanied by a reluctance of regional lenders to provide loans, investments, and other support. The purpose of this chapter is to test this hypothesis in the cases of Nicaragua and Guyana.

Promoting Electoral Democracy in Theory

The promotion of electoral democracy has been a long-term bipartisan goal of the United States. For example, Presidents Ronald Reagan and Jimmy Carter, two very dissimilar U.S. leaders, were in agreement on the national importance of promoting this goal, especially in the Caribbean Basin. Yet there remains a lack of accepted definitions as to what democracy and democratization entail, and also on how to promote them.[1] Most useful for this chapter's focus is the procedural and measurable definition used by Samuel Huntington: the development of a routinized pattern of "elections, open, free, and fair," that have the potential to replace governments. Huntington notes that this emphasis on procedures, more so than on the less measurable "common good" arguments of the political philosophers, was made by Joseph Schumpeter in 1942 and has been strengthened by the pivotal role currently played by recent electoral monitoring missions conducted by trained international groups representing both public and private international organizations. Huntington argues correctly that "[b]y 1990 the point had been reached where the first election in a democratizing country would only be generally accepted as legitimate if it was observed by one or more reasonably competent and detached teams of international observers, and if the observers certified the election as meeting minimal standards of honesty and fairness."[2]

As we will see in revolutionary Nicaragua, the dwindling of economic assistance from the former communist bloc, the U.S. restrictions, and the indiscretion of Sandinista policymakers (augmented by the severe damage inflicted by Hurricane Joan) were key factors in inducing the Sandinista leadership to invite the Carter Center and other monitoring groups to observe their 1990 general election as it attempted to restore international legitimacy and bolster the opportunity for economic assistance. Multidigit inflation and a destructive civil war were progressively eroding middle-sector support for the government.[3] Increasingly the use of external election monitors became a necessary option for President Daniel Ortega Saavedra.

Guyana, a racially divided former British colony (called British Guiana prior to 1966), faced a similar need for increased international legitimacy. Although their most authoritarian president, Linden Forbes Sampson Burnham, had died in 1985, internationally monitored elections seemed a potentially strong option to relieve the domestic pressures for increased democratization and to satisfy increasingly strident demands of foreign lenders and potential investors. Hence elections monitoring increasingly became an attractive option for the beleaguered government of Desmond Hoyte, Burnham's successor. In both Nicaragua and Guyana, a major and direct intervening role into the electoral process by the U.S. government would have been inappropriate due to previous interventions. The best option for both appears to have been the Council of Freely Elected Heads of Government (CFEHG) of the Carter Center at Emory University, working in conjunction with other NGOs and IGOs.

Nicaragua and Guyana: Comparative Insights

Nicaragua and Guyana appear highly dissimilar as nations. Even racially and ethnically, they differ significantly. The Central American nation of Nicaragua is mostly Spanish-speaking and mestizo-dominated, with minorities of English-speaking Native Americans and blacks. Guyana, in northeast South America, has a slight majority (51 percent) of descendants of Hindu and Muslim indentured servants brought from the Indian subcontinent for plantation labor following the emancipation of the country's African slaves between 1834 and 1838. Most of the remainder of the Guyana populace consists of descendants of the former slaves, with small minorities of Native Americans and Europeans completing the plural pattern.

Following centuries of Spanish rule, Nicaragua joined four other Central American states in gaining independence in 1821, initially as part of the Central American Republic. Internal wars and authoritarianism predated this milestone, however. Guyana also was once on the colonial periphery, first by the Dutch and then by the English, who took control from the Dutch in 1803. The overriding aspects of English culture and law soon predominated. The Dutch institutions that managed to take root have either atrophied or were absorbed into British colonial structures. The old Dutch Court of Policy and the Combined Court, for example, were restructured "as legislative-cum-executive bodies into the British colonial framework."[4] Hence, today little remains of the Dutch influence in Guyana except a few place names and aspects of Roman Dutch law in the legal system.

Despite the obvious differences, there are also many similarities between Nicaragua and Guyana: the commonality of European colonization; their relatively small geographic and population dimensions; their economic dependence on the sale of primary extractive or agricultural products; and their surprisingly similar military usage and expenditures, both in percentage of gross national product (GNP) and on a per capita basis.[5] Moreover, of prime importance, at least during the twentieth century, both countries lie within the U.S. sphere of influence. Agriculture and raw materials are important export earners for both Nicaragua and Guyana, and both countries have suffered from severe economic mismanagement, poor credit, and brain drain. By the decade of the 1990s both countries were also experiencing infrastructural and societal atrophy. Decades of authoritarian and/or semiauthoritarian governance had also become standard in both Nicaragua and Guyana.[6]

By the end of the 1970s, both Nicaragua and Guyana had also suffered decades of authoritarian or semiauthoritarian rule that was stimulated by U.S. interventions—or Anglo-American in the case of Guyana. As will be seen, these regimes—the four-and-a-half-decade Somoza family regime in Nicaragua and more than two decades of government headed by Linden Forbes Burnham in Guyana—were notorious not only for their blatant violations of civil rights and civil liberties but also for their longevity, being among the longest-lived governments in the entire Americas. In Nicaragua the abusive rule produced a Marxist-led social revolution that was opposed by expensive covert and overt actions led by the United States. Both governments face a crisis in legitimacy, and both have been beset by major economic downturns since the late 1970s.

Democratization in Hispanic America: The Case of Nicaragua

The Council of Freely Elected Heads of Government

In November 1986 former presidents Jimmy Carter and Gerald Ford co-chaired a seminar at the Carter Center of Emory University. Participants included scholars on democratization and ten incumbent and recent heads of government from both Hispanic and non-Hispanic America. At issue was how to halt the pendulum that was swinging wildly between authoritarianism and electoral democracy, especially in Hispanic America, and what strategy should be pursued to reinforce the fragile flower of democracy when it sprouted or was replanted. A highly visible NGO specifically for this purpose was soon constituted as the Council of Freely Elected Heads of Government, with Robert Pastor, former director of Latin American Affairs on the National Security Council staff, as executive secretary. Limited assistance toward democratization soon was directed to Argentina and Haiti, and a decision was made to monitor the upcoming Panama elections.

A team for Panama assembled in May 1989 under the leadership of former presidents Carter and Ford made a sincere effort to implement free elections. Polling data gathered by CFEHG indicated high support from the Panamanian people and suggested an overwhelming opposition victory. This victory was not to be realized, however, because Manuel Noriega halted the ballot count when the electoral outcome became evident. Former president Carter could do little but to denounce this theft of the election and to request action by the Organization of American States (OAS). Although a disappointing experience, General Noriega's actions in Panama taught the CFEHG valuable lessons that would be most useful in future monitoring missions.

The Panama experience underscored four realities: (1) simply monitoring elections does not guarantee that the votes will be counted; (2) the acquisition of reasonably accurate voting lists, although a pre-election necessity, does not guarantee a free election; (3) even apparent opportunities to assemble, speak, and advertise one's candidacy are not guarantees of an open electoral process, although they too appear important to liberal democratization; and (4) there is no assurance that parties and candidates participating in the electoral activity will adhere to the electoral outcome, even when there is opportunity to count ballots at the polling site, which makes possible a quick count derived from early access to the ballots as well as accurate predictive data gathered from statistically determined key precincts. The quick count can play a pivotal role both in fraud detection and as a leveraging resource. Although all of these electoral precursors are important for producing a fair and accurate election, alone they cannot guarantee an honest and responsible electoral outcome if, as in the Noriega case, the de facto government does not honor the results of the vote.[7]

Convincing the Nicaraguan Revolutionaries

To ensure that future electoral observations were successful, it was imperative for the Carter Center to include adaptive and corrective measures in their next electoral monitoring mission. To avoid a replay of the Panama debacle, it was determined that all parties to an election must invite the monitors, appear willing to accept the process, and indicate a willingness to comply with its results. For a country to accept this intrusion into its sovereign affairs by NGOs such as the CFEHG and various IGOs, including the OAS and the United Nations (UN), they must perceive the process to be in their interest—and in the case of Nicaragua there were in fact reasons for both the leaders of the revolutionary government and the parties opposing it to perceive an internationally monitored election to be in their interest.

The opposition believed that a monitored election was the only way the government could be induced to relinquish power if it did in fact suffer an electoral defeat. It was also the only mechanism through which needed campaign equipment and supplies could be procured. Further, the physical presence of groups such as representatives from the Carter Center and other prestigious election monitors would provide some insurance against harassment by Sandinista ideologues. Overall the opposition was extremely pleased at the prospect of electoral observation by the Carter team. More important to the process, though, would be the willingness of the government to extend an invitation and present evidence of voluntary compliance with the electoral results, and especially to accept monitoring by a group headed by two former U.S. presidents. The Sandinistas were not only the leaders of a sovereign state that was exceedingly sensitive to intervention by the northern colossus, but they also were Marxist-oriented revolutionaries at best ideologically lukewarm to liberal or bourgeois electoral democracy. As this author was able to document in traveling from Managua to Bluefields and from San Carlos to Estelí on the eve of the 1989–1990 election, however, it was evident that Nicaragua was rapidly approaching economic collapse. The key to international electoral monitoring would be the level of economic vulnerability as perceived by President Ortega and his advisers.

Domestic production in Nicaragua had enjoyed a significant resurgence immediately after the end of the fighting phase of the revolution in 1979. By the end of 1980 food production had expanded by 10 percent and employment by 34 percent, and more than 12,000 landless families had been issued land allotments. Inflation had fallen from 84 to 27 percent. The popular mood appeared to parallel the propaganda poster: "*Con trabajo y sudor haremos una patria mejor*" (With work and sweat we will make a better country).[8] Then came the collapsing economy compounded by the U.S. embargo in 1983. By 1988 the official rate of exchange in Nicaragua was falling dramatically, dropping from 10 córdoba (C$) to the US$1 in February 1988 to C$250–US$1, and then to C$325–US$1 by mid-July, the fourth major devaluation in less than a month. By December of that year US$1 bought C$4,500, and by June 1989 the rate had tumbled to a disastrous C$26,250–US$1. Per capita output had fallen below that of Haiti![9]

By the late 1980s there was an obvious need for economic restructuring in Nicaragua, including technical assistance and a strong influx of capital. Growing uncertainties with ideologically oriented goals and artificially established cost parameters for the state-run factories, along with inadequate quality control in the manufacturing sector, were completely straitjacketing the economy. In the wake of an embargo pursued by the United States and a decade of costly proxy warfare with the contras that was funded by or through the Reagan and Bush administrations, Nicaragua had a desperate need for markets. It was also greatly in need of a resurgence of national and international confidence and political legitimation.[10]

Nicaragua's infrastructure was in shambles as well. Much of what had not collapsed from age and wear had been crippled in contra attacks or in the horrendous destruction of Hurricane Joan. In addition, economic difficulties in the USSR led to the loss of alternative aid from the Eastern bloc, and the USSR's renewed concentration on its own domestic crisis led to the loss of the support that had previously been engendered by solidarity with the Soviet and socialist causes. The government was indeed perceiving its vulnerability.[11] Thus the little-publicized promise by President Bush to renew U.S. trade and aid with Nicaragua if the Sandinistas would only accept international monitoring of their 1989–1990 general election by the Carter team and other IGOs significantly increased the likelihood that the government would accept international observers. One of Carter's discussions with the Sandinistas, in fact, focused on how an election that was considered fair by Washington would likely contribute to resumption of the U.S. assistance so long denied to the revolutionary country. "President Alfonsín and I and others can certify," Carter told Ortega in February 1989, "this [monitoring action] would almost ensure . . . an immediate improvement in relations between the United States and Nicaragua."[12]

In July 1989 the Carter Center sent Robert Pastor to Nicaragua for discussions about the potential for international observation of the upcoming election and about CFEHG procedures. The prestige of the CFEHG representatives apparently was perceived quite positively by the Sandinista government, and in early August 1989 President Ortega personally requested that the CFEHG join with the OAS and UN teams in monitoring from beginning to end the general election scheduled for February 25, 1990, in Nicaragua.[13] Thus both Ortega and the fourteen disparate groups that formed the opposition party coalition solidly agreed to international monitoring of the 1989–1990 election.

Voting out a Revolution

The monitoring groups would have to do more than simply implement procedural lessons learned in the Panamanian experience if open and free elections were to be successfully effected. In Nicaragua's favor was that the 1984 general election conducted after the 1979 revolution had been judged to be as fair as those in most Latin American countries by observer teams from groups such as the Latin American Studies Association (LASA)—despite allegations, especially by the Reagan administration, of Sandinista intimidation of opposition voters and candidates. Also in its favor was that seldom, if ever, was internal violence employed to the degree that it has been used in El Salvador, Guatemala, or Guyana (our second case study). However, because of the ongoing military conflict in Nicaragua, thanks largely to Washington, Nicaragua was still in the midst of civil war. The potential for the still-simmering military conflict to escalate made it imperative that the electorate and electoral officers accept the monitors and that the several monitoring groups engage in a cooperative effort.[14]

The CFEHG set up a permanent office in Nicaragua and engaged in five visitations, including one jointly led by President Raúl Alfonsín of Argentina and Jimmy Carter in September 1989. Their discussions with the Supreme Electoral Council reiterated assurances that the CFEHG's observer corps, plus those of the UN and the OAS, would have complete access to the entire electoral process. It was also established that they would receive copies of the final *actas* or vote tallies. A second CFEHG visit, led by former president Rafael Caldera from Venezuela and former U.S. governor Bruce Babbitt, was scheduled for one month later to coincide with and partially monitor the registration program then under way. The registration drive, conducted on each Sunday of October 1989, enrolled 1,752,088 people, or 89 percent of a total electoral population of 1.9 million. Former presidents Carter and Daniel Oduber (Costa Rica) visited Nicaragua in December on a mission that coincided with the party campaigning segment of the election that began in earnest in November 1989. In other visits Carter was accompanied by both Republican and Democratic senators from the United States and by Latin American political leaders such as Alfonso López Michelsen of Colombia.

By December it had become apparent that the monitoring mission would face ongoing security problems since it was now clear that the contra war, although under negotiation as a result of the peace plan of Costa Rican President Oscar Arias, would not be resolved prior to the election scheduled for February. An additional security problem flared with the expulsion of U.S. diplomats from Nicaragua following the December 20, 1989, invasion of Panama by the United States. As a conciliatory gesture prior to the election, however, the Ortega government released 1,190 Nicaraguan prisoners, many of whom were perceived as political prisoners by Washington. On the whole, campaign rallies were peaceful from the beginning to the end of the electoral period. The closing rallies for both the National Opposition Union (UNO) coalition and the governing Sandinista National Liberation Front (FSLN) attracted huge crowds (100,000–300,000). This reinforced polling data suggesting a very large voter turnout, perhaps as high as 85 percent.[15]

A CFEHG delegation of thirty-four arrived in Managua on February 23, 1990, to join with larger OAS and UN delegations in preparation for monitoring the actual balloting activity. Despite an initial reluctance to work in concert, the UN and OAS teams eventually complemented not only each other but also the Carter team. It was primarily the UN team, in fact, with assistance from a few members of the OAS team, that facilitated the crucial quick count, based on an 8 percent sample, that made possible an early prediction of the election. And it was the OAS group that collected copies of the tally sheets from every voting site in the country. "Had there been violence, a close vote, or any significant irregularity," writes one key member of the Carter team, "this operation would have been essential to sort out who had actually won."[16]

Despite a few irregularities generated by the continuing security problems—such as armed police being stationed at *Juntas de Receptoras de Votos* (JRVs), the registration and voting sites in the sensitive Region V (Chontales) and Region IX (San Carlos) districts—only 5 percent of the 4,383 JRVs experienced any problems and election monitors were able to provide quick counts from the statistically chosen sites in all nine regions. Based on data derived by the OAS and Carter teams, it was ascertained by 10:00 P.M. on February 25 that the UNO amalgamation had 56 percent of the presidential vote, and the FSLN approximately 40 percent. By the next day, with 70 percent of the official returns reflected, there was a 55–41 spread. Thus on April 25, 1990, the UNO-backed Violeta Barrios de Chamorro, widow of the popular publisher of *La Prensa* who had been slain during the Somoza regime, became the country's new president.[17] Chamorro was not a stranger to government; she had been part of the original junta but departed the revolution when she perceived its leadership veering sharply to the left.

Political Change and Economic Uncertainties

In a state as badly polarized as Nicaragua, it was remarkable that the balloting produced few instances of crisis. There was concern once when returns seemed to stall, but the fears were premature. A more serious moment may have occurred when, as the result of a misunderstanding, it was uncertain whether Daniel Ortega would bestow the presidential sash on the newly elected president. This concern, too, proved to be unfounded, although it did necessitate special negotiating skills on the part of President Carter and others on the CFEHG team.

Perhaps the most enlightening statement about the role of the three election monitoring groups in Nicaragua was one made by Robert Pastor, the executive secretary of CFEHG: "The international observers helped expand the boundaries of civility in a country filled with mistrust. The three groups would listen to UNO's charges, distill the hundreds of complaints down to the few that were most serious, and then take them up directly with the senior levels of the Sandinista government. In virtually every case, Ortega responded . . . and almost every issue was resolved." Suspicion had dominated the country's political history, but "in the early morning hours of 26 February 1990," Pastor writes, "the first tentative signs of a new spirit of conciliation and comity emerged in Nicaragua."[18] Before then the government and its opposition each believed the worst about the other and repeatedly acted in ways that helped to confirm those beliefs and justify mutual distrust. The extremes on both sides fueled this demeanor by exaggerating negatives and discounting positives.

The international monitors of the 1989–1990 election in Nicaragua exposed that nation to some positive activities and thinking. But the positive attitudes have yet to become internalized in this still-disillusioned country. In the words of a scholar who recently conducted field research there, Nicaragua remains a country in which an inordinate number of nationals feel a strong sense of victimization and betrayal, both those associated with the Chamorro government and those associated with the Sandinista opposition. This finding, which is verified by former Sandinista minister Father Miguel D'Escoto,[19] combined with ongoing sharp ideological divisiveness, intensifying class divisions, sporadic military activity (with perceived potential for renewal), economic uncertainties, and metropolitan neglect, especially from the United States—largely the result of an almost personal vendetta by Senate Foreign Relations Chairman Jesse Helms—make positive development in post–Cold War Nicaragua exceedingly difficult.

In 1995, just a year before the next scheduled election in Nicaragua, the U.S. Agency for International Development (AID) suspended funds for Ixchen, a Nicaraguan nongovernmental organization that has been offering alternative health services for low-income women since 1989. This resulted from pressure by Senator Jesse Helms in the United States and the right-wing Catholic organization *Opus Dei* in Nicaragua.[20] As the United States had intended, the war and a decade of economic embargo were very costly for Nicaragua.

Nicaragua's real gross domestic product (GDP) growth rate dropped to a negative level during the middle to late 1980s, a trend that has continued through every year since the 1990 election, with the exception of 1992, which reflected positive growth, although only 0.4 percent. Nicaragua's external debt, a manageable US$2.1 billion in 1980, ballooned to US$11 billion in 1996 and is the most difficult to manage of any developing country, according to the World Bank. The Nicaraguan Center for Human Rights (CENIDH) estimates that 75 percent of the nation now lives in poverty, with nearly half (44 percent) "living in extreme poverty." Some desperate and unemployed Nicaraguans are migrating, creating a crisis with neighboring Costa Rica. In the opinion of one specialist, "the strict application of the neo-liberal development model is the direct cause." And if these problems are not sufficient cause for distress, mid-1995 found the Nicaraguan legislature mired in a constitutional stalemate as the result of policy demands by internal factions, diplomats, and international lenders.[21]

The preceding assessment reveals mixed results for the hypothesis presented at the beginning of the chapter. There is little doubt that the monitoring activities have contributed remarkably to the legitimacy of the leaders of Nicaragua, both locally and internationally. Moreover, because of the international legitimacy, it is more realistic now to expect the necessary foreign economic support to help relieve the economic deprivation. The human rights situation, however, leaves much to be desired, partly because improvements in civil and political rights are closely related to improvements in economic and social rights—and the situation in the latter area has been unsatisfactory. Nicaraguans have few fond memories of either the final months of their experiment with socialist revolutionary democracy or of their current exposure to liberal democracy, in each instance largely as a result of the country's badly malfunctioning leadership and economy, and it is likely that the relatively positive growth rates during the Somoza regime or the euphoria of the early stages of the revolution will gain a renewed appeal, thus undermining the opportunities for liberal democracy afforded by the monitored election of 1990.

Rectifying Three Decades of Electoral Malpractice: The Case of Guyana

Cold War–Induced Authoritarianism

A second leadership change in the Caribbean Basin in the early 1990s—on October 9, 1992—also involved a Marxist leader. This time, instead of an electoral loss for revolutionaries, it was an opportunity for electoral victory for a revolutionary, Dr. Cheddi Jagan. Indeed, it was something of a vindication for Dr. Jagan, the twice metropole-deposed Marxist in the Cooperative Republic of Guyana. As in Nicaragua, there was opportunity for key assistance from the Carter Center and other NGO and IGO monitoring teams.

Jagan, a presidential candidate in 1992 at age seventy-four, has been a self-proclaimed Marxist since his student days in Chicago during the 1940s.[22] By 1945 he had organized the multiracial, independence-promoting Political Affairs Committee (PAC). Afro-Guyanese Forbes Burnham joined PAC in 1950 following his return to Guyana (then British Guiana). By 1951 PAC had been transformed into the People's Progressive Party (PPP),[23] soon to be a mass institution that was instrumental in electing a PPP government in 1953. This government was led by Jagan but included Burnham as minister of education, under the first constitution in the colony permitting full adult suffrage and modified home rule. Burnham became head of the colony's oldest and largest trade union, the British Guiana Labor Union (BGLU), following his return from law school in England. Both he and Jagan, who also headed a trade union, had brought their respective groups into the PPP.

The struggle had paid off, and independence was within sight under a government in which the leadership positions included members of both the country's Afro-Guyanese and its Indo-Guyanese populations. The Jagan-led government was toppled from power after only 133 days in office, however, due to the PPP's professed Marxist ideology and growing fear of communism in Britain and the United States in the wake of the newly dropped Iron Curtain. Britain, in executing this "coup" with strong supportive backing from Washington, also suspended Guyana's new constitution and imprisoned Cheddi Jagan for six months. His removal from organizational activities during much of 1954 was crucial in the breakup of the multiracial PPP. It encouraged the ambitious Burnham to break with Jagan to lead a largely Afro-Guyanese "Burnhamite" wing of the PPP that would compete against Jagan and the remaining mostly Indo-Guyanese "Jaganite" wing.[24] Thus instead of the benefits of a broad-based party that could crosscut the country's increasingly sharp ethnic and racial divisions, the party system that emerged reinforced the divisions. This pattern of institutionalized racial separation largely continued into 1992.

Despite this reversal, Jagan's now Indianized PPP managed to win an electoral majority in 1957 over Burnham's newly formed People's National Congress (PNC), and again this U.S.-trained dentist became the government's leader, albeit with the less important title of "chief minister" and with reduced constitutional authority. By 1961, however, Jagan's title again became "premier," and the office was accorded some additional powers. Despite the restrictions with which Jagan—still "unacceptable" to the metropole—was required to operate between 1957 and 1964, including travel restrictions imposed by the United States and several British Commonwealth colonies, his government's accomplishments were substantial: the first inventory of Guyana's considerable natural resources; a major expansion of Guyana's capacity to generate electricity; the establishment of the University of Guyana; the general enhancement of public education at all levels;

and a serious mixed-economy plan for development.[25] Such accomplishments were to serve him well in 1992.

But because of the Red Scare in the United States, continued fears of communism in the United Kingdom, and Jagan's increasingly hard-line position, he was once again pushed from power, this time by a collusion of American and British intelligence agencies that sponsored destabilization activities.[26] Between 1962 and 1964 violence, arson, and political and racial confrontations served to prevent Jagan from governing and helped to undermine his legitimacy during the twilight months of British colonialism. According to Vere T. Daly, this was a costly destabilization in which 176 persons were killed and 220 injured and 1,400 buildings were destroyed.[27] Finally, in 1964, in what has been called the last free election in Guyana prior to 1992,[28] a Colonial Office–induced referendum won voter approval, largely as a result of the period of sponsored destabilization. This referendum changed the constitution from a system of election used throughout the region and in the United States—based on single-member districts, which was viewed as favoring the PPP—to a system of proportional representation, which would favor the PNC. This change, and the manipulation of the process, effectively removed the PPP and Jagan from power for more than a quarter of a century.

An Undemocratic and Divisive Legacy

More urgent than the partisan advantage fostered by this constitutional change was the resulting damage to the state and the country's political culture. "The decision on the part of Forbes Burnham . . . to declare the ruling party paramount in its relationship to the state was particularly unfortunate" and resulted in "the establishment of a racially based dictatorship," concludes Selwyn Ryan.[29] His research demonstrates that the resulting institutionalized racism in Guyana is an equal opportunity destroyer, causing harm to all that it touches.

Ironically, the PNC government of Burnham was probably as socialist as Jagan's PPP government. Burnham's paramountcy brought increased authoritarian policies, plus racially divisive and liberty-restrictive values, with "membership of and loyalty to the PNC becoming the passport to office and to economic and social resources."[30] This paramountcy produced its own logic: If the party is all-important, it also is all-important that it prevail in election after election. This made it justifiable to taint every Guyanese election between 1964 and 1992: 1968; 1973; the referendum of 1978; 1980; and even the election at the end of 1985. The PNC's "anything-goes" election strategy contributed significantly to the accretion of serious cases of semiofficial violence in Guyana, which in turn seriously damaged the country's reputation.[31] The fraud became less blatant after the installation of Desmond Hoyte, who succeeded the deceased Burnham as president.[32]

But between 1962 and 1992 the PNC leadership utilized several electoral ploys, ranging from badly skewed voting lists to the stuffing of ballot boxes as they were being transported for counting, "assisted" voting for non-English-speaking constituents, and violent intimidation. Between 1991 and 1992 this author not only uncovered evidence of previous voter manipulation but also heard several accounts of violent intimidation. In conversations leaders of the Working People's Alliance (WPA), a multiracial party that then held a single parliamentary seat, recounted the stories of WPA workers and candidates who had met violent ends. The most notorious case involves the murder in 1980 of WPA founder Dr. Walter Rodney, a former University of the West Indies and University of Guyana history professor. There was never any public investigation into the circumstances surrounding Rodney's death during the Burnham and Hoyte periods, but by 1996 the Jagan government had announced plans for an inquiry. It was against this backdrop that the Carter Center was initially contacted by opposition leaders requesting participation by the CFEHG in the election then scheduled for 1990–1991. Before such activity could be initiated, however, the Carter Center also needed an invitation from the government.

President Hoyte and the Press: Harbingers of Change

Burnham's death in August 1985, purportedly at the hands of his own physicians while undergoing minor surgery, produced little initial hope for significant policy change among the most hard-pressed Guyanese. Desmond Hoyte, the incoming president, after all had just promised to adhere closely to the Burnham program. Further, only four months later Hoyte and his PNC government were returned to power in landslide numbers, winning forty-two of fifty-three seats in the December 1985 general election that many considered to be just one more unfree and unfair exercise. Official returns credited the PPP with just eight of the fifty-three elected seats. The PNC also controlled an additional ten appointive seats reserved for the regional districts, although Indians make up a majority of the Guyanese population and polling data indicated a majority of the voting-age electorate comprised PPP supporters. Two elected seats went to the United Force (UF) and one to the WPA.[33]

Nevertheless, it soon became apparent that President Hoyte was presenting a gentler face than his predecessor in relation to the openness of both markets and the political process. While Hoyte's detractors accused him of merely adapting to crisis, did not such adaptation represent "good" politics?

By the late 1980s there was simply no choice other than to adapt to the severe crisis at hand. Burnham's policies had failed miserably, not only in the area of human rights but economically as well. Despite the fact that Guyana has one of the most extensive resource bases in the Caribbean Basin, it had become nearly as beset as Nicaragua by massive inflation, a plummeting gross domestic product, and the inability to attract international loans.

Guyana experienced a protracted period of deficits during the 1970s, 1980s, and early 1990s that saw its per capita GNP of nearly US$800 in 1975 plummet to only $547 in 1988, the lowest in the Caribbean Community (CARICOM). The Guyanese dollar had also just been devalued 56 percent. The economy continued to suffer steady declines, registering minus 3 percent and minus 4.5 percent, respectively, in 1988 and 1989. By 1990–1991, the country's per capita GDP had collapsed to approximately US$300, and the *Economist* was placing Guyana in alleged competition with Haiti for being the poorest country in the Americas.[34] A status quo Guyana was increasingly untenable, especially after bankers and the U.S. government began making loans contingent on free and open elections. This author conversed with several businessmen from Guyana in Barbados and in Trinidad during 1991 who reported that their search for business loans had been repeatedly thwarted with the terse proclamation that there could be "no loans until free and fair elections were held." Thus President Hoyte had little choice but to attempt to secure the services of the Carter Center and the London-based Commonwealth Secretariat. Selling this to his government was difficult, but he convinced the PNC that endorsing such an invitation was in its long-term interest.

When Carter was invited to Guyana in October 1990, he forged an agreement on electoral reform. The agreement provided for a reasonably accurate voting list—within the 10 percent error range that had become a threshold for Carter—on-site counting of ballots, an end to overseas voting, and acceptance of in-the-field election monitors, including their presence, when required, in polling booths. These stipulations were placed under the direction of Rudy Collins, Guyana's newly appointed chairman of the Elections Commission—an appointment that represented a very solid act of presidential leadership, given Collins's reputation for integrity and independence. The general election date was established as December 16, 1991.

The election had to be postponed repeatedly due to difficulties in purging a very inaccurate registration list that remained more than one-third in error even in midcourse. Despite resistance, especially from the PNC hard-liners, the conditions were eventually met. And the implementation of this electoral democracy had been legitimated, especially for the large percentage of Afro-Guyanese who were generally associated with PNC, by the restructuring actions sanctioned by President Hoyte and Chairman Collins.

Resistance by the hard-liners in Guyana, as in so many of the least developed arenas of the world, hinges on the fact that those who have ruled for decades hate to expose themselves to the risk of stepping down. The most hard-line resisters in Guyana were Prime Minister Hamilton Green and, though to a lesser extent, former president Burnham's widow, Viola, and his son-in-law and the minister of health, Richard Van-West Charles. Here President Hoyte's leadership was strongly visible as he forced Van-West Charles from office, stripped the Burnham family of many perks, and reduced Green's portfolio to little more than responsibility for athletics. Randi Chandisingh, then general secretary of the PNC and a governmental vice president, also seen as an impediment to change, was dispatched to Moscow on diplomatic assignment.[35] Hoyte also responded positively in Guyana's negotiations with other governments and with the International Monetary Fund (IMF). His efforts to attract foreign investment achieved a higher level of cooperation with the United States, Venezuela, Britain, Canada, and the IMF, and he downsized the Guyanese government by eliminating seven ministries. In exchange, the United States forgave a portion of Guyana's debt.[36]

During this period of adjustment in Guyana the editorial policies of the government-owned *Chronicle* newspaper remained largely intact, in all probability because both Hoyte and his party needed its support in their forthcoming campaign. Yet, in general, the press in Guyana played an important role in the country's predemocratization. Foremost was the inauguration of the *Stabroek News* in September 1986, which, according to one Guyana specialist, probably contributed more to setting the stage for democratization than any activity Guyana had experienced in more than two decades. While both the state-owned *Chronicle* and the PPP's *Mirror* reflected their respective partisan positions, *Stabroek News* courageously offered an alternative perspective by making available uncensored space to opposition parties, preparing and publishing national surveys in 1991 and 1993 despite the temporary jailing of some pollsters, and publishing numerous letters to the editor. At the same time it presented some of the most balanced news in the region.[37]

At Last, a Free and Fair Election

The elections that were constitutionally due by 1990 had to be postponed nearly two years while electoral preconditions were implemented. As in Nicaragua, the Carter Center's CFEHG had established a permanent office in the capital following its official invitation to participate. It had strengthened its presence in Guyana with the appointment of George Price, prime minister of fellow CARICOM member Belize, as co-chair of the delegation and sent four delegations to Guyana during this lengthy delay. Of these official visits, none was more important than the first, led by Jimmy Carter, that defined and clarified the conditions and initiated the focus on Guyana's faulty elector list. In late March 1991 a team led by Price visited Guyana to monitor the registration process. A subsequent team led by former Costa Rican president Rodrigo Carazo concluded that the elector list remained badly flawed. Work associated with cleansing the list to meet the well-publicized announcement that the CFEHG could not certify a fair election unless the error level was reduced to an acceptable 10 percent was under the jurisdiction of the Guyanese Elections Commission. This level was finally achieved and accepted by all parties in August 1992, and on August 29 the election date was announced as October 5, 1992.

By this time sufficient structural changes were in place to make a fair election possible. Despite this progress many concerns and rumors surfaced as election day approached regarding the potential for sabotage of the electoral process or bringing about its overturn either by the pro-PNC Guyana Defense Force (GDF) or by the courts. There were also unsubstantiated rumors of a boycott by polling officials, and the hospitals were alerted to anticipate massive casualties, presumably from voter insurrections. Two particular activities designed to induce confusion were positively addressed by the Elections Commission. The first was an apparent alteration of the PPP-Civic coalition name on the official printed ballot to read only PPP. The second was an order to election officials that forbade election monitors from viewing ballot boxes or entering polling sites before the start of the balloting.

All that remained was for the Guyanese people to vote and for the sixty-five international monitors from Carter's CFEHG and the approximately equal number from the multinational Commonwealth delegation, plus small independent contingents from the CARICOM states, to earn the acceptance of the Guyanese electorate by demonstrating their sincere effort and their fairness.[38] Upon their arrival in Georgetown, the capital, CFEHG monitors and some representatives from the Commonwealth were briefed by Carter and his staff at a meeting to which leaders of the eleven competing Guyanese parties had been invited to discuss their concerns. Following a review of communications tactics, the monitors were dispersed to the field to begin their official duties.[39] In general, it was an orderly election on the polling day. The international monitoring teams were in place and there was a high turnout. More than 90 percent of the polling sites had at least three officials show up for the 6:00 A.M. opening, with only 2 percent reporting absences, dispelling the rumor reported by government radio and the official government paper that there would be a strike of polling officers. Nearly all who voted (93 percent) followed procedures approved by all poll watchers.

But there also were incidents of scattered violence connected with the balloting, including partially PNC-orchestrated mob action that erupted at two sites: in Linden, a bauxite mining town and PNC stronghold (named for Linden Forbes Burnham), and in Georgetown, where most of the violent demonstrators came from the lower income area called Tiger Bay. The Linden demonstration occurred nearly simultaneously with the action in Georgetown. In Linden, several hundred youthful protesters, led by a known PNC activist who was at least circumstantially linked with the disruption/protest tactics of Prime Minister Green, attacked polling officials, who fled to the police station, and trashed the office of the region's election commission, destroying furniture, equipment, and ballot boxes as they protested that Afro-Guyanese were being denied the right to vote.[40] The election monitor was able to negotiate a truce by securing authorization from election headquarters to extend voting privileges. The perpetrators in Georgetown included some alleged voters whose names were not on the revised electoral list. In addition to mobbing the election headquarters, there was looting of shops on several downtown streets.

In both Linden and Georgetown the potential election stoppage was averted and the clamor to disallow the election was defused by a quick response from Elections Chairman Collins along with effective action by elections monitors, especially President Carter. The former president displayed genuine courage and leadership in curtailing the mob activity in Georgetown, where the most persistent attack centered on the national election headquarters. When Carter was notified that the central elections office in Georgetown was under mob attack, its windows being smashed and the workers fleeing, he immediately interrupted a press conference and proceeded to the area under assault and helped to quell the action.[41]

A Positive Future?

The racially mixed government of Cheddi Jagan and the PPP-Civic coalition governs with thirty-six seats. Twenty-six seats were won by the PNC, with two for the WPA and one for the UF. None of the remaining smaller parties secured more than 0.5 percent. The international monitors found a common resolve to participate by a high percentage of voters throughout Guyana, with an election day turnout in excess of 80 percent. Once again it was the people who demonstrated the greatest tenacity and courage. As in Nicaragua, it is they who won in Guyana.

Most important for the survival of the fledgling electoral democracy in Guyana is the fact that during the 1990s major improvements are occurring in the economy, a reality that has not yet transpired in Nicaragua. Some credit for this economic growth must be given to President Hoyte; even though the economy bottomed out under his watch, it also began its ascent in 1991 under his rule.[42] Guyana's per capita GDP in current prices increased to US$500 in 1992, up by 8 percent from 1991, the highest growth rate among CARICOM states and third highest in Latin America. This growth continued in 1993, when at slightly more than 7 percent Guyana again was the highest in the subregion, with substantial output increases recorded for rice, gold, and timber. Indications of significant activity in the construction and distribution sectors suggest that these sectors also are "righting" themselves. Bauxite sales also climbed in 1993, although the world price for this commodity is depressed.[43]

Guyana now leads the CARICOM nations in per capita GDP growth. Its growth is anticipated to continue with expectations that inflation can be controlled. This positive activity, together with expected strong support from the Caribbean Community and metropolitan countries, makes continued movement toward economic development and increased democratization appear probable in Guyana. This is a very positive sign not only for democratization in Guyana but also for Jagan's leadership, which had a 70 percent approval rating, according to mid-1990s polling data.[44]

Reflections and Conclusions

In the spring of 1990 and the fall of 1992 there were changes of government and an opportunity for increased electoral democracy in two authoritarian or semiauthoritarian states that have rarely experienced electoral overturns or democracy. In the case of Nicaragua in 1990, it was change via an election that billions of U.S. dollars, countless injuries and thousands of sacrificed lives, and violations of civil and international law could not accomplish. In Guyana in 1992, it was the first regime change since the Cold War intervention by the United States and its British ally and the first free election in almost three decades. In one of the ironies of the Cold War, it returned to power a Marxist leader who had twice been removed from office and jailed by the metropole. As one newspaper appropriately headlined its column: "Doggedness? Toppled in '53, He's Top Dog Again."[45]

These case studies demonstrate the enormously important and cost-effective role of employing NGOs and IGOs to monitor crucial elections in authoritarian or semiauthoritarian systems and thereby to displace regimes by ballots rather than by bullets. Thus the major hypothesis of this chapter is tentatively proven: that monitoring activities by NGOs such as the Carter Center and appropriate regional and global IGOs not only help to provide international legitimacy but also represent an efficient and economical means for promoting electoral democracy and addressing human rights issues. This transpired in both Nicaragua and Guyana, two countries with incumbent governments that were authoritarian or semiauthoritarian in nature, each of which had experienced a pattern of U.S. or allied intervention, and each of which was severely affected by negative economic growth and a reluctance of regional lenders to provide loans, investments, and other financial supports.

One or two free elections do not produce deep democratization, of course. Democracy suggests a process in which there is openness, genuine "people power"; where there are guaranteed civil liberties, especially a free press, free speech, and the right to assemble without the intimidations that have considerable historical precedent in both Nicaragua and Guyana. These changes do not come easily, especially in societies in which there are large blocs of people who feel victimized. Such attitudes change slowly, especially in times of economic crisis such as now beset Nicaragua. Unless these economic constraints can be quickly ameliorated, the many sacrifices and progress of recent years might be for naught. Both countries have known more than their share of violence and metropolitan intrusion, but both now have the potential to enjoy political change that emanates not from force or threat of violence but from ballots cast freely and openly by ordinary people. Democracy, with all its imperfections, is a powerful check on any government. To paraphrase Winston Churchill, boring and inefficient though the process of democratic participation may be, it is still better than any other available form. This is change that is well deserved by the long-suffering citizenry of both Nicaragua and Guyana.

In sum, in both Nicaragua and Guyana there are now opportunities to install liberal democracy with free and open elections that involve the participation of a courageous electorate. It appears that an increase in positive attention and assistance from metropolitan governments would be beneficial in promoting its advancement and overall development, especially in Nicaragua. U.S. attention was riveted on much of the region when it had strategic value in the Cold War, but there is a strong possibility the Caribbean Basin will again fall out of the U.S. political radar scope in the post–Cold War era. Such a reversal would appear to be an unwise strategy for the stressful 1990s. In the end, however, both Nicaragua and Guyana must internalize their own long-term democratization and development options. Only when this is done will there be realization of true legitimacy.

Notes

1. See Guillermo O'Donnell, Philippe C. Schmitter, and Laurence Whitehead, eds., *Transitions from Authoritarian Rule: Prospects for Democracy* (Baltimore: Johns Hopkins University Press, 1986).

2. Samuel Huntington, *The Third Wave: Democratization in the Late Twentieth Century* (Norman: Oklahoma University Press, 1991), pp. 6–8. The definition of liberal democracy is enlarged by Dietrich Rueschemeyer, Evelyne Huber Stephens, and John D. Stephens in their *Capitalist Development and Democracy* (Chicago: University of Chicago Press, 1992), pp. 43–44 ff., to include "first, regular, free and fair

elections of representatives with universal and equal suffrage, second, responsibility of the state apparatus to the elected parliament (possibly complemented by direct election of the head of the executive), and third, the freedoms of expression and association as well as the protection of individual rights" that presumably include freedoms of association, of speech, and the enjoyment of a free press.

3. See W. Marvin Will, "Storms over Nicaragua's Caribbean Coast," *Caribbean Studies Newsletter and Notes*, vol. 15 (Winter 1989):4–6.

4. See Gordon K. Lewis, *The Growth of the Modern West Indies* (New York: Monthly Review Press, 1968), p. 258.

5. According to Ivelaw L. Griffith, "[o]ut of a list of the 23 largest defense spenders in the region in 1988, Guyana spent 14.6% of its gross national product (GNP) to support its military, making it second only to Nicaragua, which allotted 17.2% of its GNP for that purpose. . . . This militarization was not solely to meet actual and/or potential threats to the nation. Guyana [and Nicaragua are] . . . societies where political elites make little distinction between the security of the nation and the security of their own political regime[s]." Ivelaw L. Griffith, "The Military and the Politics of Change in Guyana," *Journal of Interamerican Studies and World Affairs*, vol. 33, no. 2 (Summer 1991):146.

6. See Evelyne Huber, "The Future of Democracy in the Caribbean," p. 88; Selwyn Ryan, "Structural Adjustment and the Ethnic Factor in Caribbean Societies," p. 140; and Jorge Domínguez, "The Caribbean Question: Why Has Liberal Democracy (Surprisingly) Flourished?" pp. 5, 10; all three in *Democracy in the Caribbean: Political, Economic, and Social Perspectives*, ed. Jorge I. Domínguez, Robert A. Pastor, and R. Delisle Worrell (Baltimore: Johns Hopkins University Press, 1993). In the late 1980s, however, Carl Stone categorized both Nicaragua and Guyana as equidistant between "democratic-populist" and "authoritarian." See his *Power in the Caribbean Basin* (Philadelphia: Institute for the Study of Human Issues, 1986), p. 64.

7. Council of Freely Elected Heads of Government (CFEHG), *Observing Nicaragua's Elections, 1989–1990*, Special Report No. 1 (Atlanta: Carter Center, 1990), pp. 9 ff.

8. Patricia Edmisten, *Nicaragua Divided: La Prensa and the Chamorro Legacy* (Pensacola: University of West Florida Press, 1990), pp. 108–109; and Peter Passell, "For the Sandinistas, Newest Enemy Is Hard Times," *New York Times*, July 6, 1989, p. A6.

9. Edmisten, *Nicaragua Divided;* Passell, "For the Sandinistas, Newest Enemy Is Hard Times." The Inter-American Development Bank (IADB), *Inter-American Development Bank Annual Report 1993* (Washington, DC: IADB, 1994), p. 2.

10. In an interview by the author in Tulsa, Oklahoma, in 1982, following a speech opposing U.S. aid to the contras, Alfonso Robelo Callejas, a wealthy businessman who was part of the junta that took over from Somoza, but then left it as it became authoritarian, reiterated his fear that civil liberties in Nicaragua would surely be curtailed if the war expanded, and electoral freedom would thus be forfeited.

11. Will, "Storms Over Nicaragua's Caribbean Coast," and Passell, "For the Sandinistas, Newest Enemy Is Hard Times."

12. "Carter Coaxing Nicaragua on Free Elections," *Atlanta Journal and Constitution*, September 17, 1989, p. A3. Carter may not have anticipated the ideologically

inspired blocking procedures pursued by Senator Jesse Helms, then minority leader of the Foreign Relations Committee, now its policy-controlling chair.

13. Robert A. Pastor, "Nicaragua's Choice: The Making of a Free Election," *Journal of Democracy,* vol. 1, no. 3 (Summer 1990):13–25.

14. This election would serve as a test of the Kirkpatrick thesis. Shortly before Ronald Reagan had appointed Jean Kirkpatrick his ambassador to the UN, she had generalized that left-wing countries neither democratized nor relinquished power via the ballot, while right-wing authoritarian states had the potential for both.

15. CFEHG, *Observing Nicaragua's Elections,* pp. 12–21.

16. Pastor, "Nicaragua's Choice," p. 18.

17. Though it is standard practice to assign responsibility for Chamorro's death to the late dictator, and certainly to the conditions he spawned, Edmisten (*Nicaragua Divided,* p. 9) quotes Edgar Chamorro, who acknowledges that it could have been the communists, or even the CIA.

18. Pastor, "Nicaragua's Choice," pp. 19–20.

19. Interviews by the author with Jan Urban, January 25–26, 1994, and with Miguel D'Escoto, November 10, 1994, both in Tulsa, Oklahoma.

20. The AID funding would have allowed Ixchen to expand into twenty-two rural areas where communities had begun to organize basic gynecological services and health training related to cancer and sexually transmitted diseases (it now has nine clinics). "Weekly News Update on the Americas," *Usenet News,* Issue #268, March 19, 1995. Factors in Nicaragua that have most upset Senator Helms are Sandinista control of the legislature in 1990 and the sense of obligation induced by this reality that led President Chamorro to retain General Humberto Ortega as head of the Nicaraguan Army, a post he relinquished on February 21, 1995.

21. "Nicanet Hotline," Nicaragua Network Hotline, *Usenet News,* February 13, 20, 27, and March 6, 13, 1995 (quote from Topic IV, March 13).

22. In 1982 this author asked Jagan how he, the son of relatively conservative Indian farmers, could have become a Marxist. "Ah," he replied, "it was your country that made me one. I was a student at Howard University when I experienced my first strong incidence of racism in the United States. This made me rethink some of my attitudes toward your country and its values. From Howard I went to Northwestern University's Dental School, and there an American exposed me to my first readings on Marxism. So my ideological migration was a made-in-the-USA phenomenon." The American "teacher" in question was Janet Rosenberg, who became Jagan's bride in 1943. Although still suspected of being a Marxist, Jagan advocates for Guyana a mixed economy that seeks Western investment.

23. Anthony P. Maingot indicates that, although open to all races and ideologies, the PPP, which espoused a tripartite emphasis on independence, labor, and socialism, had a decidedly Marxist orientation. Anthony P. Maingot, *The United States and the Caribbean* (Boulder: Westview Press, 1994), pp. 83–87.

24. Although Burnham accompanied Jagan to Britain in the aftermath of the "coup" to protest the 1953 suspension, he immediately began to undermine Jagan, according to his own account, avoiding imprisonment with help from the colonizer even as most of the PPP leadership faced incarceration. He promoted party (and increased racial) separation. A useful background on this period is found in Leo A.

Depres, *Cultural Pluralism and Nationalist Politics in British Guiana* (New York: Rand McNally, 1967).

25. See political biographies by Percy C. Hintzen and W. Marvin Will in Robert J. Alexander, ed., *Biographical Dictionary of Latin American and Caribbean Political Leaders* (New York: Greenwood Press, 1988), pp. 227–230.

26. Arthur Schlesinger, Jr., who in the 1960s was a cold warrior in the Kennedy White House, has admitted to his role in the second toppling and extended an apology to Cheddi Jagan in the June 4, 1990, issue of *The Nation*. Photocopies of this apology were widely used by Jagan in his 1992 campaign.

27. Vere T. Daly, *A Short History of the Guyanese People* (London: Macmillan Education, 1975), pp. 13–21.

28. Baytoram Ramharack, "National Opinion Polling and Surveys in Guyana," *The Round Table*, vol. 332 (October 1994):433–434.

29. Ryan, "Structural Adjustment," pp. 140–143; and interview by the author with George "Ken" Danns, Georgetown, Guyana, January 1992.

30. Ryan, "Structural Adjustment," p. 140. See also Andrew Graham-Yooll, "Guyana: The Newspaper *Stabroek News*," *The Round Table*, vol. 332 (October 1994):448–449.

31. This is the view of George "Ken" Danns (interview by the author, Georgetown, Guyana, January 1992), whose research data reflects a 7–10 percent annual escalation in homicides during the 1980s. Though certainly the economy was a significant contributor, this author believes that much blame may be assigned to PNC policy.

32. See Graham-Yooll, "Guyana: The Newspaper *Stabroek News*," pp. 448–449.

33. Griffith, "The Military and the Politics of Change in Guyana," p. 150; Georges A. Fauriol, "Guyana: Government and Politics," in *Guyana and Belize: Country Studies*, ed. Tim Merrill (Washington, DC: Library of Congress, 1993), pp. 119, 314. See also Graham-Yooll, "Guyana: The Newspaper *Stabroek News*," p. 449.

34. Though reported per capita GDP for Guyana and Haiti (and also Nicaragua) may have become roughly similar in 1989—and even in 1990, when GDP fell an additional 3.3 percent—Guyana was still well ahead of Haiti in infrastructural positioning and in political and socioeconomic institutions in place (IADB, *Annual Report 1993*, p. 2).

35. Ivelaw L. Griffith, "Conflict Reconciliation in Guyana" (paper presented to the thirty-sixth annual conference of the International Studies Association, Chicago, February 21–25, 1995), pp. 4–5.

36. Ibid.

37. Ramharack, "National Opinion Polling," pp. 435–438; see also Graham-Yooll, "Guyana: The Newspaper *Stabroek News*," pp. 451–454.

38. The CFEHG monitoring group included government leaders, former ambassadors, academics, and journalists, among others, from the United States, the Commonwealth, Latin America, and the Caribbean. I sensed strong support for CFEHG when lecturing at the University of Guyana in January 1992. A typical student response was that the Carter Center had achieved more in Guyana in just a few months than had previously been achieved in years.

39. Assignment of monitors to polling sites did not appear to be on an entirely random basis. For example, Carter, Price, and other dignitaries tended to be assigned

to key urban districts, and anthropologists who were specialists on Native American issues were dispatched to areas populated primarily by Amerindians.

40. "PNC Says Hammy Supporters Were Disorderly," *Stabroek News* (Guyana), January 15, 1993, p. 1.

41. W. Marvin Will, "Carter Observes Guyanese Election," *Washington Report on the Hemisphere,* vol. 12, no. 24 (October 21, 1992):1, 6–7. In the words of fellow election monitor Ambassador Angier Biddle Duke at the reception hosted by the United States, British, and Canadian embassies after the balloting, "the election monitoring and reconciliation missions being conducted by former President Carter may be his most important work."

42. Hoyte also negotiated with the IMF for needed capitalization that was delivered in 1993 in the form of IMF loans equivalent to SDR17.72 million—or US$25 million. *IMF Survey,* "Guyana: Enhanced Structural Adjustment Facility," January 25, 1993, p. 23.

43. Caribbean Development Bank (CDB), *Annual Report 1993* (St. Michael, Barbados: CDB, 1994); and IADB, *Annual Report 1993.*

44. Ramharack, "National Opinion Polling," pp. 442–445.

45. Howard W. French, "Doggedness? Toppled in '53, He's Top Dog Again," *New York Times,* November 3, 1992, p. A5.

5

Drugs and Democratic Governance in the Caribbean

Ivelaw L. Griffith and Trevor Munroe

The Caribbean drug phenomenon revolves around four separate but related issues: drug production; consumption and abuse; trafficking; and money laundering. These and the problems they precipitate are regionwide but not uniform; they are problematic for the entire region but are not manifested the same way throughout the region. They also are multidimensional, with ripple effects on almost all aspects of life in the region. This phenomenon presents threats and challenges that extend beyond the economic, social, or security arenas to democracy itself. As one respected scholar has observed, "[i]t endangers the capacity of the democratic state to uphold the rule of law because of its corrupting influence on the state apparatus and because of the widespread resort to violence by those involved in the drug business."[1] Yet there are critical challenges to democracy other than corruption and violence involved,[2] as the analysis of the nexus between drugs and democracy in this chapter illustrates.

Drug Operations in the Caribbean

Production and Consumption/Abuse

The three main "danger drugs" in the Caribbean are cocaine, heroin, and marijuana. However, only marijuana is produced there, and it is not cultivated throughout the region. Cultivation also varies from place to place. Belize, Guyana, Jamaica, St. Vincent and the Grenadines, and Trinidad and Tobago are among the countries with the highest levels of marijuana production. Belize and Jamaica have had the highest levels of production and export of marijuana. In both countries, marijuana has at times been the largest cash crop, once producing some US$350 million annually in Belize and about US$2 billion in Jamaica.[3]

Marijuana is cultivated mostly in the north and west of Belize, in small plots of about one acre or less. By the early 1980s Belize was the fourth largest supplier to the United States, behind Colombia, Mexico, and Jamaica. But production has plummeted since 1985, largely due to counter-measures by the Belize government, often under pressure from the United States. Most of the marijuana that is discovered is destroyed immediately by aerial eradication, or by hand where it is in close proximity to residences or to legitimate crops. The U.S. Department of State reported in 1994 that "Belize, once the fourth largest producer of marijuana in the world, has reduced production to negligible levels through an aggressive aerial eradication campaign."[4] Nevertheless, Belize halted aerial eradication in January 1995 because of environmental concerns. According to the 1996 *International Narcotics Report* marijuana seizures in 1995 totaled 2.8 metric tons, down from the 1994 figure of 4.8 metric tons. However, 135,216 marijuana plants were destroyed, a dramatic increase over the 1994 figure of 10,751.

Jamaica's subtropical climate makes the entire island ideal for cannabis cultivation. *Ganja*, as marijuana is popularly called there and elsewhere in the Caribbean, traditionally is harvested in two main annual seasons of five to six month cycles. However, the *indica* variety matures in three or four months, making four harvests possible. Large-scale cultivation of five-to-fifty acre plots were once common, but because of eradication measures, most cultivation is now done in plots of one acre or less, with yields of about 1,485 pounds per hectare.

As in Belize, the marijuana eradication agenda has been driven largely by U.S. efforts to deal with drug source countries as part of its supply-side strategy. Most of the eradication has been done under a program called Operation Buccaneer. The results of Operation Buccaneer have been quite uneven. Only 456 hectares of marijuana were destroyed in 1993, far short of the goal of 1,000 hectares. The eradication shortfall is partly the result of diminished resources for eradication and new strategies adopted by cultivators. On the latter issue the national security minister reported to Parliament in 1993 that the eradication program "has driven ganja farmers to new tactics: they now interplant ganja with other crops and grow the herb in almost inaccessible places."[5] The 1996 *International Narcotics Report* states that in 1994 some 692 hectares of marijuana were destroyed, and in 1995, 695 hectares.

Aerial spraying of ganja in Jamaica is more controversial than in Belize because marijuana is an even larger source of income there. One estimate for the 1980s placed the number of farmers cultivating the crop at 6,000. During that same decade, ganja was once said to have contributed between US$1 and $2 billion to Jamaica's foreign exchange earnings, surpassing all other exports, including bauxite, sugar, and tourism.[6] The United States complained in 1994 that "for environmental reasons and because of political opposition, the GOJ [Government of Jamaica] has failed to accept the alternative suggested by the USG [United States Government] of eradication by aerial spraying."[7] In commenting on that statement one Jamaican official indicated that Jamaica will continue to spray only young plants and nurseries. Otherwise there is a high risk of contaminating legitimate produce and groundwater supply.[8]

Economic pressures, the lucrativeness of the drug market, and the "balloon effect" of countermeasures in Belize, Jamaica, and Latin America are among reasons that other Caribbean countries have taken to significant marijuana production (and export). One gets a sense of the increased production elsewhere in the region by tracking the frequency and size of plots destroyed. In Grenada, for example, 10,862 plants were uprooted in 1992, 9,323 in 1993, and 20,000 in 1994. Police officials there indicated that the high-cultivation areas are Grand Etang, St. Andrew, St. David, St. Patrick, and Upper Homitage. These are in the central part of the island, which has mountainous terrain. They are also in rural areas where there is high unemployment and many abandoned sections of land, all of which drug operators exploit.[9]

In Dominica, 11,880 plants were destroyed in 1992, 11,140 in 1993, and close to 49,000 in 1994. The 1995 figure was 126,000. In St. Lucia, 87,760 plants were reportedly destroyed in 1992, with a dramatic increase in 1993 to 181,500. The 1994 figure was 81,923, and in 1995 the number almost tripled to 235,000. Still in the Eastern Caribbean, St. Vincent and the Grenadines eliminated some 2 million ganja plants between October 1991 and February 1992. The figure for 1993 was a mere 12,000, but with the seizure of 881 kilograms of marijuana in 1994, the 1995 *International Narcotics Report* called St. Vincent and the Grenadines the Caribbean's second largest producer of marijuana, after Jamaica. According to the *International Narcotics Report* for 1996 a combined eradication mission carried out with U.S. air support in February and March 1995 resulted in the eradication of 7 million marijuana plants and the destruction of some 8,000 pounds of processed marijuana.

Guyana has two features that are accommodating to the conduct of all sorts of clandestine activities: its physical geography and its population density of four people per square kilometer, one of the lowest in the world. It is therefore surprising that major marijuana cultivation did not begin there before the late 1980s. Marijuana seizures haven taken place mostly in the Demerara-Mahaica, Mahaica-Berbice, and East Berbice–Corentyne regions, in the northeastern and eastern parts of the country. One of the largest seizures recently was in July 1994 in the Mahaica area, where ninety-four acres of the crop were destroyed. The following month the same area was raided, and more than fifty acres of marijuana were destroyed.[10] Military intelligence sources indicate that marijuana cultivation is also undertaken in the Cuyuni-Mazaruni, Upper Demerara–Berbice, Essequibo Islands–West Demerara, and the Upper Takatu–Upper Mazaruni regions, in west-central, east-central, northern, and southwestern Guyana, respectively.[11] In 1995 about 100 hectares of marijuana were eradicated and 10.9 metric tons of the product were destroyed.

Trinidad and Tobago police officials indicated that most of the country's ganja cultivation is done in the forested northern and central ranges and along the coast.[12] As in Guyana and elsewhere in the Caribbean, joint police-army operations are the center of eradication and confiscation countermeasures. The 1996 *International Narcotics Report* indicated that over 5.4 million metric tons in mature trees were eradicated in Trinidad and Tobago in 1995—compared to 0.8 million in 1994—and 1,634 kilograms of cured leaf were destroyed—compared to 3,977 kilograms in 1994. Elsewhere in the Caribbean, ganja cultivation takes place in the Dominican Republic, French Guiana, Montserrat, St. Kitts-Nevis, and Suriname. There is variation in the size of plots cultivated. In some places, ganja production is primarily for domestic use, but in most, the product is also exported.

The problem of narcotics consumption and abuse in the Caribbean involves mainly marijuana and cocaine, with heroin becoming problematic in some places. Drug consumption and abuse in the Caribbean are not limited to any single social class or economic or ethnic group, although the consumption of certain drugs is higher in certain groups. Marijuana, for example, is predominantly a working-class drug of choice. Crack cocaine is widespread among lower and middle-class people because it has the attributes of being "hard" and a "status" drug, yet it is cheap. Heroin, on the other hand, is a rich man's drug. Apart from the cost factor, the impact of heroin abuse in the region has been mitigated by what one Bahamian psychiatrist called a Caribbean "needle phobia."[13] However, there is concern in many parts of the region that the ingestible liquid heroin that is now available in parts of Latin America will spread to the Caribbean.

Like drug production, drug use differs from place to place. The greatest concern is in Jamaica, the Bahamas, Dominican Republic, Guyana, Trinidad and Tobago, and in parts of the Eastern Caribbean. Although marijuana is abused in many places, it has had a long history of accepted socioreligious use, dating from the introduction of indentured workers from India following the abolition of slavery. Indeed, the word *ganja* is itself a Hindi word.[14] Marijuana's socioreligious use pattern has changed over the years. This use is now associated primarily with the Rastafarians, Afrocentric social-religious sects that identify with the late Ethiopian emperor, Haile Selassie. Hence the socioreligious use pattern is found in places with large numbers of Rastas, including Jamaica, Guyana, Trinidad and Tobago, and Grenada. Quite important, though, not only Rastas use ganja.

Cocaine abuse in the Caribbean results largely from the illicit cocaine trade. Crack cocaine is also readily available in many places. According to the United Nations International Drug Control Program (UNDCP), evidence of crack production in the Caribbean first came from Trinidad and Tobago. This problem is found mainly in the principal transit states: the Bahamas, Jamaica, Belize, Dominican Republic, Guyana, and Trinidad and Tobago. Needless to say, cocaine addiction can lead to singularly devastating acts, as in Guyana, where a thirty-year-old deranged crack addict murdered six people, including his own mother, in one swoop in a cutlass attack on December 9, 1994, at Buxton-Friendship, a village along the Atlantic Coast.[15]

Trafficking and Money Laundering

Apart from trading their own ganja in the United States, some Caribbean countries are important transshipment centers for South American cocaine, heroin, and ganja bound for Europe and North America. For more than two decades the Bahamas, Belize, and Jamaica dominated this business, but recently Barbados, Dominican Republic, Guyana, Haiti, Trinidad and Tobago, and Eastern Caribbean countries have featured more prominently.

In Barbados, for instance, a joint army-police interdiction operation on July 4, 1992, confiscated over 2,000 pounds of marijuana, worth about B$6 million, and arrested two Barbadians and one Canadian with arms and ammunition. Later that month 26.5 kilograms of cocaine, worth about TT$35 million, were seized at Cali Bay, Tobago, following transshipment from Venezuela. Three couriers were caught in 1993 trying to use Barbados to transport Colombian heroin from Venezuela to Europe. In January 1993, 2,761 pounds of cocaine—worth some US$17 million—were seized in St. Vincent following a raid on a family residence in Glamorgan, just outside Kingstown. In Antigua, over 150 kilograms of cocaine bound for the United Kingdom were seized on a private boat in the spring of 1994.[16]

In Guyana 1993 cocaine seizures were 1,000 percent higher than in 1992, amounting to 463 kilograms. In 1994 the amount dropped to 80 kilograms, and still further in 1995 to 51 kilograms. However, this certainly does not mean that less trafficking occurs; it indicates only that less is being seized. On January 4, 1995, 5,000 pounds of marijuana valued at US$2 million were discovered behind a false fiberglass wall of a container about to be shipped from Georgetown to Miami.[17] Trinidad and Tobago had its biggest single cocaine seizure on June 10, 1994, when a 41-foot cabin cruiser bound for Antigua, the *Aquarius,* was intercepted with 226.2 kilograms of cocaine—worth an estimated US$18 million—in plastic fuel drums. Three

Antiguans were arrested and later indicted on conspiracy and trafficking charges.[18] Between January and November 1995 authorities in Trinidad and Tobago seized 110 kilograms of cocaine—compared to 311 kilograms in 1994—and arrested 246 people for trafficking.

In the U.S. Virgin Islands 860 pounds of cocaine worth about US$10 million were seized on August 25, 1994. The same month, two seizures in St. Martin netted 2,185 pounds of cocaine, and two months later fishermen found 1,766 pounds of cocaine on a small uninhabited island between St. Barthelemy and St. Martin. In November 1994, 1,320 pounds of cocaine were seized in Guadeloupe. Also in November 1994, 121 pounds of cocaine were found in the home of the two sons of the deputy prime minister of St. Kitts-Nevis at the time, Sidney Morris. This discovery was followed by a series of events that affected the elites' ability to govern in that state.[19] (This is discussed in more detail later.)

The geography of the Bahamian archipelago makes it an excellent candidate for drug transshipment, given its 700 islands and strategic location in the airline flight path between Colombia and South Florida. Anthony Maingot once observed: "In a way, geography had always been the Bahamas' main commodity, and they had always marketed it with great skill."[20] This, of course, is true of other countries as well. When the Bahamas first became a transshipment center, the drug involved was mainly marijuana, with a few consignments of hashish. Evidence dates drug trafficking as far back as 1968, when 250–300 pounds of marijuana were flown from Jamaica to Bimini. One of the earliest cocaine seizures was made in 1974: 247 pounds of pure cocaine, with a 1974 street value of US$2 billion, at an airport in George Town, Exuma. The same year, the Bahamas police discovered off Grand Bahama a store of marijuana over six feet high and more than two miles long.[21]

The geography and topography of Belize also make that country ideal for drug smuggling. There are large jungle areas, sparse settlements, and about 140 isolated airstrips that facilitate stops on flights from South America to North America. Moreover, there is virtually no radar coverage beyond a thirty-mile radius of the international airport at Belize City. Recently, though, there has been an increasing use of maritime routes. Crack has also been featuring more prominently. According to the 1994 *International Narcotics Report*, "for the first time [in 1993], there was evidence of Belizean export of crack cocaine to the United States." Cocaine seizures in 1995 totaled 840 kilograms.

Several features of the Dominican Republic also make that country a prime trafficking candidate: proximity to Colombia, the Bahamas, Puerto Rico, and the southern United States; a long, often desolate, border with Haiti; and poorly equipped police and military authorities. The scope of their problem is reflected in the fact that in 1993, the country's National Anti-Drug Directorate, supported by the navy, seized 1,073 kilograms of cocaine, 305 kilograms of marijuana, 1,444 grams of crack, and other drugs. Also confiscated were 183 vessels, 222 motorcycles, and 164 firearms. These were the results of 812 antidrug operations in which 5,635 people were arrested. In 1994 the seizures were 2.8 metric tons of cocaine—a 160 percent increase over 1993—and 6.8 metric tons of marijuana. Arrests numbered 3,000. In 1994 about 3.6 metric tons of cocaine were seized.[22]

Jamaica has long been key to the drug trade, given its long coastline, its proximity to the United States, its many ports, harbors, and beaches, and its closeness to the Yucatan and Windward Passages. Trafficking takes place by both air and sea. Marijuana seizures in 1993 were 75 metric tons, up from 35 metric tons the previous year. The actual amount of cocaine seized in 1993 was 160 kilograms, down from a 1992 high of 490 kilograms. The 1992 figure was exceptional because of one dramatic operation in which 412 kilograms were confiscated. Heroin and hashish oil continue to be transshipped, with confiscations of the latter amounting to 235 kilograms in 1993. There were 1,416 arrests in 1993, an increase over the 1,149 arrests made in 1992. According to the 1995 *International Narcotics Report*, 179 kilograms of cocaine, 47 kilograms of hashish oil, and one kilogram of heroin were seized in 1994, and 886 people were arrested for trafficking. The amount of cocaine seized in Jamaica in 1995 was 571 kilograms, triple the 1994 amount.

Money laundering is another aspect of the narcotics phenomenon. The countries known to be implicated are Aruba, the Bahamas, the Cayman Islands, and Montserrat. Indeed it is partly the money laundering "reputation" of the Caribbean that made Anguilla the choice for Operation Dinero, a major money laundering sting operation that began in January 1992. By the time the operation ended in December 1994, American and British authorities had seized nine tons of cocaine and US$90 million worth of cash and assets, including expensive paintings, one of which was Pablo Picasso's *Head of a Beggar*. They also made 116 arrests and gathered a wealth of intelligence on worldwide drug operations.[23]

There is also evidence of Puerto Rican involvement. According to the U.S. Department of State, one major cocaine/heroin group in Puerto Rico laundered over US$7 million through casinos. Drug money is also said to be "structured" using United States postal money orders sent to Colombia.[24] Apart from Aruba, where Aruban Exempt Corporations (AECs) and bank secrecy are said to have facilitated massive money laundering,[25] most of the money laundering allegations point to the British dependencies. A 1989 study by Rodney Gallagher of Coopers and Lybrand revealed some telling reasons for this development. According to the Gallagher Report, over 525 international financial companies have had offices in one of these territories, the Cayman Islands. The Caymans accommodated forty-six of the world's fifty largest banks, including Dai Ichi Kangyo and Fuji, Japan's two largest banks; Bank America; Barclays of the United Kingdom; Swiss Bank Corporation; and Royal Bank of Canada. Banking sector assets in 1987 were US$250 billion.

The Caymans and other dependencies provide many incentives and benefits for doing business there. The Caymans, for example, have no income, corporate, or withholding taxes. Hence there are no international double taxation treaties. Companies that operate mainly outside the Caymans can register there as nonresident companies or incorporate as exempt companies, with the ability to issue bearer shares to nonresidents, and thus avoid disclosure of beneficial owners. In addition, bank secrecy is guaranteed under the 1976 Preservation of Confidential Relations Act. The offshore financial industry itself is critical to the economic security of the Caymans, having grown to US$360 billion since the 1980s. It provides one-third of the jobs in the Caymans and about the same proportion of their gross domestic product.[26]

Anguilla, another dependency, was home to 2,400 registered companies in 1988, including 38 banks and 80 insurance companies. The inducements are freedom to move capital without exchange controls, no domestic taxes, minimum disclosure requirements, and the availability of professional services. The British Virgin Islands (BVI) has a tax regime, although a light one. They had 13,000 companies registered in 1988. Although the BVI now have only six major banks, money launderers reportedly use their services extensively. However, BVI and U.S. authorities have been able to obtain vital bank records and to freeze drug-related money. In 1991, for example, over US$3 million were transferred to the United States for forfeiture and sharing between the United States and the BVI.[27]

Hence the observation by two investigators into the BCCI debacle about how the Cayman Islands have been caught in the money laundering matrix is an indictment that, unfortunately, is applicable elsewhere in the Caribbean as well: "Beneath the veneer of respectability carefully polished by the big banks with offices there, the islands thrive on three principal commodities: money laundering, money from drug sales and other criminal activities, and illegal capital-flight. . . . The criminal element simply slid in comfortably behind the reputable corporations and used the same mechanisms for their own ends."[28]

Part of this assessment is reflected in the fact that several Caribbean countries continue to be placed high up on the money laundering "hot list" published in the *International Narcotics Report*. The 1996 report placed Aruba, Cayman Islands, and Netherlands Antilles in the "high priority" category; Antigua, the Bahamas, Belize, Dominican Republic, Montserrat, and St. Vincent and the Grenadines in the "medium priority" and "medium-high priority" categories; Cuba and Trinidad and Tobago in the "low-medium priority" category; and Anguilla, Barbados, Bermuda, Haiti, Jamaica, and several Organization of Eastern Caribbean States (OECS) countries in the "low priority" category.

From Liberal Democracy to Narco-Democracy?

Performance of Liberal Democracy

To appreciate some of the actual and potential dangers to Caribbean democracy of the operations described in the preceding sections and the problems they generate, we need first to review the background and status of democracy in the region. The discussion here applies essentially to the Commonwealth Caribbean.

The 1994 Freedom House rankings place 91 percent of the anglophone Caribbean states in the "free" category and the remaining 9 percent in the "partly free" category.[29] This distribution places the CARICOM region significantly above the global average and reconfirms the anglophone Caribbean as one of the most developed zones of democracy in the modern world. Relative to other states, Caribbean states have over the last fifty years been exceptional in the consistency of fair and free elections, the observation of political rights and civil liberties, competitive party systems, and the rule of law.

The formal institutions, political behavior, and cultural values of democratic governance therefore have relatively deep roots and a long tradition in the Commonwealth Caribbean. Liberal democracy emerged in the aftermath of popular protest in the 1940s and 1950s. The period of decolonization saw the consolidation of the system based on a version of party clientelism and state welfarism that generally improved the standard of living of the people and facilitated the upward social mobility of the underclasses. On this foundation, the postcolonial state, democracy, and constitutional government retained significant legitimacy and performed fairly effectively until the early 1970s.

Between the Black Power Revolt in Trinidad in 1970 and the implosion of the Grenada Revolution in 1983, significant social sectors in the region turned toward radical left alternatives, within and outside the framework of liberal democracy and market-driven economies. The successive administrations headed by Michael Manley in Jamaica (1972–1980), the People's Revolutionary Government in Grenada (1979–1983), and the Forbes Burnham government in Guyana represented the highest development (and deformation) of these tendencies.

This turn to the left was influenced by the reality as well as the perception in the 1960s that democratic governance and state interventionist market economies in the region had deepened rather than reduced economic and social inequalities. In this context, the underclasses, the black majority, and the youth benefited less than minority social sectors from the economic growth and social development in the postwar period. Dissatisfaction led to social protest and civil commotion. Reinforced by a global context friendly to anti-imperialism and statism, socialist currents in the Commonwealth Caribbean showed a relative vitality not far out of step with significant similar tendencies in the Third World of the 1970s.

In the early 1980s, however, a combination of factors caused majority opinion to shift away from left radicalism; important among these were worsening economic conditions, heightened internal social-political conflict, and an international climate increasingly hostile to statism of whatever variety and aggressively promotive of economic liberalization. The International Monetary Fund (IMF) structural adjustment agreements and World Bank stabilization programs initiated in the 1970s became generalized throughout the Caribbean in the 1980s.

This return to market-driven economics and the rejection of socialism has been accompanied by a mixed record of performance. In general, rates of economic decline were reduced, low-income employment increased, rates of inflation dropped, and party political tension and confrontation abated. At the same time, social expenditures fell, debt grew, external aid steadily declined, and, most important, inequalities again deepened by the end of the 1980s. In sum, under both left and right dispensations since the early 1970s, the people of the Commonwealth Caribbean have experienced either no significant improvement or declines in living standards and some deterioration in the quality of life.[30]

Within this general framework, there has nevertheless been some differentiation between the performance of the larger Commonwealth Caribbean territories and the smaller states, particularly those within the OECS. The latter have done relatively well in comparison to the former in relation to growth, inflation, unemployment, and indebtedness. For example, in 1990 the territories that experienced double-digit inflation were Jamaica, Trinidad and Tobago, and Guyana. In the same year, these more developed countries (MDCs), including Barbados, also experienced overall negative growth, while the lesser developed countries (LDCs) continued to experience moderate growth. Debt service ratios in the latter were well below 5 percent whereas in the more populous territories they averaged 20 percent.

Post–Cold War democratic governance in the Commonwealth Caribbean can therefore be said to have arisen on a mixed foundation. On the one hand, the region's people have actively participated in over 100 national elections based on universal adult suffrage and given varying degrees of support to over 130 parties and movements in the period of decolonization and postcolonial development. Military rule has been unknown; revolution and

extraconstitutional changes of administration were confined to Grenada between 1979 and 1983; the only coup attempts were in Dominica in 1981
and in Trinidad in 1990; and one-party regimes are rare.

Moreover, competitive party systems and constitutional government as
well as popular attachment to freedom and justice survived and did relatively
well into the end of the 1980s. At the same time, so did a larger number
of IMF and World Bank programs per capita than perhaps in any other region in the world. Hence while popular expectations of the state and of the
political system remain relatively high, the role of the state has changed and
its capacity to deliver has declined. Concurrently, the private sector is dis-
playing, at best, a mixed record in taking the lead in bringing about economic growth with social equity. In this context, democratic governance in
the Commonwealth Caribbean, long institutionalized and deeply legitimated, is undoubtedly in a state of malaise and very probably in a process of
decay.

One clear indicator of malaise and possibly of decay is the state of the electoral process in the region. Traditionally, rates of voter turnout have been
among the more important measures of confidence in the effectiveness of
the Caribbean political system and of the faith of the people in the capacity
of government to perform. Conversely, significant declines in rates of electoral participation often signal trouble and on occasion, in specific circumstances, a turn to nonelectoral forms of manifesting popular disaffection.
Thus, for example, in Grenada, the turnout in the 1976 election (65.3 percent), the eve of the 1979 popular insurrection, was significantly below rates
of participation in elections going back to the early 1960s, and below the average participation in elections from the inception of universal adult suffrage. In Trinidad and Tobago, the Black Power Revolt of 1970 was preceded by elections in 1966 in which turnout was lower than in any previous
election save the first vote under adult suffrage in 1946.

In this context, popular participation in national elections across the
Commonwealth Caribbean reveal a remarkably uniform pattern, despite the
continuing diversity from one territory to another. In thirteen of the eighteen territories in which general elections were held in the 1990s (up to December 1996), voter turnout has registered a decline in comparison to the
average for the 1980s.[31] In Jamaica the decline in turnout in the March
1993 election represented almost 30 percent of the average turnout in the
elections held during the 1980s, whereas in Grenada the equivalent of 20
percent of the 1984 electorate did not participate in the 1990 vote. In other
territories the decline has been noteworthy but less dramatic.

The significance of this incipient trend increases when examined against
the turnout profile in the period of modern political development in the region. With few exceptions across the region, rates of participation in the
1980s were lower than in the 1970s. In only two territories—Grenada and

St. Vincent and the Grenadines—did participation peak in the 1980s. In nine others participation peaked in the 1970s, and in one—Trinidad and Tobago—it did so during the 1960s. In other words, electoral turnout in the Commonwealth Caribbean has been on the decline from the decade of the 1980s and the trend has continued into the 1990s. In fact, the average turnout across the region so far in this decade appears lower than that of forty years ago when adult suffrage and democratic elections were new to the Caribbean and popular involvement relatively limited.

Were data for the entire region readily available they probably would reveal other trends, consistent with declining voter turnout, which have certainly been confirmed. In the Jamaican experience, nonregistration levels, particularly among the youth, have increased; the age cohort from which election candidates and members of Parliament are drawn is rising and becoming increasingly out of step with the profile of the electorate. Among those who do participate in elections, voting on the basis of party loyalty has declined dramatically. Public interest in parliamentary proceedings has dropped significantly and the frequency of parliamentary sittings leaves much to be desired. Undoubtedly, the inability of the state, under conditions of significant downsizing and of economic liberalization, to deliver levels of welfare typical of the 1950s, 1960s, and 1970s is undermining both its effectiveness and legitimacy.

Dangers to Democracy

It is against this background of a debilitated state system and the increasing magnitude of the drug phenomenon that the dangers of narco-democracy in the region become real. The 1992 report of the West Indian Commission put it this way: "Nothing poses greater threats to civil society in CARICOM countries than the drug problem[s]. The damage . . . to democratic society itself—from the drug problem[s] is as great a menace as any dictator's repression. . . . CARICOM countries are threatened today by an onslaught from illegal drugs as crushing as any military repression."[32]

These assessments are supported by other appraisals. U.S. government evaluations, dating back to at least the 1986 Anti–Drug Abuse Act, held that "[o]f the many threats which the international drug trade poses the greatest is its almost unlimited capacity to corrupt legitimate political institutions."[33] The United Nations Development Program (UNDP) sees the narcotics trade not only as a danger to political institutions but also as "one of the most corrosive threats to human society."[34] Clearly, political, economic, and social institutions are threatened when drug money can be used to bribe or eliminate, depending on their perspective, customs officials, police officers, prison guards, politicians, ministers, judges, bankers, jurors, witnesses, prosecutors, and, not least, voters. Inherent in this situation is the emergence of a new "powder elite" and the possible transition to what has been appropriately designated "narco-democracy."

Such dangers are hardly far-fetched in a CARICOM context in which the decline in economic and political performance of state and private sector elites, from the popular standpoint, is dissolving the postwar social order, undermining the hegemony of the post-independence middle strata, and opening up space for the emergence of drug dons and "powder elites" to share, take, or corrupt power. The impact of drugs on democracy becomes more obvious when one considers some recent episodes affecting different levels and segments of state power in the region.

Police and Constituency Politics

Corruption can be described as endemic. It permeates all ranks . . . corruption . . . also includes the protection of drug dealers, their supplies and their supply routes. This is where the corrupt core of the police service get its money. At the top is direct participation in crime or, more specifically, drug racketeering . . . police officers have been involved in the importation of cocaine in growing marijuana, in transporting drugs, and selling them. . . . [35]

The recent admission concerning drug-related criminal elements by Edward Seaga, Jamaica's leader of the opposition and a former prime minister, is revealing: "I have no control over these persons, no control whatsoever. . . . I have no intention of presiding over any area in which people can tell me that they are not listening to what I have to say when I have the moral right to tell them that, and I have no reason to stay in a constituency in which people are being brutalized by men who are totally out of control, with a massive police station right in the middle of the whole thing."[36]

The connections exist with various drug gangs. For example, one police intelligence report noted the following about the Jamaica Gang in Eastern Kingston:

A very sophisticated group seemingly with political connections. Its aim is to acquire most if not all the business community in Eastern Kingston. Whenever its offer of purchase for any business . . . is refused, the business is systematically plagued with robberies, burglaries, and general intimidatory tactics by this group . . . betrays . . . an interest in political office . . . their threat level bordered on national security concern.[37]

The police intelligence report indicated that the Cassie or Aallo gang was "a politically affiliated group, financed mainly from the proceeds of its robberies, drug distribution and trafficking." Of the Maverly Crew or Patrick Mouth gang it said: "highly political in nature . . . financed mainly by robberies and political handouts . . . their threat level was high, bordering on national security."[38]

Major Political Parties and Political Elites

The point has been made in one of Jamaica's leading newspapers that the People's National Party (PNP) "is deep in debt, owing about J$33 million to various creditors, according to informed sources. . . . There were also rumors that the JLP [Jamaica Labor Party] was flat broke."[39] In St. Kitts-Nevis there is evidence to suggest that both major parliamentary parties are connected to drug money. Moreover, government ministers have been implicated in or convicted for involvement in the illicit drug trade in Antigua-Barbuda, the Bahamas, Montserrat, and the Turks and Caicos Islands.

The 1994 St. Kitts-Nevis experience mentioned earlier dramatized some of the dangers to democracy at several of the levels noted in the preceding sections. Particularly since 1993 people in the leadership of the People's Action Movement (PAM), which ruled the country from February 1980 to July 1995, and of the St. Kitts Labor Party (SKLP), which won power in July 1995, have been connected to people known to be involved in the drug trade.

In the 1980s the ambassador to the United Nations, Dr. William Herbert, had been implicated in money laundering and drug trafficking. In July 1994 Herbert and his family disappeared mysteriously at sea. There was strong suspicion of foul play related to drugs. On October 1, 1994, Vincent Morris, one of the sons of Deputy Prime Minister Sidney Morris, disappeared along with his fiancée, Joan Walsh. Later they were both found murdered—in the trunk of a burnt vehicle abandoned in a cane field. The following month, two other sons of the deputy prime minister were arrested for trafficking 121 pounds of cocaine and for the possession of illegal weapons. They were also implicated in the murders. In the interim, on October 13, Superintendent Jude Matthews, head of Special Branch—the agency that protects top government officials—and the chief investigator into the murders, was himself assassinated on the way to work.

The Morris brothers were granted bail after arraignment. A public protest and a prison riot ensued as a result of the perception that the family and political connections of the Morris brothers influenced the granting of bail, manifestly violating equal treatment norms. Sidney Morris was forced to resign as deputy prime minister. The prison riot resulted in the complete destruction of the central prison and the escape of over 150 prisoners, necessitating the invitation of troops from the Regional Security System (RSS) to help restore order.

Given the erosion of public confidence, the PAM government was forced to concede to a call by the opposition SKLP and a coalition of civic groups for new elections within a year. The elections were held on July 3, 1995—three years before the government's term of office was due to end. The opposition SKLP was victorious, winning almost 50 percent of the popular vote and seven of the eleven elected legislative seats. Predictably, a major issue in the elections campaign was the escalation of narco-crime and drug-related violence in the country and the perceived complicity of government officials in drug trafficking.

At the same time, the leadership of the SKLP, which formed the new government, was not without its own skeletons in the closet. In May 1993, for instance, just six months before the controversial November 1993 general elections, Noel "Zamba" Heath, a long-standing business partner of both Dr. Denzil Douglas and Sam Condor, SKLP leader and deputy leader, respectively, was arrested and charged with illegal possession of drugs and ammunition. Heath subsequently pleaded guilty to the illegal weapons charges and was fined. Hence in St. Kitts-Nevis drugs have tarnished the credibility of the country's leadership and contribute to the erosion of confidence, all of this clearly undermining good governance.

Policy Issues in the "War Against Drugs"

It is clear that the "war against drugs" is being lost both in the region and on a global basis. On this there could hardly be a greater consensus amongst scholars, government bodies, multilateral agencies, and informed journalists. The reasons are fundamental and have to do with ill-conceived priorities and a gross inadequacy of resources devoted to the drug problem. Consideration of several aspects of policy clearly reveal these shortcomings.

Inadequate Focus on Demand Reduction   From time to time U.S. policymakers voice recognition of the centrality of reducing U.S. demand for illicit drugs. For example, at the special UN General Assembly Session in February 1990, Secretary of State James Baker acknowledged that "curbing domestic consumption [of drugs] was the most critical challenge" facing the United States. He noted that as long as demand for drugs by Americans remained voracious, his country would face an endless, uphill struggle to halt supply. "American users act as paymasters to organized murderers. Profits from every kilo of cocaine bought in the streets of America buy bullets that rob democracies of their dignity and freedom."[40]

This declaration was neither matched by deeds, nor was it consistently articulated. Instead, the number of illicit drug users continues to grow in the United States, and the 1994 *International Narcotics Report* notes that "rampant cocaine use, which was once a peculiarly American phenomenon, is now a world-wide scourge." According to the UNDP, "The real solution has to lie in addressing the causes of drug addiction—and in eradicating the poverty that tempts farmers into drug production. As long as the demand persists so will the supply."[41] Yet anticrime legislation in 1994 in the United States allocates relatively limited resources to the balance between demand control and law enforcement.

Along with perverse prioritization, demand reduction mechanisms and strategies in the Caribbean have hardly attracted the resources on the scale necessary to address the consumption/abuse problem. For example, the Integrated Demand Reduction Project in Jamaica has achieved good results and is regarded internationally as a model for demand reduction programs. Yet this project and other associated programs attracted US$4.3 million in aid between 1989 and 1993 from the UNDCP, AID, and the European Community. This is approximately 1 percent of Official Development Assistance (ODA) received by Jamaica in 1993, and 2.5 percent received in 1992.[42] It is no wonder, then, that this program with all its potential is only able to touch fifteen communities nationally. A major policy goal should therefore be the formation of coalitions and networks nationally, regionally, and hemispherically to give central priority to demand reduction, both in the United States and in the Caribbean. Some such coalitions and networks exist, but they give more attention to the supply side, at the expense of the demand side.

Resources and Capability According to the U.S. General Accounting Office, in fiscal year 1993 the U.S. Congress approved $147.8 million for worldwide narcotics control. This was reduced to $100 million in fiscal year 1994. At the United Nations, the budget for drug control projects was approximately US$82 million, made up of voluntary contributions from seventeen major donor nations. Clearly, the drug control programs are grossly underfunded. Renewed effort should be put into greater resource allocation, for otherwise there can be no truly significant impact. The UNDP assessment is obviously correct: "Despite the magnitude of the threat, the international community has yet to produce a coherent [and adequately funded] response."[43]

Legislation providing for asset seizure and forfeiture already exists in a number of CARICOM states, including Jamaica, Antigua-Barbuda, the Bahamas, Barbados, Dominica, St. Kitts-Nevis, and St. Vincent and the Grenadines. Other states must be encouraged to introduce such legislation. And, more important, the legislation must be used by the relevant agencies. Efforts to professionalize the police forces and to reform criminal justice systems should be accelerated. Existing Joint Information Coordination Centers (JICCs) need to be strengthened. Most of all, in the post–Cold War context, the proposals by A.N.R. Robinson and Michael Manley for an international narcotics court and an international antinarcotics strike force should be revisited. Given the importance of all these initiatives, the need for adequate resource allocation is all too obvious.

Substitution and Decriminalization   The Jamaican South West St. Ann Agricultural Rehabilitation Project, begun in 1988 with funding from the European Community, has been successful in providing alternative income-earning activity for ganja farmers. A new grant proposal, *Alternative Systems for an Illegal Crop*,[44] which would have an impact on the lives of thousands of ganja farmers in a range of rural parishes, should be pursued urgently. Though earnings from substituted crops are not as high as those from cannabis cultivation, the removal of the risk factor in the context of aggressive ganja eradication programs has made substitution attractive to farmers, and hence more crop and income substitution programs are needed.

As for decriminalization, particularly of marijuana, a task force should be established with Caribbean and hemispheric, including U.S., participation to review the decriminalization option. Persuasive arguments and advocates exist for and against decriminalization, with supporters and opposers coming from ranks that one would normally not expect. For instance, conservative economist Milton Friedman is one of many people supportive of it. On the other hand, Charles B. Rangel, a liberal Democratic member of Congress from New York, opposes it.[45]

Politically, it may not now be a feasible option for the region. Certainly the hostile response of the U.S. policymaking community to the decision of the Colombian Supreme Court to decriminalize possession of "personal doses" of narcotics suggests that any level of legalization may well be a nonstarter. However, this option should be kept on the back burner, if not put on the agenda, particularly if the "war on drugs" continues to be so obviously futile and if the necessary massive infusion of resources is not forthcoming for integrated demand control and/or increased law enforcement. One interesting version of this—a more oblique, less confrontational approach—now being attempted by the Ernesto Samper administration in Columbia is to negotiate surrender settlements with the "dons," whereby cartels are dismantled in return for relatively light prison sentences.

Political Reform and Economic Remodeling

The goal should be to strengthen the independent capability and popular accountability of political parties and state institutions. For this goal to be achieved and for Caribbean democracy to be better insulated against corruption by drug money, several reforms must be considered, including some public funding for bona fide political parties and election campaigns; laws and regulations requiring some degree of transparency in the sources of party finance; the diffusion of power into more independent legislatures and judiciaries, and the populace; and electoral reform to facilitate more representative parliaments while avoiding the danger of unstable coalition governments. In this regard there is an urgent need in all CARICOM states for strategic elites to become more familiar with the wealth of material and experience accumulated in recent years on reengineering constitutions and political systems in pre- and postcrisis situations. Should reform be either cosmetic or, if radical, too long delayed, Caribbean democracy will sink into deeper malaise.

There is, finally, a need for a redesigned economic model that better combines several factors: growth in production with social equity, the downsizing of the state with its strengthening, export orientation with production for the domestic market, and economic growth with social equity. On this redesign depends largely the increased levels of human development and the social well-being that can provide a sounder foundation for coping with drugs and for promoting economic democracy.

Conclusion

In the final analysis, human development and social well-being, in the Americas as well as globally, are indivisible. Both the people and the political elites in the United States should appreciate that, as sure as night follows day, renewed waves of illegal migration to the United States and Caribbean narcocrime in U.S. cities are among the inevitable consequences of a continued failure to make the necessary policy shifts to deal effectively with the drug phenomenon. For many people in the United States the impact of Caribbean drug problems is merely collateral, but to the people of the Caribbean, the impact is direct. Our analysis suggests that drugs present some clear and present dangers to democracy in the Caribbean.

Notes

1. Evelyne Huber, "The Future of Democracy in the Caribbean," in *Democracy in the Caribbean,* ed. Jorge I. Domínguez, Robert A. Pastor, and R. Delisle Worrell (Baltimore: Johns Hopkins University Press, 1993), p. 83.

2. For discussions of drug-related corruption and violence, see Ron Sanders, "Narcotics, Corruption, and the Smaller Islands," *Caribbean Affairs,* vol. 3, no. 1 (January-March 1990):79–92; Ivelaw L. Griffith, "Drugs and Security in the Commonwealth Caribbean," in *Size and Survival: The Politics of Security in the Caribbean and the Pacific,* ed. Paul Sutton and Anthony Payne (London: Frank Cass, 1993), pp. 70–102; and Anthony P. Maingot, *The United States and the Caribbean* (London: Macmillan, 1994), pp. 142–162.

3. Scott B. MacDonald, *Dancing on a Volcano* (New York: Praeger, 1988), p. 89.

4. U.S. Department of State, *International Narcotics Control Strategy Report* (Washington, DC, April 1994), p. 137. Hereafter, this document is referred to as *International Narcotics Report*.

5. Government of Jamaica, Parliament, *Presentation of the Hon. K. D. Knight, Minister of National Security and Justice*, Budget Sectoral Debate, July 15, 1993, p. 19.

6. MacDonald, *Dancing on a Volcano*, p. 90.

7. *International Narcotics Report* (April 1994), p. 197.

8. Interview by Ivelaw Griffith with Captain Douglas Edwards, military intelligence officer, Jamaica Defense Force, Up Park Camp, Jamaica, December 19, 1994.

9. Interview by Ivelaw Griffith with Assistant Police Commissioner Maurice Darius and Superintendent Ray Raymond, head of the Special Service Unit, Fort St. George Police Headquarters, Grenada, July 11, 1994; and *International Narcotics Report* (various years).

10. Mohamed Khan, "Four Held in $720M Mahaica Marijuana Bust," *Stabroek News,* July 28, 1994, pp. 1, 24; and "Cops Raid Mahaica Marijuana Fields," *Stabroek News,* August 23, 1994, p. 1.

11. Interviews by Ivelaw Griffith with Winston Felix, Assistant Commissioner of Police (Crime), Eve Leary Police Headquarters, Georgetown, June 28, 1994; and Lieutenant Colonel Edward Collins, Chief of Military Intelligence, Guyana Defense Force, Camp Ayangana, Georgetown, June 30, 1994. The 1995 figure is from *International Narcotics Report* (March 1996), p. 175.

12. Interview by Ivelaw Griffith with Commissioner of Police Jules Bernard, Police Headquarters, Port-of-Spain, July 8, 1994.

13. Interview by Ivelaw Griffith with Dr. Nelson Clark, Doctors Hospital, Nassau, the Bahamas, December 21, 1994.

14. See Vera Rubin and Lambros Comitas, *Ganja in Jamaica* (Garden City, NY: Anchor Books, 1976), p. 16.

15. Ronald Waddell, "Deranged Man Murders Mother, Five Others," *Stabroek News,* December 10, 1994, p. 1; and Waddell, "'Baby Arthur' Was a Crack Addict," *Stabroek News,* December 11, 1994, pp. 1, 24.

16. Janice Griffith, "$6M Ganja Haul," *Sunday Sun,* July 5, 1992, p. 1; "Trinidad and Tobago Police Make Big Cocaine Seizure," *Stabroek News,* July 29, 1992, p. 7; "Cops in US$12M Cocaine Timehri Haul," *Stabroek News,* September 12, 1992, p. 1; and UNDCP, *Subregional Program Framework for the Caribbean 1994–1995*, Bridgetown, Barbados, October 1994, p. 8.

17. See *International Narcotics Report* (1994), p. 189; Alim Hassim, "Marijuana Container Valued at US2M," *Stabroek News,* January 6, 1995, p. 1; "Three Charged for Trafficking," *Stabroek News,* January 16, 1995, pp. 1, 24; and *International Narcotics Report* (1996), p. 175.

18. Sherrie Ann de Leon and Rita Taitt, "T&T Biggest Drug Haul Seized at Sea," *Sunday Express* (Trinidad and Tobago), June 12, 1994, p. 3; Robert Alonzo, "Third Antiguan Charged with Trafficking in 'Coke,'" *Trinidad Guardian,* June 14, 1994, p. 1; and *International Narcotics Report* (1996), p. 195.

19. See Kenneth Anderson, "$10M Coke Haul off St. Thomas," *St. Croix Avis* (USVI), August 27, 1994, pp. 3, 23; Daniel Hierso, "Two Bodies Found in St. Martin," *Daily News* (USVI), November 2, 1994, p. 7; Lisa Ham, "St. Kitts Scandal Re-

flects Regionwide Drug Problem," *Daily News,* November 21, 1994, p. 7; and "U.S. Investigates St. Kitts Drug Scandal," *St. Croix Avis,* November 22, 1994.

20. Anthony P. Maingot, "Laundering the Gains of the Drug Trade: Miami and the Caribbean Tax Havens," *Journal of Interamerican Studies and World Affairs,* vol. 30 (Summer-Fall 1988):168.

21. Government of the Bahamas, *Report of the Commission of Inquiry into the Illegal Use of the Bahamas for the Transshipment of Dangerous Drugs Destined for the United States,* Nassau, 1984, pp. 7–8.

22. *International Narcotics Report* (1994), pp. 184–185; *International Narcotics Report* (1995), pp. 168–169; and *International Narcotics Report* (1996), p. 170.

23. *International Narcotics Report* (1995), p. 483.

24. *International Narcotics Report* (1994), p. 513.

25. See Claire Sterling, *Thieves' World* (New York: Simon and Schuster, 1994), pp. 230–231.

26. *International Narcotics Report* (1991), pp. 366–367. See also Steve Lohr, "Where the Money Washes Up," *New York Times Magazine,* March 27, 1992, pp. 27 ff.

27. *International Narcotics Report* (1991), pp. 367–368; and *International Narcotics Report* (1992), pp. 421–422.

28. Jonathan Beaty and S. C. Gwynne, *The Outlaw Bank* (New York: Random House, 1993), p. 113.

29. See "1994 Freedom Around the World," *Freedom Review,* vol. 25, no. 1 (February 1994):6, 20.

30. For a discussion of political and ideological changes in the Caribbean since the 1970s, see Ivelaw L. Griffith, *The Quest for Security in the Caribbean* (Armonk, NY: M. E. Sharpe, 1993), pp. 217–242; and Anthony Payne and Paul Sutton, "Introduction: The Contours of Modern Caribbean Politics," in *Modern Caribbean Politics,* ed. Anthony Payne and Paul Sutton (Baltimore: Johns Hopkins University Press, 1993), pp. 1–27.

31. See reports of directors of elections for CARICOM states. See also Patrick Emmanuel, *Governance and Democracy in the Commonwealth Caribbean: An Introduction* (Cave Hill, Barbados: Institute of Social and Economic Research, 1993).

32. *Time for Action: Report of the West Indian Commission* (Black Rock, Barbados, 1992), pp. 343, 351, 352.

33. *International Narcotics Report* (1994), p. 3.

34. United Nations Development Program, *Human Development Report 1994* (New York: Oxford University Press, 1994), p. 36.

35. Scotland Yard report on drug corruption in the Trinidad and Tobago Police Service, excerpted in *Trinidad Guardian,* December 1, 1993, pp. 9–10.

36. Edward Seaga in an interview on the "Breakfast Club," *KLAS FM89,* Wednesday, September 28, 1994 (published in the *Herald* September 30, 1994).

37. Excerpts from Intelligence Report, Commissioner of Police, Jamaica, in *The Sunday Gleaner,* October 2, 1994, p. A8.

38. Ibid.

39. *The Daily Gleaner,* October 20, 1994, p. 1.

40. *UN Chronicle,* June 1990, p. 57.

41. *Human Development Report 1994,* p. 37.

42. Planning Institute of Jamaica, *Economic and Social Survey 1993*, Kingston, 1994, chapter 26.

43. *Human Development Report 1994*, p. 37.

44. Government of Jamaica, Ministry of Agriculture (in collaboration with Rural Agricultural Development Authority), *Alternative Systems for an Illegal Crop*, Kingston, 1994, p. 7.

45. For a discussion on this subject, see *Time*, May 30, 1988, pp. 22–28; Chester N. Mitchell, *The Drug Solution* (Ottawa, Canada: Carleton University Press, 1990); and Ethan A. Nadelmann, "Drug Prohibition in the United States: Costs, Consequences, and Alternatives," in *Drugs, Crime, and Social Policy*, ed. Thomas Mieczkowski (Boston: Alwyn and Bacon, 1992), pp. 299–322.

PART B

Case Studies

6

Democracy and Human Rights: The Case of Cuba

Damian J. Fernandez

Contrary to the popular perception that Cuba's political system remained unchanged in the midst of global transformation, the mid-1980s brought significant changes in state-society relations on the island. Not only was the relationship between the island and its benefactor, the Soviet Union, redefined, contributing to a dramatic tailspin of the economy, but also in the domestic arena agents of change coalesced outside of the state's purview. This development marked a watershed in the history of Cuban socialism. The first human rights association and its precursors became key political actors, not because of any physical attributes or access to material resources, but as a result of their ability to accrue less-tangible resources and pursue particular strategies that have guaranteed their survival.

Since the mid-1980s the human rights groups have been instrumental in sparking a small but steady and unprecedented chain reaction of independent group formation inside the one-party system. In doing so, the human rights activists planted seeds of civil society and called into question, at least symbolically, the entire political system. Cuba is a valuable case through which to study the relationship between human rights and democracy. Part of its value stems from the theoretical and methodological difficulties in approaching the topic given the particularities of the Cuban regime. The point of departure, the connection between democracy and human rights, is fraught with conceptual challenges, not least of which is the question of how to incorporate socialism in this dyad. One possibility is to approach the topic from the perspective of socialism, democracy, and human rights. To do so is to recognize that the praxis of socialism (if not the theory) has been in most cases quite different from the experience of liberal democracies (however wide the spectrum of the socialist regimes and traditional liberal democracies has been).

The inclusion of socialism by necessity must be grounded in the actual structures and practices of the Cuban version. Any other approximation of the topic that deals with the theoretical rather than the historical dimension of the issue would be of interest but off target if the aim is to find out how a particular state has faced a challenge that many other states have faced in the late twentieth century. Democracy and human rights present difficult definitional challenges, as does socialism. Scholar after scholar have approached the concepts, generating a myriad of definitions from which to choose.[1] In this chapter I will employ a simple definition: Human rights, whatever else they might include, must incorporate a respect for the individual's prerogative to exercise civil political rights—such as the free expression of ideas and participation in sociopolitical groups of their choosing—without state reprisal.

A minimalist and partial, yet broad, interpretation of democracy is also useful for my objective in this chapter. I will argue that civil society—defined as autonomous social groups that are positioned between the individual and the state—is a requirement and a characteristic of contemporary democracy regardless of the specific trappings of the democratic system.

The approach of this chapter will be that of state-society relations in a transnational context—that is, how the state (meaning here the legal framework and the bureaucracy, including the leaders) has acted on and reacted to the issue of human rights. The focus will be on the challenge posed by the human rights actors and how the state has responded to it. The interplay between the state and the society is dynamic, contesting and shaping social relations and social values. The process of contestation takes place in an internationalized setting, which brings external forces to bear on the state and domestic social actors. In examining human rights from the perspective of state-society relations several levels of analysis are considered: the personal (human rights activists), the subnational (human rights groups), the national (the legal and political structures governing human rights), and the international (other governments, international organizations such as the United Nations and Amnesty International, and the international human rights regime).

Although in theory and in practice human rights groups may be differentiated from opposition organizations, in the case of many authoritarian regimes the line separating one from the other is blurred. In the Cuban case, the government perceives human rights associations as inherently counterrevolutionary, labeling them "*grupusculos*" (a pejorative term meaning small groups). Not all of these groups have defined themselves as political opposition, some casting themselves rather as defenders of the civil and political rights of individuals. Yet parallel to and largely as a result of the human rights groups, budding political associations such as political parties have sprung. They frequently share leadership and ideological perspectives.

In this chapter I argue that the human rights groups in Cuba, albeit small and fragmented, have been a pivotal force in the political development of the island. They constitute an emerging social movement that is a vital part of an embryonic civil society. In spite of the difficulties encountered, the movement has succeeded. First and foremost, it has been able to survive. Second, and intimately related to the first factor, it has become internationalized. The contribution of the human rights movement goes beyond breaking the official monopoly of the state and state-linked institutions in the political sphere. Human rights groups are changing the rules of the political game by injecting a measure of civility into the political praxis of civil society. Moreover, they have offered the possibility for many citizens to regain agency by participating in a grassroots movement.

In tracing the interaction between the state and the human rights groups, I first present a brief sketch of the legal context in which the issue is being contested. A historical analysis of the evolution of the human rights movement follows. Thereafter, I analyze the state's response to the movement and the contribution of the human rights groups to political change, and possibly democratization, on the island.

The Legal Context

At first glance, the Cuban Constitution, the supreme law of the land passed in 1976 and reformed in 1992, seems to guarantee a host of civil and socio-economic rights (such as the right to assembly and the right to work) that few other documents claim for the citizens. Under scrutiny, however, the constitution reveals a central contradiction that impinges not only on the theoretical conception of human rights but also on the political praxis of the state.

The document stipulates that the republic is "unitarian and democratic," guided by the Communist Party of Cuba (Partido Comunista de Cuba, PCC) to construct a socialist society along Marxist-Leninist principles (Articles 1 and 5). The purpose of the republic is to promote "the enjoyment of political liberty, social justice, collective and individual well-being" (Article 9). According to the document, every citizen is entitled to participate in the running of the state, to equality before the law, and to the exercise of civil freedoms. These rights and freedoms, however, are conditional, not absolute. They are upheld as long as the exercise of the rights does not go against the consolidation of the revolution and the socialist system.[2] What this means in practice is that the limits placed on civil and political rights are clear. Fidel Castro's 1970 dictum, "within the Revolution everything, against the Revolution nothing," delineated the boundaries of what is permissible in terms of expression and political behavior.

Cuba's legal code operationalizes the limits for individual and collective behavior. One such law, the "*ley de la peligrosidad*" (law of dangerousness), epitomizes the state's attempt to control the parameters of political correctness. The law allows the government to imprison individuals suspected of being "dangerous," even if they have not have perpetrated any crime.

The one-party system established by the constitution in conjunction with the mass organizations (linked to the state and the party) negates the possibility of citizens organizing alternative political associations to articulate different interests. The socialist conception of human rights is biased toward collective rights (as defined by the state), which the party and the mass organizations promote in theory. Marxism-Leninism, the ideology undergirding the constitution and the state, sets narrow parameters for civil-political rights and broad parameters for economic rights.

Marxism as an ideology has a teleological underpinning that makes it fixed. It is based on the notion of social harmony stemming from the common interest of the working class and on the dialectical unfolding of history as prescribed by some law of history. At a basic level it is this ideological assumption, enshrined in the constitution, that human rights groups have contested. At the level of political practice, any discussion of the rights of citizens will bring to the fore the use and legitimization of power, the allocation of values in society, and as a consequence, the appropriate role of the state in both political and economic affairs.[3] In the context of the ideological and economic crisis in Cuba after the mid-1980s, a debate over economic and social rights promises to shake the pillars on which the socialist state has been constructed.

The Evolution of the
Human Rights Movement

The struggle for socioeconomic and political rights in Cuba has long roots in the nation's history. By world standards, the Constitution of 1902 (establishing the Republic) was a progressive document in that it recognized key civil and economic rights of the individual citizen. The "frustrated" revolution of 1933 also resulted in an expansion of economic guarantees for workers and a legal strengthening of the civil liberties of the people. The culmination of this trajectory of expansive socioeconomic and civil legislation reached a zenith in the Constitution of 1940, one of the most advanced legal documents of any time. In terms of human rights, the 1940 document was particularly favorable to labor and women.[4]

To be sure, problems in the arena of rights continued to exist. The question of race was not resolved, and the legal word did not always carry through in actual practice. Nevertheless, these documents constituted an ideal culture that embodied the normative aspirations of the Cuban people. Any judgment on the human rights situation on the island before and after the revolution of 1959 must be reached through comparative analysis from the perspective of specific world time, not by the standards of any other historical moment.

Progress in human rights was the fruit of an energetic civil society. Of particular significance were the activities of labor organizations, the women's movement, and liberal and leftist political sectors. Progress was not linear, however. The dictatorship of General Fulgencio Batista (1952–1959) under-mined the Constitution of 1940 and, as a result, the protection of individual and collective rights. Groups opposed to the dictatorship launched a civil, and eventually an armed, campaign to topple the military from power, pledging to restore the Constitution of 1940 and to redress many of the po-litical and economic grievances of the people.

From this current of social activism would emerge the human rights ac-tivists of revolutionary Cuba. The tradition of struggle for individual and collective rights in civil society continued in a different fashion under the post-1959 regime. Almost immediately after the triumph of the revolution-ary forces, groups from the right of the political spectrum launched attacks against what they perceived as antidemocratic tendencies on the part of the new government. But overwhelming popular support for Fidel Castro and the social revolution silenced (through repression, exile, or alienation) many of these minority voices that clamored for the traditional civil liberties of in-dividuals. The revolutionary process meanwhile expanded the state's com-mitment to the socioeconomic rights of the collectivity.

Although the state was successful in defending its agenda against the con-servative opposition, the human rights challenge that surfaced in later years sprang from the ranks of the left. Individuals sympathetic with the revolu-tion became the leaders of the human rights movement. The first formal human rights association in post-1959 Cuba, the Comité Cubano pro Dere-chos Humanos (Cuban Committee for Human Rights or CCPDH) was es-tablished in 1976 by a handful of individuals who had supported the Marx-ist-Leninist course the revolution took after the early 1960s. The social and historical origins of the movement are of significance. The individuals who organized the group were professionals who had at one point worked in mid-levels of the state. Many of them had long-standing Marxist credentials as a result of their affiliation with the Partido Socialista Popular (Socialist Popular Party or PSP), the old-time pro-Soviet Marxist party and the pre-cursor of the PCC.

The personal history of one of the founders of the CCPDH reveals the process through which a political insider is transformed into an outsider. Ri-cardo Bofill grew up in a working-class family of committed socialists. He at-tended the University of Havana, where he eventually taught Marxist ideol-ogy after 1959. His political credentials allowed him to travel to the Soviet Union and Eastern Europe in 1966, where he came into contact with dissi-dents and reformists during the period of liberalization under Nikita Khrushchev and the Prague Spring in Czechoslovakia. In 1967 he was among a group of individuals sentenced to prison after being accused of planning to orchestrate a putsch against Fidel Castro's leadership. The offi-cial explanation offered for the incident, known as the Microfaction Affair, claims that these men where attempting to pursue a closer pro-Soviet course. Bofill indicates that being pro-Soviet at that time meant being part of a liberalizing current within socialism.[5]

The seven years he served in prison revealed to him a side of the regime that he had not suspected of existing and convinced him that individual human rights had to be defended in a civil manner. Once out of prison, Bofill and several other individuals in similar positions—Elizardo Sanchez and Eduardo Lopez, among others—and with the cooperation of Marta Frayde, an erstwhile associate of Fidel Castro, decided to establish the CCPDH in 1976.

The personal profile reveals important dimensions of agency as well the roots of a social movement. The personal plays an instrumental role in political activism. A family tradition of political consciousness (in Bofill's case, a tradition of defending the rights of workers), the stories heard from survivors of Stalin's gulag, the conversations with socialist reformers in the Soviet bloc, and the discovery of the state's repression while in prison predisposed this individual to take the actions he did. His cohorts in the first human rights group shared similar personal experiences that pushed them toward taking a position that carried with it great risks. The process is neither automatic nor linear, nor is it entirely up to the individual, for situations arise to which the person reacts without knowing what will be the consequences. It is not an atomized phenomenon; although it is personal, it occurs in a social context, with others. Moreover, although it is a local phenomenon it is tied to the international stage.

Since 1976 the human rights movement in Cuba has undergone several stages: from 1976 to 1980; from 1980 to 1988; and from 1988 into the early 1990s. The initial stage began with the establishment of the CCPDH and ended with the committee abandoning the secretive, anonymous activism for a more open and identifiable denunciation of abuses. The decision to identify themselves as members of the CCPDH and to expand their activities came in 1980 as a result of the abuses committed during the Mariel boatlift, when over 120,000 Cubans left the island.

During the initial period the handful of founders never met in plenum, so as not to risk their anonymity or their safety. Activities revolved around issuing press releases to the foreign media on the island and visiting the diplomatic corps. This stage was possibly the most delicate one for the movement. It did not have a constituency (usually not even their family members supported or knew of their decision to form a group), and they could not count on the attention of the foreign press or diplomats. Some foreign diplomats turned a blind eye to the members of the group, suspecting them of being provocateurs. Ironically, such was also the response of the U.S. Interest Section in the late 1970s under the leadership of Wayne Smith.

President Jimmy Carter, who had negotiated the exchange of interest sections with the Cuban government, had unfolded the banner of human rights to guide U.S. foreign policy. Yet the U.S. Interest Section in Havana did not nurture the activists who knocked at its doors. Years later, Presidents Ronald Reagan and George Bush reversed the policy, to the point of using the human rights issue to conduct an international campaign against the Cuban government.

During the movement's embryonic period the members of the CCPDH carried out the tasks of monitoring and compiling cases of human rights abuses quietly, running great risks by visiting embassies and foreign reporters to release information. From its very beginning the human rights "movement" on the island was internationalized. Not only did the activists seek support from diplomats and foreign media, but also they gained moral capital with the Helsinki Accords and the Charter 77 process in Europe. In addition, they wrote letters to international organizations and prominent individuals asking them to publicize the human rights situation on the island and denouncing specific cases of abuse.

The international community did not receive the human rights effort with open arms; indeed, some critics claim that "nobody listened." The reasons behind this deafness stem principally from the romanticism with which different groups abroad perceived the Cuban Revolution. Although after the late 1980s the human rights movement in Cuba received increasing international attention at the United Nations (UN) and from organizations such as Amnesty International and Americas Watch, no Cuban human rights activist has received a major international award in recognition of his or her work.

The second stage of the human rights movement signaled a new strategy and a strengthening of the organization. Confronted by the events surrounding the Mariel exodus (including the infamous *actos de repudio*, officially sanctioned mass attacks against individuals who wanted to leave the island), the members of the CCPDH increased their activities and in the process shed their anonymity. The new course of action carried with it repression, including imprisonment. The Cuban prisons became the center of human rights activism as the leaders of the movement made contacts there with others who eventually joined the ranks of the human rights movement.

Two international developments during these years point to the growing international credibility of the Cuban human rights movement. First, through the mediation of the French government of François Mitterrand some of the human rights activists were freed from prison, but they did not abandon their activities. Second, the interest of the United States in promoting human rights and discrediting Cuba at the same time fueled a campaign in the UN Human Rights Commission. Havana, not expecting the consequences, allowed the commission to visit the island in 1988 to conduct interviews.

The Human Rights Commission's visit inaugurated a third stage in the evolution of the human rights movement in Cuba. Over a thousand Cubans sought the commission's delegates to detail instances of abuses. As a result the commission produced one of the longest documents in UN history describing human rights abuses. The popular turnout, thanks in part to the publicity generated through the Voice of the America's Radio Martí broadcasts, caught the government by surprise and legitimized the human rights activists. Dozens of Cubans allegedly requested membership in the CCPDH after the commission's visit. The leaders of the CCPDH opted to establish a political party to channel this grassroots support, the Partido Pro Derechos Humanos (Party for Human Rights).

Another international factor of great importance, the reform programs initiated by Mikhail Gorbachev in the Soviet Union after 1986, energized the human rights movement in Cuba. Perestroika and glasnost became the guiding lights for activists, who all of a sudden found their base of support expanding. The success of erstwhile dissidents such as Lech Walesa and Václav Havel provided additional moral capital. Although the origins of the human rights movement were autochthonous, the symbolic value of political change in the Soviet Union and Eastern Europe for the development of the movement cannot be overestimated. The fall of communism in Eastern Europe and the Soviet Union left Cuba with fewer allies willing to defend the island's human rights record. For the first time since 1959, the United States found the necessary votes in the United Nations to investigate the Cuban case. On several occasions since 1988 the majority of the member states have voted in favor of the U.S. resolution to send a special rapporteur to the island. Havana, in an act of defiance, has refused to allow the rapporteur's visit.

The third stage is characterized by the multiplication of human rights associations. A variety of groups emerged after the late 1980s, espousing slightly divergent ideological proclivities and articulating different interests (both personalistic and group-based). Some were narrowly defined human rights associations that splintered off from the CCPDH or were established by newcomers. Others were created by artists, students, women, environmentalists, and religious believers to promote sectoral interests. In spite of their diversity, they were all united under the umbrella of greater political rights. From the perspective of the state, all were illegal counterrevolutionary associations. Some groups have asked for legal recognition but their demand has fallen on deaf ears.

The dynamics of group formation during that period resembles that of a chain reaction. Once a group of individuals coalesced to defend moral claims that carried resonance for many on the island, it showed that civil resistance was possible. Others imitated the example soon thereafter.

As of 1994 the principal human rights groups were the CCPDH, the Comisión Cubana de Derechos Humanos Y Reconciliación Nacional (Cuban Commission for Human Rights and National Reconciliation), and the Movimiento Cristiano Liberación (Christian Liberation Movement, which has unofficial ties to the Catholic Church). Two umbrella organizations have been established to bring together the scattered human rights associations: the Coalición Democrática Cubana (Cuban Democratic Coalition) and the Concertación Democrática Cubana (Cuban Democratic Convergence). The dividing line between the two is drawn by their positions on two issues: the embargo and negotiations with the Cuban government. Whereas the Coalición supports the U.S. embargo and rejects any dialogue with Cuban authorities, the Concertación opposes U.S. policy and supports dialogue with the government.

The umbrella organizations are also divided over their ties with exile groups. The Coalición is associated with the conservative Cuban American National Foundation, the most influential Cuban-American lobby in the United States. The Concertación, at one point the one with the most members, is linked to the Plataforma Democrática (Democratic Platform), an exile organization led by liberal intellectuals. Although the symbolic value of unity is strong, in practice both umbrella associations are rather weak due to internal divisions and structural obstacles such as their lack of access to the national media and their inability to organize openly. The politics of Cuban exiles, fraught with bitter acrimony and divisions, was a complicating factor for intergroup relations. The likelihood of unity among the activists decreased once they started to pick sides among contending exile organizations.

As of 1993 there were over 100 human rights, opposition, and independent groups inside Cuba, many with counterparts in the United States and elsewhere in the world. The proliferation should not be understood as a massive social movement. On the contrary, the human rights activists remain a tiny minority of the Cuban population. Most of the leaders are unknown to the population and do not command a following. Some of them, however, have gained exposure through the international media, particularly Radio Martí. As the activities of the individuals become known and the situation on the island worsens, the leaders and the groups increasingly receive support from neighbors and strangers alike. They constitute a social movement insofar as they are like caps of waves, with strong currents running below the surface.[6]

Women have been important actors in the human rights movement since the beginning. In addition to Marta Frayde, who was instrumental in the organization of the CCPDH, several others have held prominent roles. The writers Tania Díaz Castro and María Elena Cruz Varela achieved international notoriety for their activism, paying a steep price for their activities. Both were dismissed from their state jobs, harassed, assaulted, and imprisoned. Women have been active in the Asociación Pro-Arte Libre (Association for Free Art) and in other human rights groups as well as in recently formed women's groups such as the Asociación de Madres por la Dignidad (Association of Mothers for Dignity).

In spite of their heterogeneity, the human rights groups in Cuba are united under the banner of individual civil liberties and the rejection of the status quo. In this sense they are all liberal but are revolutionary in their context. Though many of these organizations stake their legitimacy in the Universal Declaration of Human Rights, others emphasize the national traditions of their political thought (emanating from diverse patriots such as José Martí, a founder of the Cuban nation, and Julio Antonio Mella, a young communist leader of the 1920s). Other groups (such as the Amigos de la Perestroika) found their inspiration in the reform process of the former Soviet Union. Under the broad unity of purpose among these groups lies ideological and personalistic differences.

The ideological spectrum of the human rights movement in Cuba ranges from conservative democrats who favor a market economy to center-left socialist sympathizers. Most agree on the value of competitive elections and on the need for some measure of free enterprise in the economy. Though the fragmentation of the movement into a number of groups might be understood as a source of weakness, it can also be considered a source of strength since a variety of groups with particular agendas and different leaders is a prerequisite to the emergence of a civil society on the island. At the heart of the matter is whether the movement will become atomized to the point of losing effectiveness or merely be pluralized, which could only add to the democratic grounding of Cuban society in the future.

An important shift occurred in the scope of the politics of human rights in the late 1980s and early 1990s. At this stage the groups, instead of limiting their objectives to the promotion of human rights, demanded a fundamental change in the essence of the political game; in other words, the agenda expanded from a minimalist to a maximalist one. In 1987 one of the leading human rights associations, the Comité Cubano pro Derechos Humanos y Reconciliación Nacional, headed by Elizardo Sanchez Santa Cruz, called for a plebiscite and gathered 11,000 signatures in three months in support of the initiative. A year later the CCPDH established a political party.

The relationship between human rights groups and the emergence of opposition political parties has been an intimate one. The human rights activists proved that opposition was possible in Cuba. The impact of their example on the behavior of others should not be underestimated. In addition to its symbolic contribution, the human rights movement provided leadership to the newly established political parties and independent organizations.

The case of the Corriente Socialista Democrática (Socialist Democratic Current), a left-of-center political association, suggests that longtime regime supporters (including the son of one of the founding members of the old socialist party of Cuba, the Partido Socialista Popular) may continue to abandon the PCC to establish alternative political associations. The Corriente Socialista found support among human rights activists such as Elizardo Sanchez Santa Cruz, who became a member. This is typical of the crosscutting networks of leadership between human rights groups and opposition parties. The social base of the leaders of both types of organizations are quite similar.

Conjunctural factors of the late 1980s came into play in the emergence of organized opposition parties. Organized opposition to the regime spread at the time when the regime was most vulnerable. The transformation of the communist world and the ensuing economic catastrophe catalyzed closet critics and liberals within the party to manifest their discontent.

The State Responds to Human Rights Groups

The Cuban state has always defended its position on human rights. Before the 1980s the government had touted the progress made in education, health, employment, sports, and general social equity as evidence of the regime's commitment to socioeconomic rights. From the Marxist perspective, the guarantee of social welfare is fundamental, in turn guaranteeing the political access of all citizens. In defense of its human rights record, the official discourse pointed to the reeducation campaign for political and common criminals as a sign of the progressive nature of Cuban penal system. Furthermore, it has denied the use of torture or disappearances, all too common in other countries of the region. Victims and activists, however, have challenged the glowing official accounts.[7] Amnesty International, for example, reported in 1994 that Cuba was holding at least 500 political prisoners in jail and that dozens of human rights activists have been victims of repression.[8]

To understand the conflict between the state and human rights advocates one must resort to the foundational views of politics that each holds. For the state, both the revolutionary experience and Marxist ideology conceive socialist politics normatively as free of conflict. The revolution of 1959 was supposed to embody the will and the aspirations of the Cuban people. Unity of purpose resulted in the victory of the revolutionary forces. Unity was instrumental in guaranteeing the consolidation and the continuation of the regime. The people, or the masses, were the subjects of the construction of socialism. Besieged from outside and from within, the revolution required cohesion and could not tolerate diversions that could place the survival of the revolution at risk. In sum, the Cuban state defined itself as a harmonious entity that embodied the will of the people in one single party. The state equaled the nation. Without the revolutionary state the nation was impossible.

The unitarian conception of the state (with its appendages of mass organizations) explains several things. First, it explains the facade of monolithism prevalent in contemporary Cuban politics. Second, it helps one to understand why dissidents have been attacked frontally, treated as outsiders, as the "others" who attempt to bring down the house of all the people. And third, it reveals why the emergence of human rights organizations has been significant. The establishment of autonomous groups and the human rights discourse shook the premises on which the state and the regime were erected.

The individuals who started the human rights movement on the island hold a strikingly different view of politics, both in the normative and practical dimensions. Their premise is a simple one: The state has not respected the rights of individuals. By professing to be everything for everyone, the Cuban state has not acknowledged that different interests exist within Cuban society and that they deserve a voice, representation, and equality in face of the law. According to them, the official monolithism is a facade that hides pluralism. What is stopping pluralism from emerging is a recalcitrant state led by a dictator and an ideology that harps on centralism. The agency conveyed by citizenship has been stripped; mass organizations are forms of state control through mobilization.

At the basis of this perspective is a particular view of the place of the individual in society. Whereas the Cuban political system focuses on the collectivity, the activists emphasize the importance of granting the individual a fundamental place in society, guaranteed by the rule of law and the institutions of civil society. This perspective derives from traditional liberalism, which perceives absolute power as corrupting and hence advocates a separation of powers and independent intermediate organizations between the people and the state. This is not to say that human rights activists in Cuba fit perfectly in a liberal mode of thought or practice, either consciously or unconsciously. To be sure, their ideological makeup is far more polychromatic than what this interpretation might lead one to believe. Although the philosophical foundation of their actions shares commonalities with the liberal current, they are members of a political community with a specific political culture not emblematic of liberalism. Yet they are part of a strand of political thought running throughout the island's history that is akin to liberal ideology.[9]

The other principal current of political thought on the island, akin to corporatism, emphasizes centralization of authority and goals rather than means. It is this current that runs through the discourse and practice of Fidel Castro and Cuban socialism. From this vantage point, the ideology of the human rights movement on the island is not new or alien to the Cuban context. What is innovative within the context of domestic politics is the praxis of civil resistance as a form of dissent. This civil action also has roots in prerevolutionary civil society.

In sharp contrast to paramilitary groups operating outside the island and to the propensity evident in the island's history to resolve conflicts through violence, the human rights groups have espoused Mohandas Gandhi's and

Martin Luther King's strategies of peaceful opposition. The adoption of this strategy stems not only from the cost/benefit calculus that small numbers of individuals cannot defeat militarily a well-armed state but also from a deeper conviction that bloodshed should not be accepted as the only way to resolve political crises on the island. Another, less painful, way of conducting the business of negotiating political society must be found. Civil resistance as a strategy to deal with social conflict bodes well for the construction of civic society.

The state has responded to the challenge of human rights in a variety of ways, from brutal repression to co-optation. Human rights activists in Cuba have suffered intimidation, cessation of employment (until recently the state was the only sanctioned employer), incarceration, beatings, separation from family and friends, psychological abuse, and exile. The state's security apparatus has kept close tabs on the activists and has infiltrated the movement in an attempt to dismantle it. As traditional mechanisms of repression met with partial success, the government devised alternative forms of dealing with the *grupusculos.* In the early 1990s a new security force, known as the Brigadas de Respuesta Rápida (Rapid Response Brigades), was established to deal with the opposition. The Brigadas are composed of security officials dressed as civilians whose purpose is to break any public manifestation against the regime and to attack the members of the independent groups.

The most interesting official response to the human rights movement has been the attempt to co-opt its message (and at times its leaders as well). To do so the state has adopted discourse echoing that of the activists. In the domestic arena the discourse has been accompanied by policy changes. In the early 1990s the government opened controlled spaces for "free" political discussion (such as the call for the Fourth Congress of the Communist Party of Cuba in October 1991) and implemented "liberalizing" reforms (such as reforming the electoral procedures and allowing religious believers to join the PCC). Reforms in the economy also point to an *apertura.* However, the slow opening of the Cuban economy is less a response to pressure stemming from the opposition and the grass roots than the state's realization that the only way out of the crisis is market reform and reintegration into the world economy.

The Cuban government has also responded to the human rights challenge in the world arena, partly because the challenge has been an international one. Human rights is one of the priority issues in Cuba's foreign policy agenda. To counter the setback dealt by UN human rights resolutions endorsing a special rapporteur to visit the island to follow up on the Human Rights Commission's 1988 visit, the Foreign Ministry orchestrated a public relations campaign abroad as well as at home. The purpose of the defensive maneuver is twofold: to acquire international moral capital by debunking the image of Cuba as a pariah state and to appropriate some of the language of the human rights movement. By doing so, the regime is attempting to disarm the internal and external opposition by co-opting parts of its lexicon. The image Cuba wants to create abroad requires a new vocabulary at the very least. That is why in the 1990s the government has incorporated into its official discourse such *en vogue* terms as *democracy* and *human rights*.[10]

The campaign has also included defamation of the activists, who are caricaturized as a handful of puppets manipulated by the enemies of Cuba (read the United States). The government portrays itself as besieged, yet struggling to guarantee economic rights to all. Cuba, from the government's perspective, embodies the most democratic system of all. Foreign Minister Roberto Robaina, speaking at the World Human Rights Conference in June 1993, claimed that Cuba did not agree with the definition of human rights espoused by Amnesty International and the UN. Instead Cuba interpreted human rights as tied to development and geopolitics. He argued that once "foreign threats [against Cuba] end, we will have to reconsider many things in Cuba."[11]

After several refusals to allow the special UN rapporteur to travel to the island to collect testimonies of human rights violations, Havana permitted the UN High Commissioner for Human Rights, Jose Ayala Lazo, to visit the island and meet with activists in November 1994. The visit was preceded by arrests and intimidation of human rights activists, revealing the government's two-tiered policy: openness to the international community (which has been applying increasing pressure on the government for its human rights situation) and, at the same time, repression at home.

That the regime feels threatened by the human rights issue domestically and internationally is confirmed by the level of official force employed against the activists.[12] Every time a UN resolution passes against Cuba's objection, a wave of repression washes over the activists. It is as if Cuba is showing the international community that it will not accept its intervention in what the government considers a domestic matter. The violence with which the government reacts hurts Cuba's image abroad and undermines its public relations campaign. International Human Rights Day (December 10) has become a painful day for the individuals involved in human rights promotion on the island, with the government routinely incarcerating several of them in reprisal for their activities.

Human Rights and the Emergence of Civil Society

Civil society, understood as autonomous groups representing particular social interests vis-à-vis the state, is a vital aspect of democratic systems. The relationship between human rights and the emergence of civil society in Cuba is directly linked to the possibility of democratization of politics in a variety of ways. The formation of independent human rights associations constitutes the seeds of a civil society on the island. Their ability to contest openly the power of a one-party state is a major accomplishment that sets off a chain reaction of small-group formation. This is perhaps the greatest contribution that the human rights movement has made to the process of democratization.

Two other strategies are helping the emergence of a civic culture. First, the human rights groups have taken the government to task by demanding that the island's national and international legal commitments in defense of individual liberties be respected. By asking the government to live up to recognized legal standards sanctioned by the state itself, the human rights movement is underscoring the importance of legal (rather than personalistic) authority for society. Second, the movement has encouraged individuals throughout the island to record incidents of abuses and to report them. Human rights activists in Havana receive hundreds of these from other towns and cities, from people they do not know. The act of reporting the alleged offenses is itself a mechanism of empowerment.

The development of civil society requires both respect for the rule of law and the agency of citizens. The civility with which the groups have undertaken their political activities contributes to democratization. Social tolerance of contending points of view is a sine qua non of democratic environments. Above and beyond their operative style, the message of these groups, underscoring the rights of individuals and the rule of law, is a foundation on which to build a democratic civil society.

Conclusions

By the 1990s the Cuban human rights movement had developed features in common with other social movements throughout the globe. In spite of the constraints in which it has operated, the movement has been able to survive, challenge the state, and achieve legitimacy domestically and internationally. In spite of the moral capital it has gained through the years, it continues to face an uphill battle as it deals with repression from the state and division within the ranks. The impact of the human rights groups on political change on the island and the possibility for democratization should not be underestimated. By establishing independent associations and breaking the state's monopoly on political organizations, human rights activists have planted seeds of civil society. Their message and their modus operandi (i.e., civil resistance and citizens' agency) also contribute to the emergence of civil political society. This development is a harbinger of the possibility of democratization on the island.

However, the prospect for democracy is not as clear or as rosy as one might wish. Several factors warrant caution. In spite of the movement's contribution to opening a door to a more democratic political system, the personal rivalries and the fragmentation (if not atomization) of the human rights groups call into question the likelihood of a workable democratic political consensus. Furthermore, after three decades of a socialist state that has guaranteed a level of basic needs to all, popular expectations (and Cuba's political culture) are predisposed to favor a political system that acknowledges the economic rights of the citizens and the duty of the state to help provide them.

Given the economic crisis of the immediate and the medium-term future, it is unlikely that any state will be able to accommodate the demands for welfare. In the 1990s the socialist state is accepting its own limitations and has been in the process of whittling away at the social safety net. In the future this trend is likely to continue. The most likely scenario is that a future Cuban state will find it easier to meet the demand for civil rights than to satisfy an agenda of economic rights. Confronted with such a reality, the Cuban people, who hold high political and economic expectations, will have to renegotiate the balance between civil liberties and economic rights.

Notes

1. Jack Donnelly, *The Concept of Human Rights* (New York: St. Martin's Press, 1985); and Zehra Arat, *Democracy and Human Rights in Developing Countries* (Boulder: Lynne Rienner, 1991).

2. See Roberto Cuellar, "Human Rights: The Dilemmas and Challenges Facing the Non-Governmental Movement During a Transition in Cuba," in *Transition in Cuba*, ed. Cuban Research Institute (Miami: Florida International University, 1993), pp. 155–159.

3. Susan Waltz, *Human Rights in North Africa* (Los Angeles: University of California Press, 1995).

4. See Hugh Thomas, *The Cuban Revolution* (New York: Harper and Row, 1977).

5. Interviews by the author with Ricardo Bofill, Miami, March 1994, and with Oscar Pena, Miami, March 1994. The following discussion is largely based on these interviews.

6. See Damian J. Fernandez, "Civil Society in Transition," in *Transition in Cuba* (Miami: Cuban Research Institute: Florida International University, 1993), pp. 97–152.

7. Juan Clark, *Cuba: Mito y Realidad* (Miami: Saeta Ediciones, 1990).

8. Pablo Alfonso, "Cuba Por Dentro," *El Nuevo Miami Herald*, July 7, 1994, p. A2.

9. Rafael Rojas, "Viaje a la Semilla: Instituciones de la Anti-Modernidad Cubana," *Apuntes Posmodernos*, vol. 3 (Fall 1993):3–20.

10. *Foreign Broadcast Information Service–Latin America*, June 16, 1994, pp. 3–4.

11. Ibid.

12. Juan M. del Aguila, "The Politics of Dissidence: A Challenge to the Monolith," in *Conflict and Change in Cuba*, ed. Enrique A. Baloyra and James A. Morris (Albuquerque: University of New Mexico Press, 1993), pp. 153–195.

7

Democracy and Human Rights in the Dominican Republic

Larman C. Wilson

The related topics of democracy, elections, and politics in the Dominican Republic have received considerable attention recently. This attention, however, has largely neglected the important and relevant issue of human rights, and it generally does not include the controversial election of May 1994 or the elections of 1996—the special and run-off elections of May and June.[1] In view of the contested outcome of those elections and the *continuismo* of gerontocratic President Joaquín Balaguer and his political rule until August 1996, this is an opportune time to examine the nature and status of Dominican democracy and human rights and to consider their future course.

The "procedural" conditions of democracy and human rights include the following: the right to organize, campaign, and vote; freedom of speech; regular, free, and honest elections; right of workers to organize and strike; personal freedom, protection, and security; and equal legal rights and opportunity for an education and employment. The "substantive" democratic requirements include the acceptance of the outcome of elections by the defeated party and the military; two or more competing parties; an effective and viable legislature; and an effective judiciary. The crucial importance of economic well-being has been acknowledged and the indispensable relationship between economic and political development has been recognized.[2] None of these conditions of democracy can be achieved and maintained without a certain basic level of economic development, and the serious erosion of economic development jeopardizes the continued acceptance and practice of democracy.

In addition to applying these conditions as indicators, this chapter will also consider both the external and internal factors that have either impeded or contributed to the transition to and the development of democratic practices and institutions and the protection of human rights in the Dominican Republic. The best example of external influence in Dominican affairs lies in the policies of the United States, which has long assumed the role of "guarantor" of democracy in the Dominican Republic. The United States has exercised this role by means of military intervention and/or occupation, diplomatic and political pressure, providing or terminating economic and military assistance, and sanctions, all of which it has sometimes arranged through the Organization of American States (OAS). The OAS itself has been another external force, albeit often serving as an instrument of U.S. foreign policy—acting first as an anticommunist alliance, then as an antidictator alliance against General-President Rafael Trujillo, and later as an observer and verifier of free elections.[3]

Among the internal factors, the principal domestic obstacle to the transition to and the development of democracy and the protection of human rights was the legacy of Trujillo—a dictatorial and personalist system of absolute political control and one that remained an obstacle long after his murder in 1961. There were also cultural and racial dimensions to his legacy. Trujillo made it official policy that the Dominican identity was that of the *"Madre Patria"*: culturally Spanish, religiously Roman Catholic, and racially *"blanco."* He denigrated those who were African, practiced voodoo, and were "negro"—that is, the Haitians, whom he viewed as inferior. He institutionalized hatred and fear of Haiti, and his policies contributed to the enslavement of Haitians to cut sugarcane in the Dominican Republic.

Balaguer was a part of and a perpetuator of the Trujillo legacy of *Hispanidad* and intolerance of Haitians. Although in the 1970s he accepted the public recognition of most Dominicans' African roots and *criollo* culture, he stressed the primacy of *Hispanidad* and continued anti-Haitian feelings and the exploitation of Haitian cane cutters. The two presidents from the Dominican Revolutionary Party (PRD) who held office from 1978 until 1986—Antonio Guzmán and Salvador Jorge Blanco—moderated Balaguer's political model and reinforced the honoring of the country's African roots and attempted to mitigate the anti-Haitian attitudes.

Another important internal factor is the status of the economy, which is tied to external factors as well, such as the price of oil and sugar. A depressed economy of course has a negative impact upon the commitment to democracy on the part of those suffering economic hardship. A depressed economy also may require the government to turn to outside international financial agencies, such as the International Monetary Fund (IMF) or the Inter-American Development Bank (IADB), for financial assistance. These agencies, then, through the conditions they set for their aid, become important external influences on the economic development process as well as on political development.

The Transition to Democracy (1961–1966)

Trujillo's agents attempted to kill Venezuelan President Rómulo Betancourt in June 1960. The assassination attempt prompted a meeting of the OAS, which passed a resolution condemning Trujillo's intervention and providing for sanctions—diplomatic, economic, and trade—against the Dominican Republic. Although this first application of collective sanctions by the OAS was implemented because Trujillo had violated the nonintervention principle and not because of his dictatorial regime, the United States used the sanctions as a means of pressuring Trujillo to make democratic reforms and to accept the reforms demanded by President John Kennedy's Alliance for Progress. (The sanctions were expanded as a bargaining device for a commitment to hold free elections and were in effect until January 1962, even though Trujillo was killed in May 1961.)

In response to the OAS sanctions, Trujillo's brother resigned as president, and Vice President Joaquín Balaguer took over "to democratize" the country.[4] After Trujillo was assassinated the promises for free elections and political amnesty were taken more seriously, and Balaguer requested the lifting of the OAS sanctions. OAS and U.S. pressure continued, however, and the Inter-American Commission on Human Rights (IACHR), established in 1960, visited the country in October 1961. The following month, Trujillo's two brothers returned from abroad and attempted a takeover, but they and other family members fled when the United States threatened to intervene and engaged in a naval show of force within sight of the capital, Santo Domingo. Mounting opposition resulted in the formation of a provisional government headed by Balaguer, and elections were promised for 1962. Continuing disorder after the OAS sanctions were ended led to Balaguer's exile, after which the United States provided economic aid and increased its Dominican sugar quota as the political campaign got under way.

Juan Bosch, a well-known literary figure, returned from exile—twenty-five years in Costa Rica, Cuba, Venezuela, and Puerto Rico—and became the presidential nominee of the PRD. On a platform of "democratic socialism," Bosch won the OAS-supervised election in December, defeating his conservative opponent by a large margin. Shortly after Bosch's inauguration in 1963, the United States began to present the Dominican Republic as a showcase for the Alliance for Progress in order to prove the Alliance's efficacy in democratic reform and economic development, which served in turn to maintain political stability and prevent communist influence. Massive amounts of economic and technical assistance along with hundreds of experts were provided to bring about reform and development and to cancel out Trujillo's legacy. When Bosch was overthrown by the military seven months later, clearly the victim of Trujillo's legacy, President Kennedy broke relations, suspended all aid, and recalled most U.S. officials.

The military junta was soon replaced by civilians, and Donald Reid Cabral emerged as the "president" and received the support of the Lyndon Johnson administration. However, in April 1965 he was removed by a pro-Bosch faction in the army. This faction's effort to restore Bosch to office was strongly opposed by the bulk of the army, whose leaders had removed him and who were in favor of Balaguer's return, and a civil war ensued. President Johnson, fearing the victory of the "leftist" pro-Bosch side, sent in 22,000 U.S. troops "to prevent a second Cuba." In May, once the United States had secured the situation, it directed the OAS to create an Inter-American Peace Force, which added units from six Latin American countries to the U.S. contingent.[5] After months of negotiation the two sides agreed on an "Act of Dominican Reconciliation" and on a provisional president to prepare the country for national elections in June 1966.

The two presidential candidates were former president Juan Bosch of the PRD and former vice president and titular president Joaquín Balaguer of the Reformist Party (PR). On June 1, 1966, Dominicans voted in a generally fair and free election that was observed by the OAS and by a private group. Balaguer was elected with over 56 percent of the vote, some 236,625 votes more than Bosch.[6] A month later Balaguer was inaugurated, and the OAS Peace Force was withdrawn in September. It now appeared that progress toward the creation of a democratic system, which had begun under Bosch in 1963 but had been aborted by the military, could continue.

The Balaguer Regime (1966–1978)

Balaguer's primary concern during his first term was to establish and consolidate political control. In the process, his government suppressed and attacked critics and opponents. It even cut off the required budget payment to the Autonomous University of Santo Domingo (UASD), a center of anti-Balaguer and pro-Bosch activity. These measures were a key aspect of an authoritarian and personalist government and were strongly backed by the armed forces. Balaguer was also interested in his country's economic recovery and development, and he turned to the United States, which was willing to provide considerable aid since it was interested in stability as a Cold War issue. The United States greatly increased economic and military aid during Balaguer's first term and continued the large Dominican share of its sugar quota. Thereafter, however, the United States reduced its assistance, and Balaguer then tried to attract foreign private investment, particularly from the United States, by providing numerous economic and tax incentives, including the creation of Industrial Free Zones (IFZs).

A combination of factors ensured that Balaguer would establish his control, both authoritarian and personalist, and be reelected in 1970 and 1974. First, he permitted the suppression of dissident leaders and groups—political, labor, and student—and he promoted and gained control over officers loyal to him. Second, U.S. support, via economic and military assistance as well as political backing, was very important. Third was the great economic improvement that took place. And fourth, the PRD, the leading opposition party, became fragmented because of government suppression and internal dissension.

The dissension in the PRD followed Bosch's departure from the country in 1966, leaving radical Secretary-General José Francisco Peña Gómez in charge. A split developed between his faction and a "moderate" faction, and debate was provoked between the two groups when in 1968 Bosch made a case for a "dictatorship with popular support." As the May 1970 election approached there was mounting police violence against the opposition parties, and it increased when Bosch returned. This violence, the division of the vote among different opposition parties, the PRD's boycotting the election, and election fraud all ensured Balaguer's reelection. With a voter turnout estimated at 56 percent, Balaguer received 57 percent of the vote, and a coalition's candidate received 20.4 percent.[7]

A police-sponsored terrorist group of young men, *La Banda*, was formed in 1971 to suppress government opponents. It dealt violently with political activists and was responsible for thousands of individual attacks, resulting in about 300 deaths. During the period of *La Banda*'s attacks there was an attempted coup, the leader of which was arrested and deported. Also in 1971 and shortly thereafter, apparently in response to international criticism and pressure, Balaguer announced the dissolution of *La Banda*. This was one of Balaguer's stock political tactics—to tolerate illegal and beneficial actions by supporters (whether or not he had approved them in the first place), but when they became unpopular and/or counterproductive, to take a statesmanlike stance and end the actions.

In 1973 the colonel who had commanded the pro-Bosch side during the civil war landed with a small invasion force, hoping to precipitate Balaguer's overthrow. Although the force was quickly defeated (and the colonel killed), Balaguer used the crisis to further suppress the opposition, particularly the PRD, by implicating Bosch and Peña Gómez. He ordered their arrest, but they went into hiding and the "moderate" wing of the PRD took over. Later that year Bosch formed the Democratic Liberation Party (PLD) and Peña Gómez became head of the PRD. A coalition slate for the 1974 election placed Antonio Guzmán, a "moderate" PRD member (he had been in Bosch's cabinet in 1963), as the presidential nominee. Due to the government's continuing suppression, Guzmán recommended abstention and most opposition leaders withdrew from the election. Warning of chaos and economic collapse if not elected, Balaguer was easily reelected in 1974 with 84.7 percent of the vote (the main opposition candidate received 15.3 percent).[8]

The election and later events—a major military shake-up and the easy elimination of a small guerrilla force, both in 1975—confirmed Balaguer's firm control. His position was enhanced by the continued economic improvement, generous U.S. assistance, the flow of foreign private investment, and the high price of sugar in the U.S. market for the large Dominican quota. From 1970 to 1977, the economy's growth rates almost tripled and per capita income increased substantially, although the main beneficiaries were the middle class and especially the elite. During this period Balaguer spent hundreds of millions of dollars to improve the country's infrastructure, expand the tourist industry, restore colonial Santo Domingo, and build the Plaza de Cultura.[9] The high price of sugar was a key aspect of prosperity and Balaguer's resultant popularity, but in 1977 the price of sugar fell sharply as Balaguer was expecting reelection in 1978.

Balaguer emphasized the Spanish legacy of culture, religion, and white racial purity, and he continued the policy of hating, fearing, and exploiting "negro" Haitians. In 1966 he had renewed the contract with Haiti's dictator, François Duvalier, for recruiting Haitians to cut sugarcane on the Dominican estates run by the State Sugar Council (CEA). Although these workers were supposed to receive basic pay along with minimal accommodations and care, they usually did not and were virtually enslaved until the sugar harvest ended.[10] Balaguer glorified the Spanish colonial heritage by means of an extensive and expensive program to restore colonial Santo Domingo and construct galleries and museums of high culture in the Plaza de Cultura. A major goal was to prepare for the celebration of the fifth centennial in 1992 and finally build the long-planned *El Faro* (The Lighthouse), which would contain a permanent burial site for Columbus's remains. Despite Balaguer's focus on the Spanish heritage and his suppression of the Afro-Dominican movement, he found it politically expedient to tolerate the latter during his third term.

The Election of 1978

In a recent book chapter, Jonathan Hartlyn includes a section entitled "Balaguer's Authoritarian Period, 1966–1978: Midwife to Democracy?"[11] Hartlyn's characterization of this Balaguer period as "authoritarian" certainly seems appropriate, but the "midwife" role may be more aptly credited to the United States for its insistence on democratic procedure during the election. If the Jimmy Carter administration had not pressured and threatened the Balaguer regime to resume the counting of ballots in May, democracy would have been aborted and Balaguer's authoritarianism continued. It was justified intervention because it contributed to the institutionalization of Dominican democracy via a functioning two-party system and had wide Dominican support.

A number of economic and political developments undermined Balaguer's reelection prospects. This time the PRD rejected abstention and mounted a major electoral challenge. One major factor working against Balaguer was the declining economy, which had resulted in government cutbacks, increasing unemployment, demonstrations, and strikes. A growing and more prosperous middle class became more active and turned against the Balaguer government, attacking corruption within it and the military. Moreover, some members of the elite began to question Balaguer's competence to manage the economy and his ability and/or willingness to limit corruption, maintain order, and protect their interests.

During the campaign Peña Gómez, the PRD's secretary-general and leader of the "left" wing, became an issue, although he was not running for any office. His past radical activities were stressed by conservatives and military leaders, and a rumor was circulated that he was a dangerous demagogue who was "antinationalist," meaning pro-Haitian (his parents were Haitian immigrants). Peña Gómez's critics portrayed Guzmán, the PRD's moderate and millionaire businessman-rancher presidential nominee, as being weak and unable to control him.

There were some external factors that affected the campaign as well. Balaguer was interested in maintaining U.S. economic aid and private investment, and he emphasized his close friendship with but independence from the United States. The PRD moderated its attitude toward the U.S. government and private U.S. companies and tried to use the Carter administration's commitment to free elections and human rights to restrain and criticize the Balaguer government. At the September 1977 signing of the Panama Canal treaties in Washington, President Carter lavished special praise upon Balaguer for his restoration of democracy and pledge to restore human rights. Balaguer used this praise to associate himself with Carter, and its repetition was incorporated actively into the campaign. Despite the substance of Carter's praise of Balaguer, the PRD and other opposition parties suffered some violence at the hands of the military, the police, and young toughs. This violence increased sharply as election day approached, with military officers praising Balaguer and some police openly campaigning for him.

In preparation for the May 16 election, the Dominican government opened the electoral process and invited foreign observers to avoid charges of fraud. Observers included a mission from the OAS that included three former Latin American presidents. The Central Electoral Commission (JCE) in Santo Domingo, headed by a Balaguer appointee, was in charge of the elections. The military retired to their barracks on May 13 as required by the electoral law, and the JCE was assigned security personnel. On election eve Balaguer promised to accept the choice of the voters and indicated that he expected the military to do the same. On election day the country was peaceful, and there was a large voter turnout, giving the PRD reason to be optimistic. The early returns indicated that Guzmán had a large lead over Balaguer in the capital.

The PRD's hopes were suddenly dashed when Dominican troops forcibly stopped the ballot count on the morning of May 17. They occupied the JCE headquarters and most polling places around the country. They also closed radio and television stations that were reporting the counting. At the time about 25 percent of the votes had been counted, with Guzmán leading Balaguer by 3 to 2. The head of the JCE and his staff disappeared. Both the PR and the PRD celebrated victory, with the military celebrating that of the PR. But the attempt to steal the election had little credibility or support. Three factors contributed to saving the election: the Dominican electorate's strong opposition to a coup; external and international pressure, particularly by the United States; and widespread resistance to the plotters from their military colleagues.[12] The focus here will be on the second factor.

The U.S. response was clear and rapid. A U.S. defense attaché relayed his concern to the armed forces secretariat; Ambassador Robert Yost conveyed a message from Carter to Balaguer, reminding him of promises made at the signing of the Panama Canal treaties; a similar message was delivered to the foreign minister. U.S. officials made strong statements in Washington on May 18: Carter warned that future U.S. support would depend on the "integrity" of the elections and the results being honored by the military; Secretary of State Cyrus R. Vance warned of the "serious effect on [Dominican] relations with the U.S."; and congressional leaders deplored the election's interruption.[13] The members of the OAS observation mission, and even socialist parties in Europe, also applied pressure.

On May 18 Balaguer announced the resumption of the vote counting and promised to honor the outcome. He accused the PRD of electoral fraud and denounced the "interference" of American states threatening to cut off aid. He called for the end of protests and acceptance of the results, and he promised to maintain Dominican democracy and to support the constitution. Although the JCE began releasing incomplete election results on May 18, it was clear that Guzmán would win. However, the official returns were not made public until seven weeks later. Guzmán was declared the winner with 51.7 percent of the vote over Balaguer's 42.2 percent, a margin of around 157,000 votes, with a turnout of 73 percent.[14] The PR ended up with a 16-to-11 majority in the Senate, and the PRD had a 48-to-43 majority in the Chamber of Deputies.

Prior to Guzmán's inauguration on August 16, he reiterated his earlier promises to respect private enterprise and human rights and to continue Balaguer's Cuba policy—nonrecognition, but friendly relations. He also promised that his government would be a representative democracy and would pursue friendly relations with the United States.

The PRD Governments of Guzmán and Jorge (1978–1986)

These two presidents differed ideologically and pursued different approaches in their efforts to strengthen the civil, political, and economic rights of Dominicans and to institutionalize Dominican democracy. Whereas the conservative Guzmán stressed *"democracia política,"* the liberal Salvador Jorge Blanco focused on *"democracia económica."* Although their moderate and progressive policies did contribute to reinforcing democracy, some of their efforts in the political field were undermined by the worsening economic conditions.

Unlike Balaguer, Guzmán was a party rather than personalist politician, and he was a political moderate. At his presidential inauguration on August 16, 1978, which was attended by a high-level U.S. delegation (led by Secretary Vance), there was great optimism, and Guzmán was the beneficiary of a new Dominican pride. A military *golpe* had been prevented and the electorate had experienced the first constitutional transfer of power from one leader to a former opposition leader, even though this had been assured by foreign "electoral intervention." Ironically, the Balaguer legacy was also a part of Dominican good feeling. Though Balaguer was unpopular and his government's corruption was deplored, Dominicans appreciated that he was an intellectual and pointed to his colonial restoration, the Plaza de Cultura, and public housing projects.

In Guzmán's inaugural address, he announced a plan for the armed forces of "depoliticization, institutionalization, and professionalization." He promised to bring a "true institutionality" to Dominican democracy. He gave primacy to military over economic matters during his first six months in office, and by transfers, promotions, and retirements he gained military acquiescence to his policies. Six months after the inauguration, Guzmán delivered his state-of-the-nation address. Though he emphasized the democratic nature of his government and the positive changes in the military, he admitted the existence of serious economic problems.

His economic program and reform policies were vitiated, despite his dedicated efforts, by the declining economy and increasing political problems, including a growing division in the PRD and opposition of the Santiago business community. In the PRD there was a split over dealing with foreign private investment: The Peña Gómez wing advocated nationalization whereas the other wing and Guzmán favored regulation. Although Guzmán was from Santiago and it was his power base, the industrialists there opposed his national development plan. He tried to cope with the domestic economic situation by doubling the minimum wage (it had been frozen by Balaguer for twelve years) and imposing price controls. Tension increased between the government and business over economic and social reforms. Labor unions became politicized, and there was a threefold increase in the number of strikes, work stoppages, and other demonstrations from 1979 to 1981.[15] Guzmán was therefore forced to institute an austerity program.

Guzman's increasing political difficulties also impaired his ability to execute his economic and reform policies, and this undermined his credibility. Not only did the PRD lack full control of the government, but also its control was divided. First, as noted earlier, the PRD held a small majority in the Chamber of Deputies, but was in the minority in the Senate. Moreover, although all of the provincial governors were from the PRD, since they were appointed by the president, a majority of the elected mayors were from the PR. Second, a majority schism developed in Guzmán's own party over dissatisfaction with his major appointments. Senator Salvador Jorge Blanco, PRD president, was the most important dissenter, and he often opposed Guzmán's policies in the Senate.

Guzmán improved relations with Haiti in two fields—treatment of Haitian workers in the Dominican Republic and political-economic relations. He took much more seriously the status of Haitian sugarcane workers and the conventions of the International Labor Organization (ILO). He initiated Dominican consideration of the United Nations (UN) Convention on the Elimination of All Forms of Racial Discrimination, which was ratified in May 1983, and worked toward reducing Dominican antipathies toward Haitians. Relations with Haiti were normalized, and Guzmán met with President Jean-Claude Duvalier in 1979 and signed a cooperation agreement. Later agreements provided for a joint irrigation project and for trade promotion. An old problem between the two countries had been the use of Dominican territory by anti-Duvalier exiles trying to organize a coup in Haiti and/or to make critical radio broadcasts. Guzmán suppressed these activities.

The Election of 1982

Guzmán surprised his party by announcing that he would not run again, which left open the PRD nomination. He chose his vice president, Jacobo Majluta, as his successor but was defied by his party at its nominating convention. The PRD was divided, and after a struggle between Peña Gómez and Jorge Blanco, the latter received the presidential nomination. Balaguer was the nominee of the PR in his effort to return to power despite hearing and vision problems at the age of seventy-five. Another grand old man was a candidate as well—Juan Bosch of the PLD, who had returned to do political battle after an absence of many years.

During the campaign Jorge Blanco promised to base his government on Guzmán's "political democracy" but that he would also pursue "economic democracy." Some members of the business class viewed this goal as shorthand for socialism and more governmental control. However, what Jorge had in mind was to solve the economic and social problems of education, land distribution, and unemployment. Balaguer campaigned on the basis of the sorry state of the economy and the resultant instability, reminding the electorate of the relative economic prosperity and stability during his government in the 1970s. While Jorge appealed to the urban masses and the lower middle class, mainly in Santo Domingo, his base, Balaguer appealed to the middle class and the business community.

The campaign culminated in mid-May 1982, when around 75 percent of the electorate voted, electing Jorge and placing a PRD majority in both the Senate and the Chamber of Deputies. (Peña Gómez won the Santo Domingo mayoralty.) Jorge received 46.7 percent of the vote to Balaguer's 39.2 percent. In the Senate the PRD had seventeen seats to the PR's ten; in the Chamber of Deputies, the shares were sixty-two to fifty.[16] Majluta was elected to the Senate and soon sharply criticized Jorge, just as the latter, in the same position, had opposed Guzmán. (Two months after the election and before Jorge's inauguration in August, Guzmán committed suicide, apparently because he feared an exposé of corruption in his government attributable to the influence peddling of his daughter and some close aides.)

The Jorge Government (1982–1986)

In his inaugural address, Jorge, a progressive urban lawyer from the PRD's left wing, announced that the Dominican Republic was "financially bankrupt" and that it was a "victim" of external forces such as European and U.S. "protectionism." He announced an austerity program as absolutely necessary and he promised to maintain good relations with the United States. Also, as had Guzmán, he first took certain actions to forestall hostility by the military. While trying to expand agricultural production, his economic problems also required him to turn to the cities, which were bearing the brunt of his austerity program and where there was mounting opposition. He tried to modernize industry and engaged in public works programs to reduce unemployment, but his legislative proposals for stimulating the economy were blocked in the Senate. A prime mover in this opposition in the PRD-controlled Senate was former vice president Jacobo Majluta.

Jorge was soon confronted by a far worse economic crisis than Guzmán. The prices for the country's main exports continued to decline, and the Ronald Reagan administration had recently cut the Dominican sugar quota by 32 percent. To deal with the crisis Jorge banned the importation of luxury goods and raised taxes on capital gains and real estate, actions that antagonized the business community. The worsening economic situation forced him to turn to the IMF for credits and loans. The conditions imposed by the IMF resulted in the Jorge government's antagonizing and then losing the support of its natural constituency—urban workers and the lower and middle classes.

Jorge signed a three-year standby agreement with the IMF in the fall of 1982, gaining a credit of US$467 million. The IMF's requirements included ending most import restrictions, moderating export restrictions, devaluing the Dominican peso, and ending many government subsidies. Contrary to Jorge's desires, he found it necessary to seek foreign investment with few restrictions. Jorge was worried about the potentially dangerous social impact of the IMF's conditions on stability and democracy, which he had noted in a letter to President Reagan. His concern was prescient, for when he began implementing the restrictions, riots broke out in April 1984.

In response to limiting imports and ending subsidies on many basic food-stuffs, the business community and labor unions jointly announced a twenty-four-hour strike. Barricades went up, the police were resisted, and riots resulted, accompanied by looting and arson. Although Jorge ordered the police to end the strike and the violence, they were unwilling to use lethal force to do so. However, a special military unit was ordered in and used deadly force to end the rioting, but the result was about 100 deaths, several hundred casualties, and over 4,000 arrests.[17] A new accord was signed with the IMF in early 1985, and its implementation resulted in a general strike that closed the capital and some other cities.

The riots and violence, and their great human and economic costs, had a strong negative impact on the political system, setting the stage for the campaign and election of 1986. The Jorge government lost its legitimacy and support due to its economic policy reversals and failed social reforms; its willingness to permit the use of force to end the strikes and violence caused many of Jorge's natural supporters to consider him to be as oppressive as Balaguer had been.

The PRD entered the 1986 electoral period on the heels of a divisive nomination contest among three competitors: outgoing President Jorge, Senator Majluta, and Santo Domingo Mayor Peña Gómez. After months of factional negotiations and public squabbling, a unity deal was struck, giving the presidential nomination to Majluta and the vice presidential nomination to Peña Gómez. But Peña Gómez withdrew and later publicly stated that the 1990 nomination should be his. The other major contender was Balaguer, who at seventy-nine was legally blind and in declining health. In 1984 he had merged his PR with the Christian Social Revolutionary Party (PRSC), the merged group keeping the latter's name. Balaguer's running mate, Carlos Morales Troncoso, had considerable appeal, being young (forty-five years old), not a politician, and president of the country's largest sugar company. Juan Bosch, now seventy-eight, was also running again as the PLD's nominee.

The major campaign issue was the economy, and the PRD was on the defensive after eight years in office. Its claims of having made some social reforms, reduced corruption in government, and professionalized the military and its blaming the dependent economy rang hollow. Balaguer blamed the PRD for mismanagement, reminded the voters of the economic prosperity under him, and promised to restore the economy via a major public works program. He also emphasized the importance of Dominican sovereignty and of ending pressure from the IMF and the United States. Bosch stressed the same independence theme.

At the request of the opposition the government appointed a *Comité de Notables*, headed by the archbishop of Santo Domingo, to supervise the election. When most of the returns showed a narrow margin favoring Balaguer, Majluta stopped the counting by a legal challenge and called for a recount. The final outcome of the election was determined by negotiations between the JCE, the *Comité*, and representatives of the three leading candidates. The result was a narrow victory for Balaguer: Balaguer had 41.4 percent of the votes, Majluta 39.5 percent, and Bosch 19.1 percent. Balaguer's PRSC won a majority in the Senate, with twenty-one seats to the PRD's seven, and also in the Chamber of Deputies, fifty-six to forty-eight (Bosch's PLD won two Senate and sixteen Chamber seats).[18]

Balaguer's Return and Terms Four–Six (1986–1994, 1994–1996)

Once he returned to office after eight years of PRD government, Balaguer was interested, first, in establishing control over the military and the government bureaucracy, and second, in trying to improve the economic situation, which had continued to worsen. By key military appointments, transfers, and retirements, he made the armed forces commanders subordinate and loyal to him. Balaguer then turned to the PRD carryover government bureaucracy, which he expanded and remade into a largely PRSC one. He did not have to worry about opposition from the legislature, for he had a rubber-stamp majority in the Senate, and the PRD and PLD in the Chamber of Deputies were partisan rivals unable to unite to oppose his programs.

In dealing with the declining economy and economic problems, which he blamed on the policies and corruption of the Jorge government, he soon found it necessary to pursue some of the same policies. (In 1987, Jorge and other PRD officials were indicted for corrupt practices in the use of public funds and military purchases.[19]) The economic situation was due to deficit financing but also to the declining world prices for Dominican exports and the high cost of imported oil. By this time tourism had become the major foreign exchange earner. Despite the declining importance of sugar, the

United States delivered a major blow to the Dominican economy when it cut its Dominican sugar quota by 48 percent in 1987.

Balaguer's efforts to rejuvenate the economy included repressing wages, undertaking extensive construction and public works projects, increasing the money supply, and attracting foreign investment. The resultant rapid increase in inflation and the cost of living, along with the low wage rates, resulted in mounting protests in early 1988. Strikes and violence spread throughout the country. A major general strike in March was suppressed on Balaguer's orders, causing ten deaths, many injuries, and thousands of arrests. Balaguer responded to the strike by giving large wage increases to public employees and freezing food prices, but the protests continued, as did the attacks of the riot police, resulting in more casualties.[20]

The Church entered the tense scene and brought together for negotiations the government, business, and labor in the "Tripartite Dialogue." Shortly thereafter, the archbishop of Santo Domingo announced an eight-point program, which included changes in the Labor Code and increases in the minimum wage. A few weeks later, however, the labor confederations withdrew from the plan, charging violation by business. The government took no action. While relations between labor and the government returned to being confrontational, relations between business and the Balaguer government steadily deteriorated—mainly in response to the government's strict control of exchange rates, restrictions on imports, and its stabilization programs.

Following the departure of Haitian dictator Jean-Claude ("Baby Doc") Duvalier in February 1986 and months of instability, the Dominican-Haitian agreement for Haitian sugarcane cutters was not renewed, which led to a shortage of cane cutters on the Dominican state plantations. The Dominican military responded to the shortage by rounding up Haitians in the country and taking them forcibly to the estates; Dominicans, too, were forced to cut sugarcane. A critical report by Americas Watch in 1989 caused great controversy in the Balaguer government, where officials denounced it as a false attack on the Dominican Republic; the report brought international attention to these human rights abuses.[21]

The Election of 1990

Once again Balaguer and Bosch, now octogenarians, were the nominees of their parties, the former seeking reelection and the latter hoping to expand the 19 percent of the vote the PLD had received in the 1986 election and thereby return to office after twenty-seven years. He and his party were optimistic, in part because of the usual division in the PRD and because the PLD had over the years moved from the left to the center. Peña Gómez continued to lead the "leftist" wing while Majluta headed the "moderate" wing. After weeks of discussion and squabbling, Peña Gómez became the PRD nominee, and Majluta became the nominee of his own independent party. As usual announcing his candidacy at the last minute, Balaguer preempted the announced candidacy of another member of the PRSC—Fernando Alvarez Bogaert—who had raised a common campaign issue of age and competence in his slogan "time for a new generation." Clearly it applied to Balaguer in particular but to Bosch as well.[22]

The campaign issues dealt with the economy and Balaguer's policies. Whereas he emphasized his role in expanding IFZs and foreign private investment and tourism, the PRD stressed its diversification of the economy while in office. On economic issues these two parties had both come to favor austerity. Once again rumors circulated about Peña Gómez's being a Haitian and not a loyal Dominican. In the May election (the results were not announced until mid-July) Balaguer was reelected with 35.1 percent, Bosch receiving 33.8 percent and Majluta 7 percent). The PRSC won sixteen Senate seats, the PLD 12, and the PRD 2. The PRSC won 42 Chamber seats, the PLD 44, and the PRD 32.[23]

Balaguer's Fifth Term (1990–1994)

Balaguer began his 1990 term facing continuing economic problems and the opposition of labor and business; he implemented a stabilization plan, and in 1991 he finally signed a long-postponed agreement with the IMF. The IMF agreed to provide US$113 million, and the agreement resulted in a $926 million debt renegotiation with the Paris Club. The required liberalization program, which ended price controls and subsidies to state agencies, created the beginning of an economic "turnaround," which greatly helped Balaguer and set the stage for the 1994 election.[24]

Until the turnaround became apparent in late 1992, labor agitation and strikes continued in opposition to the austerity program. To end the protests and placate the strikers, Balaguer promised to hold national elections in 1992 and to have the constitution amended, limiting presidents to a single term. This promise, however, turned out to be another shrewd tactic to buy time and undermine the opposition. A long strike by doctors and medical workers was finally settled in 1991 by a promise to increase salaries by 50 percent.

Balaguer's plan for the official inauguration of the Columbus Lighthouse (*El Faro a Colón*) on October 12, 1992 (Columbus Day), as the culmination of the fifth centennial was also a part of his focus on *Hispanidad* and the Spanish heritage. The project had been engulfed in great controversy because of the expensive public works, estimated at US$50–70 million, and because 3,000 squatters had been forced from a razed area for the construction site. In order to hide the surrounding slum area, a wall—called the

"Wall of Shame"—was built around the lighthouse. Despite the cost and the publicity, the celebration was a disaster: Balaguer's sister died; only one invited Latin American president attended; the king of Spain, who was to preside, did not appear; and the pope, then in the country for a bishops' conference, distanced himself from the ceremony and refused to conduct mass as requested. Moreover, there were protests directed against the ceremony in general and against the lighthouse in particular.[25]

Two months after his inauguration, Balaguer responded to the critical 1989 report of the Americas Watch in relation to Haitian workers and made some improvements in that area: standardization of their immigrant status, issuance of individual contracts to cane workers, and improvements in the living facilities on the state plantations. Even a later Americas Watch report admitted that there had been some improvements. However, other major abuses continued.[26] A subsequent critical report by the U.S. Lawyers Committee for Human Rights, which focused on the treatment of Haitian children, continued the bad publicity. Balaguer responded to the critical reports in June 1991 by ordering the deportation of illegal Haitians under sixteen or over sixty years of age. Within a few months 50,000 Haitians had been deported or left on their own in anticipation of being rounded up. The deportation policy received a mixed reaction in the Dominican Republic: It was supported by the National Defense Organization but opposed by hundreds of intellectuals.[27]

Balaguer also indicated his traditional attitude toward Haiti when Jean-Bertrand Aristide, a Roman Catholic liberation theology priest, was elected president in December 1990, in Haiti's first free and honest national elections. Although Aristide was inaugurated in February, Balaguer refused to recognize him and refused to condemn the military for overthrowing him in September 1991. When the OAS approved economic sanctions against the military junta to help secure Aristide's return to power, Balaguer refused to cooperate (later he promised the United States that he would), and the Dominican border remained open for smuggling goods to Haiti, especially gasoline.[28] Dominicans were happy to take advantage of the situation, for suppliers and border guards were able to enrich themselves. However, after the UN's total blockade and President Bill Clinton's request in May 1994 (during the election crisis), Balaguer reluctantly agreed to the border presence of a UN-U.S. force. Balaguer and many Dominicans did not welcome the return of Aristide to office in October 1994—the result of U.S. military intervention.

The Election of 1994

The two octogenarians were again major contenders, with Balaguer again seeking reelection and Bosch hoping to make up for his narrow defeat in 1990. Peña Gómez was the PRD nominee and Majluta that of his independent party; this time the PRD appeared to be united. Two campaign issues were the economy and age. Balaguer was in a most favored position because the economy had recovered beginning in late 1991. Agricultural production had increased, inflation had been greatly reduced, unemployment was down, there was a new Labor Code, and tourism and the number of IFZs had increased.[29] Balaguer took credit for the economic situation and emphasized the resultant stability. Since Balaguer's increasing enfeeblement was obvious, he dealt with the issue of age by selecting as his running mate a young, energetic, and capable administrator—Jacinto Peynado.

At the start of his campaign Peña Gómez gave public support to the return to office of democratically elected President Aristide. Internally, he noted the issue of corruption in the Balaguer government, an issue of reduced importance given the trial and conviction for corruption of former PRD President Jorge and the maldistribution of the benefits of the greatly improved economy. Once again, but more racist than before, he was the victim of attacks about his being "Haitian" and practicing voodoo, and thus not being a loyal Dominican. True to form, Balaguer came out publicly during the campaign to denounce these attacks on Peña Gómez. They had apparently served their purpose and/or were becoming counterproductive.[30]

The May election was observed by a twenty-six-member delegation, headed by former congressman Stephen Solarz, which had been organized by the National Democratic Institute (NDI) as it had done for the 1990 election. There was also an OAS team and another private group of observers. As the returns started coming in, Balaguer had a large lead, but the gap steadily closed, with Peña Gómez gaining until there was a minuscule difference—less than 1 percent (around 22,000 votes), leading Peña Gómez to charge fraud and to demand a recount.

The charges of fraud rested on the fact that the JCE had issued two different voter lists, one to the polling site officials and the other to the political parties. Many names on the latter list did not appear on the former, resulting in the turning away at the polls of voters with valid voter identification cards; this appeared to work against the PRD and Peña Gómez. The members of the NDI observer mission supported this charge and issued a critical report two days after the election.[31] Most of the presidential candidates signed a Pact of Civility, agreeing not to claim victory before the final official results were announced and to respect the results. (The pact was formally witnessed by a group of prominent Dominicans, organized by the Church, called the Dominican Commission to Comply with the Pact of Civility.)

Balaguer's Sixth (Half) Term (1994–1996)

In early June the JCE created a Verification Commission to investigate the charges of fraud. However, its report in mid-July was unconvincing, for it was inconsistent and did not deal with all issues; the report was ignored by the JCE when the official returns were announced on August 2. The electoral turnout was 87 percent, and Balaguer was declared the winner with 42.3 percent of the votes with Peña Gómez getting 41.6 percent, a margin of 22,281 votes. Bosch received 13.1 percent and Majluta 2.6 percent.[32] In the Senate the PRSC kept fourteen seats, the PRD and its allies won fifteen seats, and the PLD won one seat, and in the Chamber of Deputies, the PRSC won fifty, PRD and its allies fifty-seven, and the PLD thirteen.

Charging fraud, Peña Gómez called for a general strike on August 15 and 16 (the latter day being inauguration day). The resultant negotiations, mediated by the Church and the OAS, produced the Pact of Democracy, signed by Balaguer and Peña Gómez on August 10. The pact provided for a new presidential and vice presidential election to be held on November 16, 1995, with the winners to take office on February 26, 1996. Balaguer promised not to be a candidate. This timetable of Balaguer serving 15 months, however, was not approved by the Senate and Chamber of Deputies; they approved instead a term of two years, with the winner of the special election to complete the last two years of Balaguer's four-year term. The effort to amend the constitution and to limit presidents to a single term, opposed by Peña Gómez and the PRD, was finally approved by the legislature (the amendment became effective in September 1995, thus marking the end of Balaguer's tenure in August 1996). Although there is general agreement that the May 1994 elections were not legitimate and that there was definite fraud, it was not possible to confirm that the disenfranchised voters would have elected Peña Gómez.

The Election of 1996

Unlike in 1994, the two old political protagonists—incumbent Balaguer, eighty-nine years old, and Bosch, eighty-seven—were not battling each other again; Balaguer was barred from seeking reelection and Bosch had retired from public life in 1995. This time their parties nominated much younger candidates: The PRSC selected Balaguer's vice president, Jacinto Peynado, fifty-five, and the PLD selected Bosch's 1994 vice presidential nominee, lawyer Leonel Fernández, forty-two. The PRD's candidate was once again its head, Peña Gómez, who was also the nominee of an alliance of small parties.

The campaign revolved around the economic situation and the government leadership. Whereas the PLD and PRD candidates focused on the declining economy, the ineffective and corrupt government, and the need for leaders with new, modern ideas (polls indicated that most Dominicans favored such leaders), the PRSC was on defensive. Its leaders' first approach was to ignore the 1994 political election agreement and to organize a movement to annul the election. When this failed and became counterproductive, the PRSC defended Balaguer's economic policies. In the spring and summer of 1995, there were strikes and riots over increased bus fares and limited salary increases. There was also increasing police suppression, which resulted in many arrests and injuries. In early 1996 the government aired exaggerated claims about increasing economic growth and reducing inflation. Once again Balaguer's supporters injected the race issue against Peña Gómez: that he was not Dominican but Haitian and favored the unity of the two countries. And three weeks before the election Balaguer ordered the deportation of Haitians, which resulted in a roundup of thousands of Haitians. Peña Gómez denied the rumors and appealed to the masses, stressing the theme *"primero la gente"* (the people first). Among the candidates, the most typical U.S. style of campaign was run by political novice Fernández, who for ten years had lived and attended public school in New York City.

In preparation for the May 16 election, a number of the same observer groups as in 1994—from the OAS and the UN, from the U.S. Democratic and Republican parties, former president Carter's group, and so on—were present to ensure the integrity of the process. Voter turnout was around 75 percent in what the OAS certified as a valid, reliable, and representative election. (The special election applied only to the presidency; the legislative elections are scheduled to take place in May 1998.) As expected, Peña Gómez received the greatest number of votes, with 46 percent to Fernández's 37 percent. Peynado trailed with only 17 percent.[33] Because no candidate received 50 percent, there was a run-off election between Peña Gómez and Fernández on June 30. Opinion in the Dominican Republic was that there was an emerging alliance between the PLD and the PRSC, and that because of the race factor and Peña Gómez's liberal position, he was unlikely to be victorious.[34] That thinking was confirmed when Fernández won the presidency with a mere 51.25 percent of the 2.8 million votes cast.

Conclusion

Dominican democracy has been described as both "fragile" and "crisis-prone." That would appear to be true, for both economic and political reasons. The election of May 1994 certainly seemed to validate this characterization. Considering the discussion in the introduction about the "procedural" and "substantive" dimensions of democracy and the relationship between economic and political development, the considerable democratic progress in the Dominican Republic should be noted, despite the setback of the 1994 elections.

There is agreement that "competitive elections" began with the election of 1978, which "became the first meaningful presidential contest in years."[35] The Carter administration's 1978 "electoral intervention" against Balaguer appears to have made an important contribution to assuring the development of a two-party system by enabling the PRD to hold office for eight years. Although the earlier elections were characterized by fraud and irregularities as well as suppression of the opposition, this was not the case in 1982. Unfortunately, the subsequent elections reflect a reversion to this common practice of Balaguer governments.

A number of positive developments on the political side have strengthened Dominican democracy. First, the opposition parties—the PRD and the PLD—have been strengthened and institutionalized. Their leaders, leftists or moderates, have moderated over the years—for example, Guzmán and Jorge as party leaders and then as presidents, and Peña Gómez in the late 1980s and in the 1990s. The same is true of Bosch, who after he left the PRD in 1973 to form his own party, the PLD, later moved to the center and then to the right of center on certain issues, as illustrated during the campaign of 1994. However, there is a negative side to the parties and their leaders. The parties are either dominated by a single person, making them too personalist, or they are wrought with divisions caused by battles between the leftists and moderates. The ensuing fragmentation, which weakens the viability of the party in presidential contests, is often due to personalist leaders who head a faction, such as Balaguer in the PR and PRSC and Bosch in the PLD. The PRD has been fractioned and weakened by struggles between leftist Peña Gómez and moderates Guzmán, Jorge, and Majluta. A related problem is the personal opportunism of a personalist head of a PRD faction putting his getting the party's nomination ahead of maintaining party unity.

Second, the legislative branch—the Chamber of Deputies and Senate—has become an important branch of government and one capable of challenging and opposing the executive. It is no longer a rubber stamp, as had often been the case during earlier Balaguer governments. The power of the legislature has at times been used by PRD opportunists to oppose the policies of their own party's president, for the purpose of seeking the presidency. This practice has both weakened the legislature's role and generated intraparty divisions, especially in the PRD.

Third, unions have become stronger, better organized, and unified. They regularly engage in collective bargaining and are willing to go on strike, a right widely accepted. At times they are excessively politicized. The strength of the labor movement, however, is weakened by the fact that workers in the IFZs are prevented from organizing. Fourth, the military has become more professional and has been brought under civilian control—and more committed to the democratic process. This is particularly true of the younger generation. Fifth, the class system has become more flexible, and there has been a steady increase in the size, influence, and importance of the middle class. Although most of the middle class is in Santo Domingo, the capital, it is sizable in other cities as well, Santiago being a leading example. The middle class has become very influential in the Roman Catholic Church, the government bureaucracy, political parties, and the military.

Sixth, related to the growing middle class is the improved educational system at the university level. There has been a great increase in the number of universities, public and private. Until the early 1960s there was one main university—the public Autonomous University of Santo Domingo—and the students were very politicized. In 1962 the business community and the Church established the private Catholic University Madre y Maestra (UCMM) in Santiago, which has become a leading modern and progressive university. Now are branches of UASD outside the capital and a number of other private universities. Unfortunately, public education at the elementary and junior high levels, particularly in the rural areas, is in a state of crisis.

The political side of democracy is clearly linked with and dependent on the economic, for political and economic development are interdependent. As has been illustrated in this chapter, economic crises have presented threats to democracy. The Dominican economy has continued to become more diversified and less dependent on one major export and on the agriculture sector. There is a better balance in terms of income from tourism (the top revenue generator), mining, commerce, the IFZs (now being replaced by Mexican exports to the United States since the North American Free Trade Agreement [NAFTA]), and private foreign investment. But far too many Dominicans remain virtually outside the economy, and they have been organizing at the grassroots level to improve their economic plight. They constitute what is called the Popular Movement, which was organized in and grew out of the slums in Santo Domingo.

There remains another area of concern, involving both the political and the economic, and that is human rights and racism, which are related. There continues to be a racist dimension in the country, although directed mainly toward Haitians and Haiti, especially Haitian sugarcane workers, but directed toward darker-skinned Dominicans as well. Balaguer's attitudes and policies reflect this continuing legacy, which manifested itself especially during electoral campaigns, with Peña Gómez bearing its brunt. Progress has been made in this area, however, as illustrated by the official recognition and celebration of the country's African roots and the *cultura criollo*.

The problem of the treatment of Haitian workers continues, however, even though the Dominican Republic is a party to a number of UN human rights treaties, including the Convention on the Elimination of All Forms of Racial Discrimination, ratified in 1983. Its enforcement will be difficult, but progress is being made. The General Confederation of Workers (CGT) and its sugar federation (FENAZCUR) have been making serious efforts to represent the interests of both Dominican and Haitian workers. In addition, the Church has become socially active on the issue of the treatment of Haitian workers.

Notwithstanding the progress that has been made toward an effective and representative Dominican model of democracy, there is one feature on the political side that will determine the future of democracy in that country. This is what one leading student of the Dominican Republic has called "political atrophy."[36] Two of the leading parties have been dominated by two men, now octogenarians: the PR and PRSC by Balaguer, and the PRD and PLD by Bosch. Hence the critical question has to do with the future leaders of the PRSC and PLD: Will Balaguer's and Bosch's successors be committed to strengthening Dominican democracy and providing the rejuvenation of atrophied political muscles? A qualified positive answer can be provided in view of Bosch's recent retirement and replacement by Fernández in the PLD and the more moderate and realistic position of the PRD's Peña Gómez.

Notes

1. See Jan K. Black, "Democracy and Disillusionment in the Dominican Republic," in *Modern Caribbean Politics,* ed. Anthony Payne and Paul Sutton (Baltimore: Johns Hopkins University Press, 1993), pp. 54–72; Rosario Espinal, "Dominican Republic: Electoralism, Pacts, and Clientelism in the Making of a Democratic Regime," in *Democracy in the Caribbean: Myths and Realities,* ed. Carlene J. Edie (New York: Praeger, 1994), pp. 147–161; and Jonathan Hartlyn, "The Dominican Republic: Contemporary Problems and Challenges," in *Democracy in the Caribbean: Political, Economic, and Social Perspectives,* ed. Jorge I. Domínguez, Robert A. Pastor, and R. Delisle Worrell (Baltimore: Johns Hopkins University Press, 1993), pp. 150–172. For a report on the 1994 elections, see Howard J. Wiarda, "Out with the Old, but Not Too Fast, in the Dominican Republic," *North-South* (September-October 1994), pp. 14–17; and Wiarda, *The Dominican Republic Elections of 1994* (Washington, DC: Center for Strategic and International Studies, August 12, 1994).

2. See Larman C. Wilson, "The Dominican Policy of the United States," *World Affairs* (July-September 1965):93–101; and Larman C. Wilson, "The United States and the Dominican Republic: A Post-election Assessment," in *The Lingering Crisis: A Case Study of the Dominican Republic,* ed. Eugenio Chang-Rodríguez (New York: Las Américas Publishing Co., 1969), pp. 101–127.

3. See Jerome Slater, *The OAS and United States Foreign Policy* (Columbus: Ohio State University Press, 1967). Slater examines the OAS's role as an anticommunist alliance in chapters 3 and 4 of that text and considers its later role as an antidictatorial alliance in chapters 5 and 6.

4. Balaguer had been a diplomat in Spain and had studied in France in the 1930s; he also had been a diplomat in Latin America during the 1940s and 1950s. He became a literary figure and held many educational and cultural positions under Trujillo before becoming vice president.

5. Larman C. Wilson, "Estados Unidos y la Guerra Civil Dominicana: El reto a las relaciones interamericanas," *Foro Internacional*, vol. 8 (October-December 1967):155–178. Two leading books on the subject are Piero Gleijeses's *The Dominican Crisis: The 1965 Constitutionalist Revolt and the American Intervention* (Baltimore: Johns Hopkins University Press, 1978); and Jerome Slater's *Intervention and Negotiation: The United States and the Dominican Revolution* (New York: Harper and Row, 1970).

6. Richard S. Hillman and Thomas J. D'Agostino, *Distant Neighbors in the Caribbean: The Dominican Republic and Jamaica in Comparative Perspective* (New York: Praeger, 1992), p. 112, Table 5.1.

7. Michael J. Kryzanek, "Political Party Decline and the Failure of Liberal Democracy: The PRD in Dominican Politics," *Journal of Latin American Studies*, vol. 9 (May 1977):121–129; and Hillman and D'Agostino, *Distant Neighbors in the Caribbean*, p. 112.

8. Hillman and D'Agostino, *Distant Neighbors in the Caribbean*, p. 112.

9. José del Castillo and Martin F. Murphy, "Migration, National Identity, and Cultural Policy in the Dominican Republic," *Journal of Ethnic Studies*, vol. 15 (Fall 1987):65–66.

10. James Ferguson, *The Dominican Republic: Beyond the Lighthouse* (London: Latin American Bureau, 1992), pp. 85–86. In January 1978 the Balaguer government ratified a number of the United Nations human rights treaties, including the Covenants on Economic, Social, and Cultural Rights and on Civil and Political Rights and the Convention Relating to the Status of Refugees. In April the American Convention on Human Rights was ratified, but the jurisdiction of the Inter-American Court of Human Rights was not accepted.

11. Jonathan Hartlyn, "The Dominican Republic: Contemporary Problems and Challenges," in *Democracy in the Caribbean*, ed. Domínguez, Pastor, and Worrell, pp. 157–162. Rosario Espinal has argued that competitive elections truly began with the 1978 election. See her "Electoral Politics in the Dominican Republic, 1978–1990" (paper presented at the Sixteenth International Congress of the Latin American Studies Association, Washington, DC, April 4–6, 1991), pp. 5–6.

12. G. Pope Atkins, *Arms and Politics in the Dominican Republic* (Boulder: Westview Press, 1981), p. 103.

13. Ibid., pp. 105–106, and Michael Kryzanek, "The 1978 Election in the Dominican Republic: Opposition Politics, Intervention, and the Carter Administration," *Caribbean Studies*, vol. 19 (April-July 1979):58–59.

14. Hillman and D'Agostino, *Distant Neighbors in the Caribbean*, p. 112.

15. Espinal, "Dominican Republic," p. 155.

16. Hillman and D'Agostino, *Distant Neighbors in the Caribbean*, p. 112.

17. Jan Knippers Black, *The Dominican Republic: Politics and Development in an Unsovereign State* (Boston: Allen and Unwin, 1986), p. 140.

18. See Espinal, "Dominican Republic," pp. 152–153, and Hillman and D'Agostino, *Distant Neighbors in the Caribbean*, p. 112.

19. Jorge was permitted to go to the United States for medical treatment and he was tried in absentia and sentenced to twenty years in prison. In 1991 he returned to the Dominican Republic, was tried in person, and the original sentence was reaffirmed.

20. Ferguson, *The Dominican Republic*, p. 35.

21. Ferguson, *The Dominican Republic*, pp. 58, 86–87; Americas Watch, *Haitian Sugar Cane Cutters in the Dominican Republic* (New York: Americas Watch, November 1989); and Americas Watch, *Harvesting Oppression: Forced Haitian Labor in the Dominican Sugar Industry* (New York: Americas Watch, June 1990).

22. Black, "Democracy and Disillusionment in the Dominican Republic," pp. 64–66, and Ferguson, *The Dominican Republic*, pp. 51–53.

23. Hillman and D'Agostino, *Distant Neighbors in the Caribbean*, p. 112. See also National Democratic Institute for International Affairs and the Carter Center of Emory University, *1990 Elections in the Dominican Republic: Report of an Observer Delegation* (Washington, DC, and Atlanta: NDIIA and CC, 1990), pp. 18–19.

24. Ladislao Brachowicz, "Turnaround in the Dominican Republic: Reforms Pay Off with Growth and Stabilization," in Inter-American Development Bank, *The IDB* (Washington, DC: IADB, December 1993), pp. 6–7.

25. This account is based on discussions in December 1992 in Washington, DC, with Martha Ellen Davis, an anthropologist at the Center for Latin American and Caribbean Studies, Indiana University, Bloomington, who had attended and prepared a video of the formal celebration. See also Douglas Farah, "Pope Lauds Church's 1492 Role," *Washington Post*, October 13, 1992, p. A14.

26. Americas Watch, *Half Measures: Reform, Forced Labor, and the Dominican Sugar Industry* (New York: Americas Watch, March 1991). See also the critical report of the Human Rights Commission of the OAS, *Annual Report of the Inter-American Commission on Human Rights 1991* (Washington, DC: OAS, 1992), pp. 260–261.

27. Bosch also supported the deportation policy (Ferguson, *The Dominican Republic*, pp. 88–91).

28. Wiarda, *The Dominican Republic Elections of 1994*, p. 10; and Wiarda "Out with the Old," p. 16.

29. Brachowicz, "Turnaround in the Dominican Republic," p. 7.

30. "Balaguer rechaza campaña acusa Peña práctica vudú," *Listín Diario*, April 13, 1994, p. 1. This column and others plus cartoons were sent to me by a former student, Amanda Fernández, M.A., who was working then for Catholic Relief Services near the Haitian border. My thanks to her. See also Wiarda, *The Dominican Republic Election of 1994*, pp. 10–11.

31. The NDI delegation issued a critical preliminary statement raising the possibility of electoral fraud. Its final report questioned the legitimacy of the election. Jonathan Hartlyn was a member of the NDI delegation. See his "Crisis-Ridden Elections (Again) in the Dominican Republic: Neopatrimonialism, Presidentialism, and Weak Electoral Oversight," *Journal of Interamerican Studies and World Affairs*, vol. 36 (Winter 1994):122–134.

32. NDI, *1990 Elections in the Dominican Republic*, pp. 1–3, Appendix A; and Hartlyn, "Crisis-Ridden Elections," pp. 122, 132.

33. *Diario de las Américas* (Miami), May 19, 1996, pp. A1, A13.

34. Max J. Castro, "Dominican Republic," *North South FOCUS*, vol. 5, no. 2 (1996):4.

35. See Espinal, "Electoral Politics in the Dominican Republic," pp. 5–7. Howard J. Wiarda and Michael J. Kryzanek call this the first meaningful presidential contest

in twelve years. Wiarda and Kryzanek, *The Dominican Republic: A Caribbean Crucible*, 2d ed. (Boulder: Westview Press, 1992), p. 49.

36. Michael J. Kryzanek, "The Waiting Game: Opposition and Political Atrophy in the Dominican Republic" (paper presented at the eighteenth annual conference of the Caribbean Studies Association, Ocho Rios, Jamaica, May 28, 1993), pp. 3–7, 10–11, 19–21.

8

Human Rights in the Eastern Caribbean

Francis Alexis

In Antigua and Barbuda, Dominica, Grenada, St. Kitts and Nevis, St. Lucia, St. Vincent and the Grenadines—the independent states of the Organization of Eastern Caribbean States (OECS)[1]—the constitution, "the supreme law," guarantees individuals certain fundamental human rights and freedoms, in provisions called the Bill of Rights. The legal philosophy of these rights is that they should enable individuals to nurture their talents for the advancement of themselves and the body politic. In this the courts, the legislature, the executive, the bureaucracy, society generally, and the individuals themselves all have their respective roles to play. Legal analysis measures the degree of success attained in the enjoyment of these rights, for the benefit of the individual and society, primarily on the basis of the frequency and the outcome of litigation undertaken to enforce them. This form of analysis is applied in this chapter in an examination of human rights in the OECS.

Three Basic Principles

The rule of law, the separation of powers, and the independence of the judiciary, the three basic principles characteristic of parliamentary democracy, point to a certain model of individual rights and freedoms. The model is presented in the great contemporary international statements of rights and freedoms, such as the United Nations Universal Declaration of Human Rights, the European Convention on Human Rights, and the Inter-American Convention on Human Rights. The model is reflected in OECS bills of rights as well.

OECS bills of rights mirror the liberal democracy characterizing the Westminster model of government bequeathed by Great Britain to the Commonwealth. As an outgrowth of the "Westministerial Constitution," bills of rights of the type found in the OECS are today an integral ingredient of the "rule of law," whatever the original signification of that term as popularized by Albert Venn Dicey. Adequate protection of such bills of rights requires, among other things, an independent judiciary. OECS constitutional instruments[2] safeguard the independence of the judiciary through entrenched provisions enshrining the appointment, tenure, and jurisdiction of members of the "higher" judiciary: the High Court and the Court of Appeal, and superior courts of record, which together form the OECS Supreme Court.[3]

Judicial independence is requisite to the separation between the legislature and the executive. The doctrine of the separation of powers is so fundamental to Caribbean constitutions that it is woven into their fabric, amounting to what OECS Chief Justice Sir Vincent Floissac calls "a basic principle implicit in the Constitution."[4] Hence the principle does not depend on some specialized literal provision of the constitution. As the Privy Council has said, "the Constitution of Dominica . . . takes for granted the basic principle of separation of powers."[5] The separation of powers is a cornerstone of the independence of the judiciary, guardians of the constitution.

Civil and Political Rights

OECS bills of rights guarantee the right to life. They frown upon cruel and inhuman punishment. They confer the right to personal liberty. The idea that a person's home is his/her castle is enshrined in restrictions against its arbitrary search or entry, an element of right to privacy. There are the freedoms of assembly and association; of movement; of conscience, including religious beliefs; and of expression or speech. One is also protected from discrimination on such grounds as political opinions, race, and sex. Moreover, there is relief from deprivation of property without compensation.

Buttressing such rights and freedoms are provisions enabling one to apply to the High Court for redress against their contravention. These go on to empower the High Court to enforce those rights and freedoms or secure their enforcement by making declarations or orders, issuing writs, and giving appropriate directions. These remedies provisions of the bills of rights afford a simple and expeditious facility for redressing human rights violations. They put beyond all doubt the pronouncement by Justice Lyle St. Paul in a Grenadian case that "the Court must stand as the last bastion to protect the rights and freedoms of all the people of the State. To fail in this can only lead to anarchy."[6]

This constitutional jurisdiction vested in the Supreme Court making it "the guardian" of the constitution against infringements[7] is protected by the basic principle of the separation of powers implicit in the constitution. This doctrine prohibits the legislature and the executive from depriving that court of this jurisdiction, or indeed of a significant part of the characteristic jurisdiction inherent in that court as a superior court of record; and from vesting such jurisdiction in a body whose members do not enjoy the tenure, jurisdiction, and appointment safeguards of members of the Supreme Court. Thus if a drug-trafficking charge carries a sentence of life imprisonment, only the High Court can try cases involving it,[8] so jealous is the Supreme Court of the jurisdiction vested in it by the constitution to guard the Bill of Rights against contravention.

A Rebuttable Presumption

When the violation of a human right is alleged to lie in an Act of Parliament, more so than in an administrative action, there is a presumption of its constitutionality, and the burden rests with whoever claims the violation to show that there has been a transgression of some constitutional provision or principle. Hence where an Act limits some right, "[t]he proper approach . . . is to presume, until the contrary appears or is shown, that all Acts passed . . . were reasonably required." The presumption requires the court to interpret the impugned provision as subject to "an implied term" to avoid conflict with the constitution. Both principles were stated by the Privy Council in two different cases.[9]

In the St. Kitts case, the Act requires Kittitians to first obtain the written permission of the commissioner of police to use a noisy instrument, such as a public address system, at a public meeting. It adds that the commissioner "may in his discretion" grant such permission. This is presumed to be reasonably required for public order and for protecting the rights of others, as allowed by the constitutional guarantee of freedom of expression.[10]

Further, it is presumed that administrative power conferred by an Act will be exercised in accordance with the mission of the Act, no matter how widely cast are the words enabling the exercise of that power. There is always a perspective within which a statutory power is required to be exercised, gleaned from the enabling statutory provisions read as a whole, and in light of the incongruence of absolute power subsisting under the rule of law. Thus no statutory power may be exercised in bad faith. That the discretion is framed generously need not render the Act unconstitutional, but if the power is abused in a particular case the courts may grant redress. The OECS courts and the Privy Council have spelled this out repeatedly.[11]

However, if a complainant shows that there appears to be justification for calling upon the state to answer an allegation of human rights violation, the onus shifts to the state to show that the measure is not unconstitutional. The presumption of constitutionality in favor of state action can be rebutted; it is rebuttable if a statutory provision is so arbitrary as to compel the conclusion that it does not involve an exertion of its permitted power, but instead constitutes the direct execution of a different and forbidden power. Such would have happened if an Antiguan Act requiring newspaper printers and publishers to obtain a publishing license had imposed an annual fee for the license that was so manifestly excessive or otherwise of such a character to lead to the conclusion that its rationale was not revenue generation but the prevention of newspaper publication. This would have rendered the Act not reasonably required for the raising of revenue and as such unconstitutional, violating freedom of expression, including freedom of the press.

In the well-known *Antigua Times* case[12] the OECS court thought that this had happened with two Antiguan Acts. One imposed an annual license fee of EC$600. The other required printers and publishers to deposit EC$10,000 with the state to meet damages for libel, but empowered a minister to waive the deposit and accept instead sufficient security in the form of an insurance policy or a bank guarantee. The OECS court would have struck down the Acts, but the Privy Council saw nothing to displace the presumption of constitutionality. The presumption has on other occasions been rebutted, with statutory provisions being struck down for being unconstitutional.

An associated matter is that of severing from an Act those of its provisions that violate the Constitution and leaving intact the provisions that do not offend it. In 1993 the Privy Council replaced the old test of textual severability with the new test of substantial severability. By this new test, impugned provisions will not be defeated if their substantial purpose and effect are clearly within the lawmaker's power but, by some oversight or misapprehension of the scope of that power, the text has a range of application exceeding that scope. Toward that end, the court will sever the offending clause and save the lawful provisions if that would cause no change in the substantial purpose and effect of the impugned provisions. This test of substantial severability can preserve provisions that might not have satisfied the test of textual severability.[13]

Liberty Not License

As in any other society, in the OECS liberty is not license. No right is absolute. One person's right is subject to respect for the rights and freedoms of others, to public interests such as public order and public safety, and to other limitations specified in the bills of rights.

One is certainly entitled to freedom of expression, including freedom to communicate or impart ideas and information without interference. But, as the constitution indicates, this freedom is not contravened by a law that is reasonably required in the interest of public order or for the purpose of protecting the rights and freedoms of other persons. That is why Parliament could enact a law requiring one to first obtain written permission from the commissioner of police to use noisy instruments such as loudspeakers at public meetings, adding that the commissioner may in his discretion grant such permission. Such a law was given constitutional validity in the *Kittitian Loudspeaker* case.[14]

The court observed that the use of loudspeakers making excessive noise at a public meeting by a person could at times constitute a nuisance by seriously interfering with the comfort and convenience of a substantial number of persons, improperly subjecting them to "aural aggression" that might reach unbearable intensity. This would disturb these people, thereby interfering with their rights. It could also be inimical to the preservation of public order. Hence, the OECS Supreme Court and the Privy Council reasoned, the use of loudspeakers at public meetings could validly be regulated and made the subject of the discretion of an appropriate licensing authority, such as the chief of police.

It is easy to agree with all that. But it is not so easy to subscribe to the view expressed by the majority of the Court of Appeal that the use of a loudspeaker is not essential to the exercise of the right to freedom of expression.[15] Today no one is expected to enjoy the right to communicate ideas and information to a large outdoor public assembly without the aid of a loudspeaker, especially during an election campaign, when the natural voice is strained. It is akin to saying that access to newsprint is not essential to enjoyment of freedom of the press. Freedom to use a loudspeaker is a necessary adjunct to the rights of free expression and free assembly. But, as Justice Gordon said, this does not give license to use it at a public meeting at any time and in any place; its use may still then be regulated for public order and for protecting other peoples' rights.[16] Similarly, freedom of the press included in freedom of expression is amenable to licensing as taxing measures and to cash deposits for meeting damages for libel. The Privy Council laid this down in the case *Attorney General v Antigua Times*, which was mentioned earlier.

Protecting Private Property

OECS constitutions ordain that no property shall be compulsorily taken possession of, and no interest in or right over property shall be compulsorily acquired, except under a law required by the constitution to contain certain provisions. Usually that law must provide for the payment within a reasonable time of adequate or fair compensation.[17] In one instance, Section P(1) of the St. Kitts constitution, it is sufficient that the law prescribe the principles on which and the manner in which compensation is to be determined and given.

A different requirement is shared by Grenada and St. Lucia, where the law needs to provide for "prompt payment of full compensation."[18] There is a context to the Grenada formula that requires some explanation. In 1974 Grenada became the first OECS country to graduate from the semiautonomous internal self-governing status of associated statehood to full sovereign independence. The move was controversial, with some people arguing that Grenada was not economically able to finance independence. It was also argued that the person leading Grenada into independence, Eric Matthew Gairy, would use independence to tighten the authoritarian grip he had already been establishing.

Importantly, the move fanned the old flames of the simple power struggle between working-class hero Eric Gairy and his inveterate antagonists, the propertied and professional classes.[19] Hence in the independence negotiations in London, the lobbyists of the propertied and professional classes demanded that property rights be elevated to the status of a fundamental human right with strong protection. The settlement was that expropriated landowners be entitled to "prompt payment of full compensation." Indeed, most of the human rights litigation occurring in the OECS since independence deals with the constitutional protection from deprivation of property without compensation.

Most of that litigation has attacked the law under which the OECS compulsorily acquire property as being the law referred to in the constitutional property protection clause—the Land Acquisition Act. It was enacted before the commencement of the constitution and as such is an "existing law" or a preconstitution law.

The Land Acquisition Act in Grenada does not specify the "prompt payment of full compensation" as spelled out by the constitutional property protection clause. But the country's constitution, like those of most OECS countries, has an existing laws modification clause that indicates that the existing laws shall, as from the commencement of the constitution, be construed with such modifications, adaptations, qualifications, and exceptions as may be necessary to secure conformity with the constitution. This is the principle of harmonization by construction required by the existing laws modification clause. It is just the opposite of the independence constitutional command in St. Kitts, where the constitutional property protection clause does not apply to any law that was in force when St. Kitts achieved associated statehood back in 1967.[20]

The existing laws modification clause of the Grenada type has been held by the Privy Council to be so ample as to be able to reconcile "absolute discretion, and indeed the power of a dictator" in an existing law with the "reasonably justifiable" powers in the constitution, despite the "very real difference" between them. The justices had so held in the *Reynolds Rule*,[21] regarding St. Kitts, when that country had an existing laws modification clause of the Grenada type, a clause St. Kitts abandoned on gaining independence. By doing so the judges achieved what some jurists had long said could be done,[22] but what others had considered impossible: reconciliation between the "absolute discretion" provisions of legislation and the "reasonably justifiable" powers of the constitution.[23]

The *Reynolds Rule* has been applied to the preconstitution Land Acquisition Act. In the 1993 Grenadian case *Beausejour Estates v Attorney-General*,[24] the preconstitution Land Acquisition Act was construed as providing for "prompt payment of full compensation," even though those words do not actually appear in the Act. The result has been a certain uniformity on Acts of that type under the OECS constitutions. The courts have harmonized the Act with the constitution by the process of construction to meet the constitutional requirement of prompt payment of full compensation. The Act provides that the value of land compulsorily acquired shall be fixed at a date twelve months prior to the date at which the land vests absolutely in the state, the date of the compulsory acquisition. Harmonizing this with the constitutional requirement of full payment, in a case famous within the Caribbean— the famous *Grand Anse Estates* case from Grenada—the courts construe the Act to mean that the value should be fixed at "the date of acquisition."[25] Not even provisions enacted after the commencement of the constitution may get away with fixing the value of acquired lands at a date prior to acquisition. The Parliament in St. Kitts found this out, although the constitution there does not stipulate that compensation shall be full, adequate, or fair.[26]

Again, the Act tends to fix at a certain percentage the rate of interest that may be awarded by the board of assessment to the owner of the expropriated land, often, as in Grenada, 5 percent. This has been construed as conformity with the constitutional requirement of full payment. It leaves the Grenadian Act as construed to provide for what Justice St. Bernard of the OECS Court of Appeal calls "a just equivalent of his loss and not a rigid and fixed rate whatever the loss may be"—interest "at such a rate as would compensate him adequately for any loss occasioned by him."[27]

It may be different where, as in Dominica, the constitutional instruments do not require preconstitution laws to be brought into conformity with the constitution.[28] But where those instruments require such harmonization, 5 percent interest may in some cases suffice,[29] but in others it may not. Moreover, there is the broader question of what constitutes "full" compensation. This has been defined as compensation that is "complete, entire, to the utmost extent"; or "a just equivalent of the land at the time of the acquisition plus any loss incurred by such acquisition plus adequate interest to the date of payment."[30]

Whether or not there is a difference between "full" and "adequate" compensation,[31] neither means unconscionable profiteering out of compulsory acquisition. Take the *Orange Hill Estates* case[32] from St. Vincent. A company paid a vendor the actual price of EC$4.3 million for the Orange Hill Estate on the slopes of La Soufriere volcano mountain. Two months later the estate was compulsorily acquired by the state. The expropriated company claimed EC$29.5 million in compensation. The board of assessment awarded EC$4.7 million in compensation.

The company appealed to the OECS Court of Appeal. Chief Justice Sir Vincent Floissac felt that the actual price paid for land at a time reasonably near to its compulsory acquisition is "generally presumed to be the open market value," the value set by the Act as the sum payable on acquisition. Justice Nicholas Liverpool might not have been sure of such presumption. But whether regarding the open market value, the actual price recently paid is "the best evidence," as Justice Byron thought, or is only one piece of evidence, as Justice Liverpool opined, it certainly is "evidence," as Chief Justice Floissac put it, and Justices Byron and Liverpool agreed. Chief Justice Floissac and Justice Byron increased the compensation from EC$4.7 million to EC$5.2 million, though Justice Liverpool would have raised it to some EC$6.5 million, so none of the judges would take the compensation to any figure even remotely resembling the EC$29.5 million claimed by the company.

Determination of the amount of compensation to which an expropriated landowner is entitled is a matter for a judicial forum. This may be the High Court. It may be a tribunal, usually a board of assessment, with appeals lying to the High Court. Just as a board of assessment cannot determine the legality of an acquisition,[33] so too an acquisition Act may not itself fix the limit of compensation payable, unlike what was done by an Act providing for the acquisition of financially strapped Kittitian sugar estates. The Act was voided as an unconstitutional usurpation of the court's jurisdiction.[34]

It is infinitely worse where a government simply makes a law confiscating properties without providing for any compensation. The most brazen example of this was what was done by the People's Revolutionary Government (PRG) of Maurice Bishop of Grenada while the constitution was suspended. A victim of such a law was former Prime Minister Sir Eric Gairy, whom Bishop had overthrown by force of arms in March 1979. Once the constitution was restored, following the fall of the PRG in October 1983, those confiscatory laws could not stand, as the state conceded when Gairy sought judicial relief.

But, the state argued, the court should not order the return of the properties to Sir Eric because the properties had been leased by the state to third parties, and such an order would create hardship on them. Justice St. Paul noted this and also that the arguments took on "a political flavor." He was not impressed. In pronouncements forcefully and vigorously championing the constitutionally guaranteed liberty of the individual, Justice St. Paul proclaimed that "judges must not regard political consequences how formidable soever they might be, if rebellion was the certain consequence we are bound to say '*Fiat Justitia Ruat Coelum*' [let justice be done even if the heavens fall]." In invalidating the confiscatory laws and ordering the return of the Gairy properties,[35] Justice St. Paul insisted that "those with the political power must respect the proprietary rights of the people," adding, "What goes around comes around." It therefore was entirely beside the point that the Gairy government had itself not compensated several persons whose lands it had expropriated.[36]

Confiscatory legislation need not be that brazen to be unconstitutional. Technical faults may have the same effect, even regarding antisocial behavior that jolts the judiciary no less than the wider society. Thus the courts rightly insist that an Act providing for the forfeiture of the proceeds of illegal drug trafficking must specify whether a conviction is required for such forfeiture, and if so, it should identify the offense for which a conviction carries forfeiture. When such an Act in Anguilla was tainted by these lacunae, it was voided by Justice Joseph as unconstitutionally authorizing deprivation of property without compensation.[37]

The requirement that payment must be "prompt" does not mean that the landowner should be paid when it is due in the ordinary vendor and purchaser transaction under private treaty, that is, when the land vests in the purchaser. In compulsory acquisition, the land vests in the state when the second acquisition notice is gazetted. The constitution is satisfied if compensation is paid "with alacrity," with "a degree of urgency," or "readiness of action." This is the sense in which it is said that there must be "immediate payment."[38] Payment may not be prompt if not made after two years, certainly not after twelve years, and not if made on a joint cash and bonds basis stretching out over ten years.

The "property" of which one should not be deprived without compensation applies equally to concrete as well as abstract rights of property, including rights of control and management of companies. The St. Kitts Parliament discovered this when it passed an Act providing for the dislodging of the managing director and other directors of a private company and the substituting for the majority of the directors with persons named by a minister. The managing director was thus deprived of his contract to hold the office of managing director until he resigned as managing director or ceased to be a director. He was also thus deprived of his right as a shareholder to choose the directors. No compensation for all this deprivation was provided for by the Act. The Act was struck down by the courts for violating the property protection clause.[39]

Conscience and Communication

As social beings, people need to relate to each other. They cannot relate unless in conscience they think about what is said and done by others, and about their God. Assembling and associating with others promotes communication, hopefully for mutual satisfaction and advancement. OECS constitutions are therefore quite right to elevate to the level of fundamental human rights the right to think according to one's conscience, the right to express one's self, the freedom to assemble and associate, and the related rights and freedoms.

OECS economies are small, open, and fragile. A public order scare is apt to discourage tourists and the foreign exchange revenues they bring. The OECS is certainly not without political and societal tensions.[40] The constitutions qualify the rights about thinking and communicating by making them subject to measures that are reasonably required in the interest of public order, or for protecting the rights and freedoms of others, or for other concerns stated by the constitutions, though such measures need to be reasonably justifiable in a democratic society. Invoking these exceptions, OECS countries have enacted legislation regulating rights relating to thinking and communicating. A Kittitian Act forbade one to organize or speak at any meeting or assembly; organize or take part in any procession; or use a loudspeaker to announce a meeting, assembly, or procession, without the prior written permission of the chief of police; and the chief was empowered to grant or withhold such permission. Justice Glasgow condemned that as an unconstitutional hindrance in the enjoyment of freedom of expression and of assembly.[41]

In Antigua an Act provided for the summary criminal punishment of any person who printed or distributed any false statement that was "likely to undermine public confidence in the conduct of public affairs." Prosecuted thereunder, political activist Tim Hector complained that this provision transgressed his constitutionally guaranteed freedom of expression, including freedom of the press. Justice Matthew agreed with Hector. His decision was reversed by the Court of Appeal but restored by the Privy Council in the case *Hector v Attorney-General*.[42]

The Privy Council felt that if the disseminating of false statements likely to disturb public order has to be criminalized, such statements need to be likely to cause fear or alarm to the public, or to disturb the public peace. But, the Privy Council said, in a free democratic society, those who hold office in government or public administration must always be open to criticism. "Any attempt to stifle or fetter such criticism amounts to political censorship of the most insidious and objectionable kind," Lord Bridge stated. He added that the very purpose of criticism leveled at those who have the conduct of public affairs by their political opponents is to undermine public confidence in their stewardship and to persuade the electorate to prefer the opposition to the government. Hence provisions criminalizing statements likely to undermine public confidence in the conduct of public affairs must be viewed with the utmost suspicion, are not reasonably required for public order, and offend against the constitution.[43] This was definitely a powerful and robust defense of the right of the individual openly to criticize the government, as befits the last decade of this century when societies are being increasingly democratized.

The *Hector* declaration fits rather neatly into that ambience. At the heart of all this is the cherished liberty of the individual. Assuredly, liberty is limited. But the state must abide by the constitutional limitations on liberty. Although the constitution enables the state to take measures such as arresting and detaining persons in periods of emergency, those measures must be reasonably justifiable, and the detainees must be provided with a written statement specifying "in detail" the grounds of their detention. It appears that the respondent in the Kittitian case *Attorney-General v Reynolds*[44] was detained because he belonged to an opposition party. Certainly he was not provided with any detail of the grounds of his detention, only a vague and ambiguous notice—a mockery, really—that he, within and outside the state, encouraged civil disobedience throughout the state, thereby endangering the peace, public safety, and public order. The failure to specify the grounds of detention suggested to the courts that there were no grounds, far less any justifiable grounds, for detaining Reynolds. The OECS Supreme Court and the Privy Council awarded him exemplary damages to underline their disapproval of the flagrant violation of his constitutional right to liberty.

It is of no use for a person to be assured liberty, being free to think according to his conscience and freely express his views, only to find that he risks being discriminated against for his expressed opinions, not least of all his political opinions. Rightly, therefore, the constitution prohibits discrimination based on political opinions as well as on such other factors as race, color, social origins, class, religion, and sex. Discrimination based on political opinions is particularly dangerous and explosive. Much of the societal upheaval the Caribbean has experienced during this century has been political, though mixed with industrial, economic, class, and social factors. Political misbehavior in state office has the potential to ignite societal conflagration.

Of course it is always easy for one who is displeased by state action to cry "political oppression and victimization against him and his family."[45] But the courts should, in any proper case, firmly reprimand a state functionary who discriminates against an individual because of his/her political opinions. It was refreshing that the court castigated the minister and the collector of customs of Antigua in 1971 when, on the dictation of the minister, the collector refused import licenses to the company Camacho and Sons wholly because the owners of the company had expressed political opinions opposed to the government.[46]

It makes no difference that it might be an alien claiming the transgression of the constitution. An alien detained in Grenada awaiting deportation claimed that his deportation involved the denial of these fundamental rights of conscience and communication by the state acting in bad faith. Quite properly, Justice St. Paul granted him an order nisi of habeas corpus to hear and determine his allegations. But when the matter was heard the alien failed to substantiate his allegations, and so the deportation was allowed.[47]

Closely related to the rights regarding conscience and communication is the right to vote, which, though not a fundamental human right, is nonetheless entrenched in the constitution as a right. The constitution ordains that, subject to the qualifications stipulated by it, one is "entitled to be registered as . . . a voter" and is "entitled to vote." This entails the right to an opportunity to register as a voter. Failure to properly revise the list of electors, thus denying a person an opportunity to be registered on attaining voting age, infringes his constitutional entitlement to be registered and to vote. Likewise, failure to afford reasonable opportunities for registered voters to cast their votes, such as by not providing sufficient ballot papers, is such a blatant denial of the right to vote that it vitiates the elections in a constituency so affected.

How much more, therefore, should the fundamental human rights be respected, not least where one's livelihood is involved? For example, in one case—*Hamilton v Morrison* (1977)—an Act incorporated farmers in the vital nutmeg industry in Grenada into an association and empowered them to have six of the nine members of the board of directors elected by them, except during a two-month dissolution period. The governor-general in 1975 made an order dissolving the elected board, providing for a board wholly nominated by himself, and giving his nominated board management and control of the association indefinitely, as distinct from the two-month dissolution period allowed by the Act. The judge ruled that this order violated the constitutional right to freedom of assembly and association, which enabled farmers of the association to choose who should manage them except during an allowed two-month dissolution. An Act passed to validate that order was futile, since the violation of the guaranteed rights was consummated on the promulgation of the order.

But some allegations of human rights violations seem flippant. Included here are those complaining against an admittedly lawful refusal of applications for temporary passports and those contending that violations of natural justice in dissolving an elected statutory farmers' board of directors and replacing it with a state-nominated board constitute slavery. Another example is the apparent belief by the people who murdered Prime Minister Maurice Bishop in October 1983 that they could avert their trial simply by frustrating the proceedings. They stamped, clapped, chanted, and jeered the trial judge and called him names. This forced the judge to cite them for contempt of court and sentence them to varying terms of imprisonment. He ejected them from the court for much of the jury selection process. When they returned to court they kept up the same pattern of disruptions as part of their posture of noncompliance with and nonparticipation in the proceedings, protesting that the court had no jurisdiction and competence to try them. It was necessary to keep ejecting them, and the proceedings were continued in their absence. When murder convictions were rendered—in Indictment No. 19 of 1984[48]—they repeatedly challenged their convictions on the ground that they had been tried in their absence.

The constitution certainly guarantees a person on trial for allegedly having committed a crime "protection of the law," comparable to "due process of law." This affords him various facilities, all designed to ensure him a fair trial in accordance with natural justice. One such entitlement is that he should not be tried in his absence. But no right is absolute; every right is subject to limitations in the interest of preserving an orderly society. Thus section 8(2) of the Grenada constitution says that the trial shall not take place in his absence unless he so conducts himself as not to render the continuance of the proceedings in his presence impracticable and the court has ordered him to be removed and the trial to proceed in his absence. The Grenada Court of Appeal ruled that the appellants clearly fell within this exception, so the trial proceeded in their absence.[49] Any other result on this issue would have enabled them to mock justice.

The appellants could not get their appeals to reach the Privy Council because when some of them had been PRG ministers, the PRG abolished appeals to the Privy Council through People's Law No. 84 of 1979, which the Privy Council accepted. Through People's Law Nos. 4 and 14 of 1979 the PRG had similarly delinked Grenada from the OECS Supreme Court and set up its own Supreme Court comprising a High Court and a Court of Appeal. Grenada could not unilaterally reenter the OECS Supreme Court but rather had to await fulfillment of the precondition stipulated for readmission by the states within the OECS Supreme Court—that the appeals regarding the Maurice Bishop murder be disposed of by the Appeals Court of Grenada.

When that precondition was satisfied in August 1991 Grenada promptly reentered both the OECS Supreme Court and the Privy Council and abolished the Supreme Court set up by the PRG. The appellants' claim was clearly an idle one when they persistently contended that the PRG Supreme Court was an unconstitutional court not competent to try them, that only the OECS High Court could try them, so that the PRG Supreme Court should refer to the OECS Supreme Court the question of the constitutionality of the PRG Supreme Court. Little wonder that these submissions have uniformly been rejected, as recently as 1993, as the PRG Supreme Court had jurisdiction, if only on the basis of necessity.

A certain submission involves the cynical absurdity that precisely in the small OECS communities the more sensational and heinous the crime alleged against someone, the more the social conscience is outraged and traumatized, and the more his human rights shield him from being tried. This is the paradoxical submission that pretrial publicity precludes a trial's being fair, the court's being independent, and protection of the law's being respected. The courts are therefore quite rightly very circumspect when faced with this submission. It was rejected when former prime minister Patrick John of Dominica tried to resist being retried for conspiracy to overthrow the government of Dominica by force of arms[50] and when former PRG deputy prime minister Bernard Coard and other former PRG ministers and officials were fighting against being tried for murdering PRG Prime Minister Maurice Bishop.[51]

In this context too, the courts do not fall easily for an allegation that the summoned potential jurors on array, from which the impaneled jurors were selected, exhibited open hostility and heated abuse toward the accused and were therefore biased. This allegation is especially unimpressive when, as in the Maurice Bishop murder proceedings, it is first made only before the Court of Appeal, was not brought to the attention of the trial court, and the offending jurors were not identified.[52]

Life and Death

OECS constitutions guarantee the individual the right to life, ordaining that he is not to be deprived of his life except in accordance with law. The constitutions also protect one from torture or inhuman or degrading punishment or other treatment, informally called cruel and inhuman punishment. They add, in effect, that neither the right to life nor the freedom from inhuman or degrading punishment is violated by any description of punishment that was lawful under preconstitution laws. OECS preconstitution laws provided for the death sentence, by saying that anyone convicted of murder should suffer capital punishment, death by hanging. Not surprisingly, therefore, submissions that the constitutionally guaranteed right to life and freedom from inhuman or degrading punishment are necessarily violated by the capital punishment of hanging per se have been rejected.[53]

A more sophisticated question is whether the right to life or the protection from inhuman or degrading punishment prohibits the carrying out of the death sentence long after its announcement. Three of the five Law Lords of the Privy Council who decided the Jamaican case *Riley v Attorney-General*[54] saw no such prohibition. The minority two, Lords Leslie George Scarman and John Anson Brightman, felt that inordinate delay was unacceptable. The minority was supported by this writer regarding "inordinate" or "prolonged" delay, defined as "delay longer than two years . . . after the termination of all legal proceedings."[55] OECS courts followed the majority in *Riley*, as they were bound to do.

But OECS courts now have to take a new course, fixed by the Privy Council in 1993, in the Jamaican case *Pratt v Attorney-General.*[56] For fourteen years the appellants faced death by hanging as the penalty for their convictions for murder, and death warrants for their execution were read to them on three different occasions. The Privy Council established that delay that is "unconscionable," one for "several years" or "many years," violates the guarantee against inhuman or degrading punishment. They set this delay at five years, not as an inflexible rigid timetable, but rather as what they considered to be realistic targets, in the reckoning of which time taken by an appellant in frivolous procedures and time-wasting tactics amounting to an abuse of process is excluded. Specifically departing from *Riley*, their Lordships said that after the five-year period there will be strong grounds for believing that the delay is such as to constitute inhuman or degrading punishment and calling for commutation of the death sentence to life imprisonment. It matters not that the commuting of a sentence is a discretionary matter falling within the prerogative of mercy whose exercise is vested by the constitution in administrative authorities and not the courts.

The five-year schedule comprises one year for the Court of Appeal proceedings, another for the Privy Council, yet another year and a half for international human rights forums like the Inter-American Commission on Human Rights (IACHR) and the United Nations Commission on Human Rights (UNCHR). The schedule is that tight because the Privy Council is convinced that if capital punishment is to be retained it must be carried out with "all possible expedition." The schedule does give the state roughly the two years after termination of all legal proceedings previously recommended by this writer, but this writer's formula would have been less stressful on the state. Indeed, the Privy Council intimated that domestic procedures regarding complaints to the international human rights bodies, if retained at all, might need to be revised for expedition to be better able to comply with the five-year rule. The criminal justice system will have to be professionally serviced if the new execution timetable is to be kept. Nothing less is at stake than the choice between life and death.

Conclusion

The analysis in this chapter shows that human rights in the Eastern Caribbean are vigorously asserted by a populace holding the independent judiciary to their vow that as bastions and guardians of the constitution, they "will not ration justice." Accordingly, there has been spirited litigation to ensure enjoyment of the guaranteed rights. Most of the litigation has centered on protection from the deprivation of property without compensation. Next featured has been the bundle of rights regarding conscience and communication, including freedom from political discrimination. Good balance has been struck between the enjoyment of individual rights and the preservation of collective rights in the interest of the public good. Hence, forged from the best of the liberal democratic tradition enshrined in OECS Westminster model constitutions, underpinned by the rule of law, honorably protected by a judiciary safeguarded by entrenched independence through the separation of powers, human rights are vivaciously alive in the OECS.

Notes

1. OECS also has three nonindependent members: Anguilla, the British Virgin Islands, and Montserrat.

2. Including the West Indies Associated States (WIAS) Supreme Court Order (the Courts Order) 1967, SI 223 of 1967 [UK]. The Associated States, which later became OECS independent countries, enjoyed full internal self-government and had bills of rights materially identical to those in the OECS today.

3. Strictly called the Eastern Caribbean Supreme Court, but in Grenada the Supreme Court of Grenada and West Indies Associated States.

4. Sir Vincent Floissac, CJ in *Mitchell v Attorney-General (No. 2)* (1993), CA–OECS, Motion No. 1 of 1992 [Grenada].

5. *John v D.P.P. (No. 3)* (1985) 1 CCCBR 645, 649.

6. *Gairy v Attorney-General* (1989), HC-Grenada, Civ. Suit No. 377 of 1987.

7. *Richards v Jack* (1990), HC-OECS, Civ. Suit No. 484 of 1989 [St. Vincent] (Singh J).

8. *Commissioner of Police v Davis* (1993) 4 All ER 476 (PC)[Bahamas]. See too *Hinds v The Queen* (1977) AC 195 (PC) [Jamaica]; *Farrell v Attorney-General (1979)* 27 WIR 377 (CA–WIAS) [Antigua].

9. Respectively, *Attorney-General v Antigua Times* (1975) 21 WIR 560, 574A (Lord Fraser), and *Hector v Attorney-General* (1990) 37 WIR 216, 220D (Lord Bridge).

10. *Francis v Chief of Police* (1970) 15 WIR 1 (CA–WIAS) (1973) 20 WIR 550 (PC).

11. *Francis v Chief of Police* (1970) 15 WIR 1, 7H (CA–OECS) (1973) 20 WIR 550, 559 G-H (PC); *Attorney-General v Antigua Times* (1975) 21 WIR 560, 575A (PC).

12. *Attorney-General v Antigua Times* (1975) 21 WIR 560.

13. *Commissioner of Police v Davis* (1993) 4 All ER 476 (PC) [Bahamas].

14. *Francis v Chief of Police* (1970) 15 WIR 1 (CA–WIAS) (1973) 20 WIR 550 (PC).

15. (1970) 15 WIR 1, 13E–F (Cecil Lewis JA); 18 B (St. Bernard JA).

16. Ibid., pp. 8A–B.

17. The Dominica constitution, Section (6)1, requires adequate compensation, as does that of St. Vincent, Section 6(1). Section 9(1) of the Antigua constitution requires fair compensation.

18. See Section 6(1) of the Grenada constitution, Section 6(1) of St. Lucia's. St. Kitts Section 8(2) refers to "prompt" but not "full" payment.

19. See A. W. Singham, *The Hero and the Crowd in a Colonial Polity* (New Haven: Yale University Press, 1968).

20. St. Kitts Constitution Order, Section. 2, para. 10. See *Mills v Attorney-General* (1993), CA–OECS, Civ. App. No. 3 of 1991 [St. Kitts]. The associated statehood

constitutional instruments of St. Kitts, replaced by the independence instruments, had treated preconstitution laws in exactly the way the Grenada independence instruments do.

21. *Attorney-General v Reynolds* (1980) AC 637 (PC) [St. Kitts].

22. A. R. Carnegie, "Constitutional Law" (1968), ASCL1, 121, criticizing *Charles v Phillips* (1967) 10 WIR 423 and *Herbert v Phillips* (1967) 10 WIR 435 because CA–WIAS [St. Kitts] held the reconciliation impossible, both now disapproved if not overruled by PC in *Reynolds.*

23. Francis Alexis, "When Is an Existing Law Saved?" *Public Law,* 1976, p. 256.

24. (1993), CA–OECS, Civ. App. No. 11A of 1988 [Grenada].

25. *Grand Anse Estates v De Gale* (1977) 1 CCCBR 472 (CA–WIAS) [Grenada]; *Windward Properties v Government of St. Vincent* (1993), CA–OECS, Civ. App. No. 13 of 1991 [St. Vincent].

26. *Attorney-General v Yearwood* (1978) 1 CCCBR 353 (CA–WIAS). The flawed Act was passed in 1975, during the associated statehood period.

27. *Grand Anse Estates v De Gale* (1977) 1 CCCBR 472, 479; *Thomas v Attorney-General* (1977) 23 WIR 491, 494C. See too *Modeste v Attorney-General* (1989), CA-Grenada, Civ. App. No. 4 of 1988.

28. *Blomquist v Attorney-General* (1987) 35 WIR 162 (PC) [Dominica], reversing (1983) 1 CCCBR 534 (Singh J).

29. As apparently happened in *Windward Properties v Government of St. Vincent,* cited earlier, Liverpool JA reserving on this.

30. See *Grand Anse Estates v De Gale* (1977) 1 CCCBR 472, 481 (Peterkin JA: CA–WIAS) [Grenada]. Then see Ibid. at p. 477 (St. Bernard JA); *Attorney-General v Yearwood* (1978) 1 CCCBR 353, 383 (Berridge JA: CA–WIAS) [St. Kitts].

31. Peterkin JA thinks "full" is stronger than "adequate": *Grand Anse Estates v De Gale* (1977) 1 CCCBR 472, 481. Byron JA does not suggest a difference and Liverpool JA reserves on it in *Windward Properties v Government of St. Vincent.*

32. *Windward Properties v Government of St. Vincent* (1993), CA–OECS, CIU App. No. 13 of 1991 [St. Vincent].

33. *Home Industries v Government of Grenada* (1969) 14 WIR 412 (HC-WIAS) [Grenada].

34. *Attorney-General v Yearwood* (1978) 1 CCCBR 353 (CA–WIAS) [St. Kitts].

35. *Gairy v Attorney-General* (1989), HC-Grenada, Civ. Suit No. 377 of 1987. An appeal against that order, in Civ. App. No. 1 of 1990 was withdrawn on March 27, 1992. See too *Attorney-General v Knight* (1989), CA-Grenada, Civ. App. No. 9 of 1988.

36. See *The (St. Bernard) Claims Commission Recommendations* (St. George's, Grenada, 1988).

37. *Hemisphere Enterprises v Chief of Police* (1984) 1 CCCBR 513 (HC–OECS).

38. See *Modeste v Attorney-General,* cited earlier, McKay JA; and *Grand Anse Estates v De Gale* (1977) 1 CCCBR 472, 480 (Peterkin JA: CA–WIAS) [Grenada]. Then see *Thomas v Attorney-General* (1977) 23 WIR 491, 494 C (St. Bernard JA: CA–WIAS) [Grenada].

39. *Attorney-General v Lawrence* (1983) 31 WIR 176 (CA–OECS) [St. Kitts].

40. Including the 1979 and 1983 revolutionary occurrences in Grenada; the 1993 fatal banana riots in St. Lucia; the 1993 post-election upheavals in St. Kitts; the 1994 vehicle license riots in Dominica, and the 1994 riots in St. Kitts.

41. *Chief of Police v Powell* (1968) 12 WIR 403 (HC–WIAS).

42. (1990) 37 WIR 216 (PC), reversing (1987) 10 WIR 135 (CA–OECS).

43. (1990) 37 WIR 216, 219 b–d.

44. (1980) AC 637 (PC) [St. Kitts].

45. As unconvincingly alleged by the expropriated landowner in *Mills v Attorney-General* (1993), CA–OECS, Civ. App. No. 3 of 1991 [St. Kitts].

46. *Camacho and Sons v Collector of Customs* (1971) 18 WIR 15 (CA–WIAS). But the court erred in not ordering the collector to grant the licenses.

47. *Re Fassihi* (1992), HC-OECS, Civ. Suit No. 340 of 1992. Unlike St. Paul J, the CA–OECS felt that the deportation order was bad in form, but specifically not prejudicing a fresh deportation order if validly made, Civ. App. No. 3 of 1992.

48. Fourteen were convicted of murder, three of manslaughter, one acquitted altogether, and the other not proceeded against.

49. *Mitchell v The Queen (No. 1)* (1991), CA-Grenada, Crim. Apps. Nos. 4–20 of 1986. See too *Mitchell v The Queen (No. 2)* (1991), CA-Grenada, Motion No. 1 of 1991.

50. *John v D.P.P. (No. 2)* (1985) 1 CCCBR 632 (HC-OECS).

51. *Mitchell v The Queen (No. 1)* (1991), CA-Grenada, Crim. Apps. Nos. 4–20 of 1986.

52. *Mitchell v Attorney-General* (1991), CA-Grenada, Civ. App. No. 11 of 1988.

53. *Richards v Attorney-General* (1992), CA–OECS, Civ. App. No. 1 of 1992 [St. Kitts].

54. (1983) 1 AC 719.

55. Francis Alexis and Margaret De Merieux, "Inordinately Delayed Hanging: Whether an Inhuman Punishment," *Journal of the Indian Law Institute*, vol. 29 (1987):356.

56. (1993) 4 All ER 769.

Acronyms

AC	*Appeal Cases Law Reports*
All ER	*All England Law Reports* (UK)
CA	Court of Appeal
CCCBR	*Cases on Commonwealth Caribbean Bills of Rights*
CJ	Chief Justice
HC	High Court
J	Justice
OECS	Organization of Eastern Caribbean States
PC	Privy Council
SC	Supreme Court
WIAS	West Indies Associated States
WIR	*West Indian Law Reports*

9

Democracy and Human Rights in Guyana

Ivelaw L. Griffith

The political dynamics of contemporary Guyana bear testimony to Bismarck's observation that "politics is the art of the possible." Following the 1985 death of Linden Forbes Sampson Burnham, Guyana's predominant leader for twenty-one years, the country has undergone dramatic change. In the context of this change, 1992 witnessed Cheddi Jagan's emergence from the political wilderness. Jagan, who first entered politics in 1946, was ousted from power by the British in 1953 and again in 1961, with U.S. assistance, because of his communist orientation. The processes that produced Jagan's reemergence—and indeed, his reemergence itself—have ushered in a new era in Guyanese politics, one that spotlights both the triumphs and the pitfalls of democracy and human rights. An examination of the relationship between regime change and democracy and human rights in Guyana demonstrates both change and continuity over the past decade: change in regime and regime politics and policies, and continuity in some regime policies that conditioned the political environment.

Human rights thinking in Guyana, as reflected in domestic legal instruments, statements by political leaders, and charters of human rights nongovernmental groups, has been influenced by both the liberal and the communalist philosophies. Moreover, the approach to human rights is an inclusive one, encompassing civil and political rights as well as economic and social rights. As might be expected, since independence in 1966 there have been changes in emphasis among various categories of rights, reflecting shifts both in the focus of the international community and domestic political and economic struggles. Central to the nature and conduct of these struggles has been the nature of the political regime.

Regime and Political Change

One way to examine political change is to assess change in relation to political regimes. Joe Hagan has designed a typology of regimes that is nicely suited to such an assessment in Guyana. He outlines five kinds of regimes along a spectrum running from close cohesion through high fragmentation: dominance by a single individual; dominance by a single cohesive party with established, autonomous bureaucracies and institutions; dominance by a single party with factional divisions; power sharing by a ruling party with one or more minor parties or groups; and no clear dominant group or a coalition of autonomous groups.[1] Irrespective of what regime typology is used, though, regime change can be detected by observing the dynamics of the various domestic political arenas, among them the cabinet, the legislature, and the political party of the regime leader(s).

Hagan also developed a typology of regime change. Under this schema, a Type I regime change is limited to the removal or resignation of a top political leader, but one who is not the effective head of state. A Type II change involves a change in the effective head of state, but no change in the basic political composition of the ruling group. A Type III change involves adjustments in the mix of groups or factions that comprise the ruling coalition, but adjustments that do not alter the essential political makeup of the regime. Type IV change is where one political group or set of groups is replaced by another, through routinized, constitutionally sanctioned procedures. Type V change is where the entire ruling group is forced from office by another group through illegal or irregular means, such as a coup d'état.[2]

Since the mid-1980s Guyana has experienced three sets of regime change. According to the Hagan approach, the death of Forbes Burnham on August 6, 1985, led to a Type II change, involving change in the effective head of state, but no change in the basic composition of the ruling People's National Congress (PNC). Hugh Desmond Hoyte, a member of the PNC Central Committee and Burnham's prime minister and First Vice President, was named as Burnham's successor by a joint meeting of the Central Committee and the cabinet within two hours of Burnham's death. Hoyte became simultaneously PNC leader and state president, passing over Ptolemy Reid, deputy leader and a former prime minister, as well as Randi Chandisingh, the party's general secretary. The new regime pledged continuity at the party congress held two weeks after Burnham's death, with Hoyte declaring, "The leadership of the party is pledged to continue his work."[3]

With general elections constitutionally due within seven months of his accession to the presidency, Hoyte took the opportunity to "renew" the mandate of the PNC under his stewardship at elections held on December 9, 1985. Those elections witnessed Guyana's going through motions of legitimacy without any real correlation between popular choice and political empowerment. As Perry Mars explains, Guyana's post-independence elections have been less about choice of government than about fulfilling a kind of "national ritual" in which contending parties exhibit mobilization strategies. The ruling party demonstrates its peculiar style of "never losing," if not necessarily "winning," popular elections, and opposition parties generally experiment with different coalition tactics to show their popular appeal based on voter turnout at campaign meetings, rather than at the usually controversial polls. In this situation, "the campaign is the thing, the elections a predictable anticlimax."[4]

Under Guyana's electoral system, presidential and parliamentary elections are combined, and the leader of the party with the largest parliamentary representation becomes president, having been earlier designated the presidential candidate and head of the party list of candidates. There are sixty-five seats in the unicameral legislature, but only fifty-three are contested directly. This is done using the list proportional representation system of voting. Each of the ten Regional Development Councils (RDCs) elects one representative for the Assembly, and the remaining two are identified by the National Congress of Local Democratic Organs (NCLDO). Elections for regional representation in the National Assembly and within the RDCs are held at the same time.[5] The 1985 elections were contested by seven political parties, and, according to the Elections Commission, which is the agency mandated by the constitution to supervise national and local elections, the PNC won forty-two of the fifty-three directly contested National Assembly seats. The PNC was thus "returned" to power.[6]

The circumstances just described would seem to constitute a situation of continuity rather than change. However, for reasons explained later, those circumstances set the stage for a type of regime change that, modifying the Hagan typology, could be called Type VI regime change: change in which the dominant individual ruler alters the composition of the cabinet and key governmental agencies as part of the political adaptation of his regime. This change does not occur all at once; it takes place over a period of time. The length of time would vary depending on such factors as the amount of personal authority the ruler possesses, the organizational strength or weakness of his party, the ideological matrix of the party, and local and foreign economic and political pressures. In any case, the change alters the political character of the regime, and in Hoyte's case, its ideological character as well.

The failure of so many of Burnham's prescriptions presented Hoyte with strong demands for change. Generally, the demands were for democratization of the polity, respect for human rights, reversal of the economic decline, and foreign policy conduct commensurate with the then dramatically changing climate of international politics. Hoyte responded to all these areas, introducing both substantive and symbolic measures. These included privatization; attraction of foreign investment; rapprochement with the United States, Venezuela, Britain, and the International Monetary Fund; electoral reforms; an end to the harassment of the political opposition; and removal of restrictions on the media. He engaged in challenging, often dangerous, balancing acts in an effort to accommodate domestic and foreign pressures. Essentially, Hoyte engaged in what elsewhere I have called "the politics of preservative adaptation."[7]

Among the political reforms undertaken in the quest for preservative adaptation were the abolition of overseas voting, access by opposition parties to state media for campaigning, sanitizing of the tainted voters list, reconstitution of the Elections Commission, tabulation of the vote at the place of voting, and scrutiny of the elections process by foreign observers. Hoyte also reshuffled his cabinet, cut the government bureaucracy by reducing the number of ministries from eighteen to eleven, and reduced the power of some formidable figures. In the latter regard, for example, he assigned Prime Minister Hamilton Green specific responsibility for little more than sports. He also removed Randi Chandisingh from his powerful party and government positions—general secretary of the party and a vice president of the government—and gave him a diplomatic assignment in Moscow. In addition, Hoyte was able to force the resignation and exile of the powerful minister of health, Richard Van-West Charles, a son-in-law of Burnham, who was known in political circles as "Baby Jesus."

Moreover, Hoyte redefined the relationship between the ruling PNC and the government, abandoning the principle of "paramountcy of the party," introduced by Burnham in 1973, whereby the legislative, executive, and judicial branches of the government and all organizations and institutions in the country were made subordinate to the PNC. He also reorganized the party structure, ending government funding of party operations by abolishing the Ministry of National Mobilization. The party's bureaucracy was also downsized. These actions not only constituted a Type VI regime change but were also central to the democratization of the society, ironically also setting the stage for Hoyte's own political demise and the third regime change in a decade.

The third regime change was a Type IV change. It involved the replacement of Desmond Hoyte and the "new" PNC by Cheddi Jagan and the PPP-Civic coalition by constitutionally sanctioned means. Following elections on October 5, 1992, in which eleven political parties competed, Jagan was sworn in as president on October 9, 1992. After the December 7, 1992, meeting of the ten RDCs and the December 12, 1992, meeting of the NCLDO, part of the process of constituting the National Assembly, the parliamentary power distribution that resulted gave the PPP-Civic thirty-six seats, the PNC twenty-six seats, the Working People's Alliance (WPA) two seats, and The United Force (TUF) one seat.[8]

The 1992 change is significant for several reasons. As the first time in twenty-eight years that both the international community and all the country's political parties agreed that the elections were free and fair, it was a vital step along the road to democratic reconstruction. Moreover, Guyana thereby joined the rest of South America in holding internationally accepted elections. In addition, the elections demonstrated the maturity of the Guyanese electorate in eschewing the politics of violence despite efforts in some quarters to promote this. However, they also indicated a continuation of the racial politics, since people voted mainly along racial lines. As Ralph Premdas has pointed out, "the PPP-Civic victory as well as the PNC support and indeed the entire election was animated by communal sentiments that suffused and shaped voter preference."[9]

Beyond Regime Change

Elections are key to regime legitimacy in a democracy, but they do not con- stitute democracy. Hence in assessing the democracy–human rights nexus, it is necessary to go beyond elections and examine participation and policy choice in the context of other institutional and behavioral aspects of civil so- ciety, especially constitutional reform, the military, the media, and the courts.

A well-established principle of democratic governance is that such gover- nance must be done under the rule of law. Hence the precepts and practices of democracy are often judged, and correctly so, against a country's funda- mental law—its constitution. Guyana's constitution pledges "to respect human dignity and to cherish and uphold the principles of freedom, equality, and democracy and all other fundamental human rights." It also resolves "to establish the State on foundations of social and economic justice, and ac- cordingly by popular consensus, after full, free, and open discussion, debate, and participation." But for most of the years between 1980, when the cur- rent constitution was adopted as a revision of the original 1966 law, and 1992, when the party that introduced it was vanquished, this pledge was honored mainly in the breach.

Most of the concern about actual and potential power abuse under the constitution centered on the presidency. Two noted Guyanese scholars have expressed a sentiment shared by many people within and outside the coun- try: "In a real sense the Presidential system, as indeed the Constitution of which it is part, is a product of the political and economic crises [now] exist- ing in Guyana. As such it is more likely to be an instrument for the exercise of absolute power than one of social cohesion and for solving the many problems facing the nation."[10] Thus Guyana watchers have recognized the need for constitutional change, both to remove the structural basis for the subversion of democracy and human rights and to make the constitution more consonant with changing domestic realities, especially in relation to its claims about the pursuit of socialism.

The desire for constitutional reform was shared by politicians as well as scholars. Both the PNC and PPP-Civic made this issue a central aspect of their 1992 elections campaign. The Hoyte manifesto proclaimed that "one of the first tasks of a Hoyte government would be to review the constitution of our country." The PNC argued that "the political and economic policies which have been pursued since 1985 are so diametrically opposed to those which were followed in the past that there is now an obvious need to reconsider and fashion together the kind of constitution that Guyanese need for their further evolution."[11]

For its part the PPP-Civic offered some fairly specific propositions:

The PPP/Civic Government recognizes the urgent need for constitutional reform. We propose that (a) the Fundamental Rights Section of our Constitution be preserved and strengthened wherever possible; (b) the Directive Principles be reviewed and abandoned where irrelevant, inapplicable, or inappropriate; (c) the powers of the Elections Commission be more adequately and unambiguously defined and its composition reviewed.

The PPP-Civic, if elected, will propose that the powers of the president be reduced so that both the President and the Office are more accountable to the people.[12]

President Jagan has sent mixed signals on his commitment to constitutional reform. At one time he declared that nothing was basically wrong with the constitution's provisions relating to the presidency; it was just the manner in which they were used, he said. On another occasion he announced that a constitutional review commission would be created, even mentioning the name of constitutional scholar Harold Lutchman as a commission nominee.[13] The commission was never appointed. However, a parliamentary resolution was adopted in late 1994 endorsing reform and creating a Parliamentary Select Committee on the Constitution to pursue it. Curiously, in September 1996 the committee announced that it did not anticipate presenting a report and a draft revised constitution before May 1997—just five months before the elections are due, and too late to take effect before the elections.

This foot-dragging has been a great disappointment to people who invested trust and confidence in the new regime, counting on it to create the structural and functional mechanisms for the furtherance of democracy and human rights. And what better place to have begun than the fundamental law that is both a symbol of democratic ideals and the instrument that guarantees a whole range of human rights? However, it would appear that now that the PPP-Civic has secured power Jagan is comfortable with the range of powers and immunities attached to the very "imperial presidency" he condemned while in opposition and is reluctant to take concrete measures to change them. One assessment of his first two years in office concluded: "If the Guyana society is to move from its present uneasy calm to a cohesive and dynamic entity constitutional change remains the prime item on the agenda and its absence the major failure over the last two years."[14] This remains a credible proposition today.

A 1994 controversy dealing with one constitutional guarantee highlights the need for constitutional reform. As mentioned earlier, the approach to human rights in Guyana has been influenced by both the liberal and communalist human rights philosophies. Under the present constitution, adopted when Guyana was flirting with socialism, human rights guarantees extend to civil and political rights as well as social and economic ones. Chapter 2 of the constitution addresses several matters in the latter category, providing for rights to work, medical care, leisure, housing, and free education. On the question of education, Article 27 proclaims: "Every citizen has the right to free education from nursery to university as well as at non-formal places where opportunities are provided for education and training."

University of Guyana students began receiving free education in 1975. The PNC government was thereby able to give expression to its belief about education and its place in society, even before the 1980 constitution was adopted. The government was able to absorb the full cost of education at the primary, secondary, and tertiary levels. But that was at a time of relative economic buoyancy. As the political and economic crises that later gripped the country worsened, the provision of free education became a huge burden, such that in the latter years of the Hoyte government abandonment of this social rights venture was no longer in doubt. The University of Guyana finally announced in 1993 that from the 1994/95 academic year there would be "cost recovery." Students would be required to pay the Guyana dollar equivalent of between US$1,000 and US$1,500 annually, depending upon their program of instruction. This announcement was met with condemnation, protests, hunger strikes, and litigation by student groups. Students sought judicial relief, claiming that the government was violating their constitutional rights under Article 27 by having the university, a state institution, force their payment for instruction.[15] After considerable delay, the court rendered a decision in 1996 rejecting the students' contention.

This outcome notwithstanding, the case calls into question the meaning and value of rights under the constitution. Though rights such as those to life, assembly, privacy, and property are fundamental and enforceable, economic and social rights such as those identified in Chapter 2 of the constitution are akin to expressions of societal desire, and their fulfillment is dependent on the society's level of economic development. This matter is a clear demonstration of the incongruity between the existence of constitutional social rights provisions and the patent inability of the society to fulfill those desires by honoring the pledges made under the provisions.[16] It is a matter that needs attention by way of constitutional review.

Guyana has been one of a few anglophone Caribbean countries in which the military has been used as an instrument of political rule and an agent for the subversion of civil and political rights. It is therefore important to examine how this institution fits into the contemporary political matrix. It should be remembered that the militarization that Guyana experienced in the 1970s and the 1980s did not occur in the sense of S. F. Finer's definition of militarization as "armed forces' substitution of their own policies and/or their persons, for those of the recognized civilian authorities."[17] Rather, the Guyana case was akin to Eric Nordlinger's, in which "civilian governors obtain loyalty and obedience by penetrating the armed forces with political ideas and political personnel."[18]

Consequently, the military—here referring to the Guyana Defense Force (GDF), the Guyana National Service (GNS), the Guyana People's Militia (GPM), and the Guyana Police Force (GPF)—became practically an arm of the ruling PNC, and it was compensated with accretions of money, equipment, and personnel.[19] The ruling party used the military to help subvert elections, to harass critics, and as scab labor when there were politically motivated industrial disputes. The military pledged loyalty to the PNC and the predominant leader, not to the constitution or to the ideals of national sovereignty. During the Burnham era there was little if any distinction between the security of the state and the security of the regime, and the military's role involved both.

Desmond Hoyte's rise to power in 1985 witnessed the adoption of a different conception of the role of the military in society. The military continued to have political, military, and economic security mandates, but there were appreciable policy and operational differences in these areas, plus the assignment of a new role: that of diplomatic security.[20] At the time the new direction seemed to offer the "hope that it will merely be a matter of time before those interested in full depoliticization of the military and the democratization of society win over those dedicated to Burnham's agenda and initiatives."[21]

That time has come. With the passage of power from the PNC there is no possibility of a return to the Burnham regimen, especially given the dramatic transformations pursued by his successor. Although the Hoyte regime had adopted a different approach to the military, and despite pronouncements from the military high command that the army would not meddle in or be co-opted into politics, there was still concern that the military had not been fully depoliticized—that it would display praetorian tendencies and perhaps declare martial law during the 1992 elections in order to guarantee a PNC victory. None of this happened. Moreover, after the elections army officials reached out to the government, promising to honor their pre-election pledge to abide by the popular choice, to act according to their constitutional mandate, and to be a professional, apolitical force.[22] Neither the army nor the police has qualms about working with a government formed by a party that once hurled scurrilous and vitriolic remarks at them. The heads of the army and police are conscious of the dramatic changes domestically and internationally and of the implications for their agencies and the nation of working against the popular will and the constitution. Hence they are pledged to work to uphold democracy and human rights in the country.[23]

The right to free speech is so central to the preservation of democracy and the exercise of human rights that scholars often invoke Voltaire's famous assertion, made at a time when both democracy and human rights were mere ideals: "I disapprove of what you say, but I will defend to the death your right to say it." The MacBride Commission on the Study of Communication Problems called the freedom of expression "one of democracy's most precious acquisitions," noting that "the presence or absence of freedom of expression is one of the most reliable indications of freedom in all its aspects in any nation."[24] In the Guyanese context, like elsewhere, it was accepted that this freedom extended to freedom of the press and to the freedom of citizens to criticize the government in power. The precept also included the right to hold opinions and to receive and impart ideas.

However, the reality in Guyana during most of the early post-independence years was one in which government dominance of the media, currency controls, restriction on press imports, and judicial decisions combined to create an environment in which these freedoms were curtailed rather than permitted or encouraged. Not only did this suppress political debate, but it also affected the exercise of several contingent freedoms—the rights of association and assembly and the right to demonstrate for redress of grievance, among other things. Moreover, it contributed to the development within the society of what one observer called "a sort of intellectual paralysis."[25]

As mentioned earlier, expression, speech, and the media benefited from the substantive and symbolic changes introduced after 1985 as Desmond Hoyte pursued his politics of preservative adaptation. Not only was a businessman emboldened enough to establish an independent and critical newspaper, the *Stabroek News*, in November 1986, but also he was able to say afterward: "The atmosphere of repression lightened perceptibly and the style and language of politics were noticeably more responsive and less threatening. . . . An independent newspaper was allowed to open and there has been no interference with it."[26] In its report to the U.S. Congress in 1991 the State Department reported that "in past years the Government . . . maintained varying degrees of control over the media. This control, however, has been easing since 1987."[27]

The changed political climate that began under Hoyte has continued under Jagan, being generally conducive to the exercise of rights related to expression, free press, and critical media. For example, in 1993 the Guyana

Publications Limited, publishers of *Stabroek News,* extended publication of the newspaper from twice weekly to seven days a week, having grown earlier from a Sunday-only publication schedule. Later that year they started publishing *Stabroek Review,* a weekly. Yet the PPP-Civic seems indisposed to having close scrutiny and strident criticism by the press—despite having proclaimed in its election manifesto that "[i]n the process of reconstruction and the development of a pluralist democracy, free media will facilitate wide and open debate on the choice of path for recovery" and promised an "opening [of] the media to different shades of opinion" under its rule.[28] The same *Stabroek News* that Jagan once hailed as a champion in the search for the truth and a bulwark in the pursuit of democracy and the protection of human rights in the country is now ridiculed as subversive.

Jagan's most scathing remarks followed the newspaper's report on the PPP congress in which he had affirmed his commitment to Marxism-Leninism. Later the *Stabroek News* also carried an editorial on the subject. Jagan excoriated the paper, calling it "unpatriotic and anti-national" and bent on "witch-hunting" his government. He expressed a totally befuddling view: "Despite all its disclaimers, *Stabroek News* is trying to destabilize this government. They probably did not want this party to be elected to the government in the first place."[29] One hopes that this reaction by the Jagan government is not a reflection of an inability to live up to the ideals for which it struggled all those years while in the political wilderness.

One of the criticisms made of the Jagan government by both the press and political analysts concerns its abandonment of the pledge to consolidate democracy and racial harmony by establishing a government of national unity. The PPP-Civic had made a bold and laudable offer in its elections manifesto: "The PPP/CIVIC is convinced that the true interests of all Guyanese lie in working towards national unity and the eventual elimination of ethnic insecurity. The proposal for a multi-ethnic, multi-class, broad-based national PPP/CIVIC list to contest these elections reflects the PPP's unending search of and means to promote national unity."[30] The assertion was also made that "the commitment of the PPP/CIVIC to winner-does-not-take-all politics and to the formation of a government of national unity after winning the elections, attests to our belief that national unity and ethnic security form the cornerstone on which a truly democratic system will be built in Guyana."[31]

Apart from the search for political renewal that existed within the society at the time of the elections, it was this pledge that made the PPP-Civic an attractive prospect to many sections of the electorate. However, as is often true with parties seeking power, the pledge, once made, becomes subject to subtle amendment or plain abandonment. In this case it was the latter. Having won 53.5 percent of the vote and thirty-six of the seats in the National Assembly, the PPP-Civic decided to exercise power exclusively. True, after much delay and some political histrionics, it offered the WPA one cabinet position—the Ministry of Planning and Production.[32] But given the low level of authority conferred by this position, the move seemed to have been part of a PPP-Civic tactic of making an offer that they knew the WPA could only refuse. (The Ministry of Planning and Production was never created.) Hence they were able to retain full and absolute control, a total about-face from the election commitment. Even one scholar who is usually sympathetic to the PPP was obliged to observe: "Its protestations notwithstanding, the stark elementary fact remained that the new Jagan-led government was essentially an Indian-backed regime and that power was not shared but monopolized by one partisan group alone."[33]

Allied to this hold on power is what one newspaper editorial called the "far more worrying tendency which seems to be clearly establishing itself to remove good Guyanese professionals who served in public positions before this new Government came to power. This line seems to be not very subtly changing from 'winner will not take all' to 'winner is perfectly entitled to take all.'"[34] It is true that any new government, especially one that has been in opposition for twenty-eight years, will harbor a certain distrust for the bureaucrats in the government once led by its political nemesis. It will therefore want to bring its own trusted cadre into the executive and judicial branches—and in the context of patronage politics, which is accepted in Guyana and the Caribbean as a whole, this is expected. But there is a certain callousness on the part of the new government in dealing with some professionals of the former administration, often reflected in the short notices given for termination, reassignment to positions of lesser responsibility, and suspension from duty, in many cases violating their administrative and constitutional rights. Some have sued and won, including Dr. Cedric Grant, former ambassador to Washington and later foreign affairs adviser to Desmond Hoyte, and James Matheson, former ambassador to Brussels.

In most cases their competence was not questioned; their political loyalty was suspect. Worse than the administrative and management implications of this action, given the dearth of managerial skill in the country, are the racial overtones of the policy, giving rise to charges of "ethnic cleansing" by the opposition PNC. These charges exaggerate the reality, but in most cases the people removed were Africans and their replacements were Indians. True, some top nonblack functionaries in the former government were also removed. Yet here again, their replacements were almost all people of Indian descent.[35] This is not to say that some of the replacements were not necessary, given the corruption and mismanagement that had existed in some quarters. Nevertheless, the indelicate management of the race factor in these actions is cause for justifiable concern given the country's history of ethic conflict.[36]

In recognition of the critical role of the judiciary in democratic governance and the exercise of human rights, a former ombudsman of Jamaica once asserted: "The rule of law is the fulcrum around which justice revolves; the catalyst from which emerges true protection and promotion of human rights."[37] This statement is undoubtedly relevant to Guyana, and unlike some years ago when the independence of the judiciary was compromised by the precept and practice of party paramountcy, the judiciary now exercises greater independence. It must be remembered, though, that the rule of law involves much more than an independent judiciary, and in this respect Guyana does poorly.

The dispensation of justice in Guyana is now affected by a shortage of criminal justice personnel, including magistrates and court officers, low salaries, inadequate training, poor facilities, and to crown it all, inefficiency in many quarters. Indeed, it has been reported that "the inefficiency of the judicial system is so great as to undermine due process."[38] It is common to have people detained for three and four years awaiting trial. And as outrageous as it may appear, there are people with murder indictments who in 1994 had been awaiting trial for seven and ten years. This problem was brought into the public spotlight in 1993 when several prisoners at the country's main prison in Georgetown held public protestations over their prolonged remand for trial.[39]

As noted earlier, human rights concerns extend to civil and political rights as well as social and economic rights. In referring to the issue of rights, President Jagan observed: "Some states emphasize civil and political but fail to note the centrality of economic, social, and cultural rights. Both sets of rights are essential."[40] However, despite the economic growth average of 6 percent during the period of 1992–1996 and a wealth of natural resources, Guyana's socioeconomic condition will make attainment of Jagan's economic, social, and cultural rights a Herculean task. One gets a sense of the magnitude of the task of pursuing economic democracy and economic, social, and cultural rights when it is recognized that, according to the minister of finance, "approximately 70 percent of the population is now living below the poverty line."[41] In explaining the country's socioeconomic dilemma to members of the Caribbean Group for Cooperation and Economic Development, President Jagan indicated: "Every man, woman, and child in this country is indebted to the tune of US$2,600—this in a country where more than half of the population lives below the poverty line and per capita GDP hovers around US$430."[42] Moreover, the country's roads, schools, power supply, sewerage system, health services, and other social infrastructure are in virtual collapse, the result of neglect, mismanagement, and the economic crisis that the country experienced under the PNC's watch. Guyana now has the dubious distinction of being the second poorest country in the Caribbean, after Haiti.

The Jagan government has some bold plans to advance economic democracy and fulfill some of the economic, social, and cultural rights specified under Chapter 2 of the constitution. These include promoting private sector development and public sector reform, rehabilitating the social and economic infrastructure, searching for maximum debt relief, and offering investment and production incentives. But, as might be expected, these plans will take massive resources and time. Meanwhile, to use a Guyanese adage, "While the grass is growing, the horse will be starving." And given the country's demographics, where 40 percent of the population is under fifteen years of age, children and women will continue to feel the greatest impact of the crisis. Indeed, says one source, "the severe deterioration of the public education and health care system has stunted children's futures and often cut short their lives."[43]

Conclusion

This discussion suggests that there has been both change and continuity in Guyana over the last decade. Change has occurred not only in terms of regime but also in terms of regime politics and regime policies. Curiously, though, there has been some continuity in regime policies despite regime change, for President Jagan has continued some of his predecessor's economic reforms. And he is strengthening the democratic environment that Hoyte had begun to create under domestic and foreign pressure as he pursued his politics of preservative adaptation.

The importance of economic, social, and cultural rights is not to be gainsaid. But their status as fundamental rights is both debatable and subject to economic vicissitudes in a way that civil and political rights are not, since their fulfillment is intimately bound up with the economic capability of the society.[44] Consequently, it is easier to give tangible meaning to civil and political rights in Guyana than to do so for economic, social, and cultural ones, as is so starkly illustrated in the dilemma in which the country finds itself in its constitutional ideal of free education. Hence, although political elites and interest groups in Guyana will continue to pay homage to the importance of economic, social, and cultural rights, and to their symbiotic relationship with civil and political rights, there will be few advances anytime soon in the economic and social areas.

Like elsewhere, the pursuit of democracy and human rights in Guyana is essentially a quest for security and liberty. Maurice Cranston argued over two decades that "the demand for liberty and security is not the demand for two things which can only with difficulty be balanced or reconciled; it is a demand for two things which naturally belong together."[45] But achieving and maintaining both liberty and security is often extraordinarily difficult, as the case of Guyana attests. Nevertheless, the quest in Guyana is understandable given what Guyanese have suffered under predominant leaders who often subordinated popular rights to political expediency as they pursued political power.

Notes

1. Joe Hagan, "Regimes, Political Opposition, and the Comparative Analysis of Foreign Policy," in *New Directions in the Study of Foreign Policy,* ed. Charles Hermann et al. (Boston: Allen and Unwin, 1987), pp. 345–346.

2. Ibid., pp. 347–348.

3. H. D. Hoyte, "Address to the Sixth Biennial Congress of the People's National Congress," Sophia, Georgetown, August 19, 1985, p. 7.

4. Perry Mars, "The 1985 Guyana Elections in Retrospect," *Bulletin of Eastern Caribbean Affairs,* vol. 13, no. 4 (September-October 1987):29.

5. For more on the electoral system of Guyana, see *Constitution of the Cooperative Republic of Guyana* (1980), Articles 60–80, 160–162, and 177; and Rudolph James and Harold Lutchman, *Law and the Political Environment in Guyana* (Turkeyen, Guyana: University of Guyana, 1984), pp. 75–87.

6. For assessments of the 1985 elections, see Mars, "The 1985 Guyana Elections in Retrospect"; British Parliamentary Human Rights Group and Americas Watch, *Interim Report on the Joint Mission to Investigate Political Freedom in Guyana* (New York: Americas Watch, 1985); and Americas Watch, *Electoral Conditions in Guyana* (New York: Americas Watch, 1990).

7. Ivelaw L. Griffith, "The Military and the Politics of Change in Guyana," *Journal of Interamerican Studies and World Affairs,* vol. 33, no. 2 (Summer 1991):141–173. For other assessments of the Hoyte regime's adaptation, see David de Caires, "Guyana After Burnham: A New Era or Is President Hoyte Trapped in the Skin of the Old PNC?" *Caribbean Affairs,* vol. 1, no. 1 (January-March 1988):183–198; Frank Long, "The New International Political Economy of Guyana," *The Round Table,* no. 317 (January 1991):73–80; and Dennis Watson and Christine Craig, eds., *Guyana at the Crossroads* (New Brunswick, NJ: Transition Publishers, 1992).

8. For reports on the elections, see "PPP-Civic Enters House with 3-Seat Majority," *Guyana Chronicle,* October 10, 1992, pp. 1, 6; Gary Brana-Shute, "Guyana '92: It's About Time," *Hemisphere,* vol. 5 (Winter/Spring 1993):40–44; Ralph Premdas, "Guyana: The Critical Elections of 1992 and a Regime Change," *Caribbean Affairs,* vol. 6 (January-March 1993):11–40; and Council of Freely Elected Heads of Government, *Observing Guyana's Electoral Process, 1990–1992* (Atlanta: Carter Center of Emory University, 1993).

9. Ralph Premdas, "Guyana One Year After the PNC," *Caribbean Affairs,* vol. 7, no. 3 (July-August 1994):157.

10. James and Lutchman, *Law and the Political Environment in Guyana,* p. 117.

11. *Development, Social Harmony, and Prosperity with Hugh Desmond Hoyte: The Manifesto of the People's National Congress,* 1992, p. 3.

12. PPP-Civic, *Time for Change, Time to Rebuild: Manifesto—Elections 1992,* 1992, p. 4.

13. Harold Lutchman is a lawyer and a political scientist who once served as head of the department of political science and law at the University of Guyana and as a dean at the same institution. At the time that he was mentioned by President Jagan he was professor of public administration and director of the graduate program in public administration at the University of the Virgin Islands, where he had been since 1986. Lutchman returned to Guyana in August 1996 to become vice-chancellor of the University of Guyana.

14. "Constitutional Reform Still a Priority: Faster Economic Progress Essential," *Stabroek News* (Guyana), October 10, 1994, p. 13. See also Harold Lutchman's views on the constitutional reform issue in "A Contribution to Public Education on Constitutional Reform," *Stabroek News,* June 21, 1994, p. 8; "Substantive Changes: The Presidency," *Stabroek News,* June 22, 1994, p. 8; and "Removal for Violation and Misconduct," *Stabroek News,* June 23, 1994, p. 15.

15. See George Cave, "University Fees," *Guyana Review,* no. 18 (July 1994):28–29; and Alim Hassim, "No Breach of Natural Justice Law by Introduction of Fees at UG—[Keith] Massiah Contends," *Stabroek News,* September 22, 1994, pp. 4, 12; and Alim Hassim, "Massiah Argues that 'Natural Justice' Was Served," *Stabroek News,* September 29, 1994. Massiah, an attorney general under the Hoyte administration, was University of Guyana counsel in the case. For a brief examination of the constitutionality of the right to education, see Jennifer Branche, "Tertiary Education: Free for All?" *Guyana Review,* no. 15 (April 1994):26–27.

16. If the minister of health, Gail Texeira, has her way, what little is left of free medical attention will also be abandoned. See Gitanjali Persaud, "Cost Recovery to Be Carefully Scrutinized in Health Sector," *Stabroek News,* September 30, 1994, p. 4.

17. See S. F. Finer, *The Man on Horseback,* 2d ed. (Boulder: Westview Press, 1988), p. 20.

18. Eric Nordlinger, *Soldiers in Politics* (Englewood Cliffs, NJ: Prentice Hall, 1977), p. 15.

19. For a discussion of militarization in Guyana, see George K. Danns, *Domination and Power in Guyana* (New Brunswick, NJ: Transaction Publishers, 1982); Ivelaw L. Griffith, "Guyana: The Military and the Politics of Change," in *Strategy and Security in the Caribbean,* ed. Ivelaw L. Griffith (New York: Praeger, 1991); and J. E. Greene, "Cooperativism, Militarism, Party Politics, and Democracy in Guyana," in *The Newer Caribbean,* ed. Paget Henry and Carl Stone (Philadelphia: Institute for the Study of Human Issues, 1983).

20. See Griffith, "The Military and the Politics of Change in Guyana," pp. 141–173.

21. Ibid., p. 167.

22. See "Army Aims at Feeding Itself," *Stabroek News,* February 16, 1993, p. 10; "GDF to Be Service Oriented—[Chief of Staff] Singh," *Stabroek News,* October 29, 1993, p. 4; Lynette Harvey, "Marking Time on Defense Policy," *Guyana Review,* nos. 10 and 11 (November-December 1993):7; and "[Commissioner of Police] Lewis Urges More Pay for Police," *Stabroek News,* December 21, 1993, p. 1.

23. This was quite clear from my interview with Brigadier Joseph Singh, chief of staff of the GDF, at Army Headquarters, Camp Ayanganna, Georgetown, Guyana, June 30, 1994; and with Commissioner of Police Laurie Lewis at Police Headquarters, Eve Leary, Georgetown, Guyana, on July 1, 1994.

24. United Nations Educational, Scientific, and Cultural Organization (UNESCO), *Many Voices, One World* (London: Kogan Page, 1980), p. 19.

25. Ashton Chase, "Freedom of Expression," *Guyana Review*, no. 2 (March 1993):13.

26. de Caires, "Guyana After Burnham," pp. 194, 195. For a short but informative commentary on the travails of *Stabroek News* in the context of press freedom in Guyana, see Andrew Graham-Yooll, "Guyana: The Newspaper *Stabroek News*," *The Round Table*, no. 332 (October 1994):447–454.

27. U.S. Department of State, *Country Reports on Human Rights Practices for 1990* (Washington, DC: Department of State, 1991), p. 649.

28. See PPP-Civic, *Time for Change*, p. 6.

29. "Jagan Repeats Destabilization Charges Against Stabroek News," *Stabroek News*, August 22, 1993, p. 24; and "PPP is Marxist, not Government—Jagan," *Stabroek News*, August 26, 1993, p. 1. The Guyana Press Association called President Jagan's remarks "inappropriate and intemperate in the prevailing circumstances of the government's stated commitment to press freedom." Interestingly, in the section of the PPP-Civic manifesto that deals with democracy the promise is made that "[t]he PPP/Civic will encourage constructive political debate, education, and activity, instead of abuse and denigration of political opponents."

30. See PPP-Civic, *Time for Action*, p. 7.

31. Ibid. See also Anand Persaud and Ryan Naraine, "Democracy Will Be Participatory," *Stabroek News*, December 18, 1992, pp. 1, 2. Participatory democracy was the theme of Jagan's speech at the inaugural session of the post-elections National Assembly.

32. See "WPA to Discuss Participation in Government," *Stabroek News*, October 28, 1992, p. 1; and Lynette Harvey, "Civic Pride: Cabinet Making in 1992," *Guyana Review*, no. 1 (March 1993)·10–11. The United Force party was also supposed to be offered a cabinet position; that deal fell through largely because TUF wanted the Ministry of Foreign Affairs in return for its support in the National Assembly, something to which the ruling party obviously could not agree, especially since TUF has one seat in the National Assembly.

33. Premdas, "Guyana One year After the PNC," p. 169.

34. "Winner Takes All?" *Stabroek News*, June 26, 1993, p. 6.

35. One Caribbean ambassador based in Washington made the observation to me in March 1994 that while Hoyte was president one saw Indians in the predominantly African Guyana diplomatic corps, but since Jagan's entry into power, blacks are conspicuous by their absence. Up to fall 1996, except for the high commissioner to Canada, the ambassador to Brazil, and the ambassador in Brussels, the heads of all of Guyana's ten foreign missions were of Indian descent.

36. For a discussion of ethnic conflict in Guyana, see Leo A. Despres, *Cultural Pluralism and Nationalist Politics in Guyana* (Chicago: Rand McNally, 1967); J. E. Greene, *Race vs Politics in Guyana* (Kingston, Jamaica: Institute of Social and Economic Research, 1974); and Perry Mars, "State Intervention and Ethnic Conflict Resolution: Guyana and the Caribbean Case," *Comparative Politics*, vol. 27, no. 2 (January 1995):167–186.

37. E. George Green, "The Role of Governments in Strengthening Human Rights Machinery," in *International Human Rights in the Commonwealth Carib-*

bean, ed. Angela D. Byre and Beverly Y. Byfield (Dordrecht, Neth.: Martinus Nijhoff, 1991), pp. 309–310.

38. U.S. Department of State, *Country Reports on Human Rights Practices for 1993* (Washington, DC: Department of State, 1991), p. 462.

39. See "Prisoner Caused His Own Dilemma," *Stabroek News,* May 6, 1993, p. 1; and Byron Henry, "Prisoner on the Roof," *Guyana Review,* no. 5 (June 1993): 14–15.

40. Cheddi Jagan, "The Caribbean Community: Crossroads to the Future," *Caribbean Affairs,* vol. 7 (July-August 1994):31.

41. Government of Guyana, Parliament, *Budget Speech by the Honorable Asgar Ally, Senior Minister of Finance,* Sessional Paper No. 1 of 1994, Sixth Parliament, 1st Session, March 7, 1994, p. 27. Three different poverty line figures exist. The government uses G$6,080 per month; the *Catholic Standard,* a sympathetic, independent weekly, uses G$15,000 per week, and C. Y. Thomas, a respected economist and the WPA parliamentarian from October 1992 to March 1995, cites G$10,644 per month. During 1996 the U.S.-Guyana currency exchange rate fluctuated between G$138 to US$1 and G$146 to US$1. For a good analysis of poverty in contemporary Guyana, see Clive Y. Thomas, "Lessons from Experience: Structural Adjustment and Poverty in Guyana," *Social and Economic Studies,* vol. 42 (December 1993): 133–184.

42. Cheddi Jagan, "Guyana is a Free Country Where Democracy Prevails and the Economy Is Open," *Thunder* (Guyana), vol. 26, no. 1 (1994):11. In his 1996 budget speech the minister of finance told the National Assembly that "at the end of 1995, Guyana's external debt stock amounted to US$2.06 billion, or a 3 percent rise over the previous year." See Government of Guyana, Parliament, *Budget Speech by the Honorable Bharrat Jagdeo, Senior Minister of Finance,* Sessional Paper No. 1 of 1996, Sixth Parliament, 1st Session, January 19, 1996, p. 25.

43. *Country Report on Human Rights Practices for 1993,* p. 464.

44. For an analysis of civil and political and economic and social rights in Guyana, see James and Lutchman, *Law and the Political Environment in Guyana,* pp. 123–173.

45. Maurice Cranston, *What Are Human Rights?* (London: Bradley Held, 1973), p. 85.

10

Democracy and Human Rights in Haiti

Robert E. Maguire

Once a great wrong has been done, it never dies. People speak the words of peace, but their hearts do not forgive. Generations perform ceremonies of reconciliation, but there is no end.

—From the Tiv of West Africa[1]

No to Violence. No to Vengeance. Yes to Reconciliation.

—Jean-Bertrand Aristide

By mid-1996, Haiti had been transformed from a notorious democratic and human rights nightmare to a country where fledgling democratic institutions were once again taking root, and where newly elected public officials—with considerable international aid—were engaging in the task of rebuilding a country devastated from years of authoritarian and military misrule. In a series of elections between June and September 1995, Haitian citizens chose from among their peers a first generation of municipal and parliamentary leaders dedicated to democracy, accountability to the citizens, and the decentralization of the state.[2] For the first time in its history, Haiti experienced a peaceful, democratic presidential transition when President Jean-Bertrand Aristide left office to his elected successor, René Préval, on February 7, 1996. In a scenario of governance previously unknown in Haiti, negotiations then ensued between the executive and legislative branches—with municipal officials also making their voices heard—on the shape of policies and budgetary allocations.

Also by mid-1996, human rights violations, out of control during the 1991–1994 period of de facto military rule, had declined so precipitously that the joint United Nations (UN)/Organization of American States (OAS) International Civilian Mission in Haiti (MICIVIH), overwhelmingly occupied since its creation in 1992 with charting and reporting on human rights abuse, had refocused its efforts toward training and educating civil society and elected leaders. Public security, previously a mirage for all Haitians except those abusing weapons and power, had improved markedly, becoming the domain of a freshly recruited and professionally trained national police force accountable to civilian authorities and actively mentored by a UN-sponsored corps of French-speaking international police (CIVPOL).

These indicators of a hopeful future were possible largely because of three factors: (1) the September 1994 intervention by a UN Multinational Force (MNF) that dislodged the de facto military rulers and continued its presence as a UN peacekeeping mission (UNMIH); (2) the subsequent demobilization of the Haitian Armed Forces (Forces Armées d'Haiti, FADH) and disaggregation of paramilitary operatives functioning with impunity under its protection; and (3) the unflagging determination of the vast majority of Haitian citizens to bring democratic political, economic, and social reforms to their country.

Certainly many challenges remain as Haiti proceeds to strengthen its democratic institutions and practices and maintain its relative freedom from human rights abuses. In a report to the UN Security Council in June 1996 the secretary-general identified, among the multitude of challenges confronting Haiti and its international partners, two that deserve top priority. The first is the critical need for the continued presence of UNMIH, particularly to continue to provide a secure space and mentoring for the still inexperienced Haitian National Police. The second is the urgent need to match improvements in security and democratization with advances in economic development.[3]

For Haitians, a significant challenge that remains is that of building a nation from the ruins of a state that did nothing but prey upon its people. Haiti continues to confront the deep and severe polarization and mistrust following decades—indeed generations—of misrule and abuse of power. These significant challenges notwithstanding, Haiti's citizens and legitimate leaders—with international assistance—have made significant strides toward achieving the dream of democracy harbored by most since the February 1986 fall of the Duvalier dictatorship. Current challenges should be placed in that context, examining the key positive role that organized civil society has played in Haiti's oft-thwarted struggle toward democracy as well as the extremely negative role of Haiti's military apparatus in the recent years of democracy denied and human rights abused. Understanding that context is crucial to appreciating the travails of democracy and human rights in Haiti.

A Democratic and Human Rights Nightmare

In the middle of the night of September 29–30, 1991, a violent military coup d'état occurred in Haiti, ousting the government of President Jean-Bertrand Aristide, who had been inaugurated only months earlier, on February 7. As Aristide fled into exile, his supporters sought refuge both within and outside Haiti. Hundreds who attempted to resist the military by protesting in the streets of Port-au-Prince were gunned down as the sun rose on that violent day. Others were shot near their homes in the city's strongly pro-Aristide slums. Hence, for the next three years, Haiti was victim to "a human rights nightmare."[4]

With the country run by the military during this dark period, constitutional freedoms such as those pertaining to speech and assembly were arbitrarily suspended. Movement within the country became restricted by numerous military and paramilitary roadblocks and checkpoints. Improvements in rule of law and judicial reform that had begun under the Aristide government fell by the wayside as "justice" became the exclusive domain of those with guns. A number of independent radio stations were raided and closed, others falling back on the proven strategy of self-censorship in order to avoid the same fate. The national radio and television stations were occupied by the army, which installed its own staff. The press, however, was generally not muzzled, as the military allowed newspapers, including those critical of the coup that are published in the United States and sent to Haiti, to continue publication and sale in the streets of the capital.

This apparent discrepancy in the army's control was only mildly surprising, however. Given Haiti's low level of literacy in French—with perhaps no more than 10 percent of the population, mostly in Port-au-Prince, able to read it—Haiti's newspapers not only have limited circulation but also limited impact as organs of information and opinion dissemination. Only the Creole-language, pro-democracy weekly, *Libète*, published in Port-au-Prince and circulated throughout the country, was forced to suspend publication following repeated violence directed toward its salesmen. Clearly, those who mounted the coup were more concerned about the dissemination of information in Creole, the language of all Haitians, than in French, the language of the elites.[5]

The prolonged ordeal—characterized by such abuses as murder, rape, and disfigurement, much of it painstakingly documented by human rights organizations inside and outside of the country, including at times by the joint UN/OAS-sponsored International Civilian Mission—drove Haiti's nascent democratic organizations and the process of change they sought to the brink of extinction.[6] Mixed signals and the confusing and at times contradictory policies of an international community seeking, at least officially, to reverse the coup characterized this period, exacerbating the already difficult conditions of those working for social, economic, and political change in the Western hemisphere's country of greatest despair.[7]

By September 1994, however, the signals and policies toward Haiti's coup leaders and de facto government had become more consistent, characterized by stronger economic sanctions, high-profile saber rattling, and preparation for a military intervention by a U.S.-led force sanctioned by the UN. On September 18, 1994, the leaders of the coup acquiesced to international pressure, agreeing to an eleventh-hour accord negotiated with a last-ditch delegation led by former U.S. president Jimmy Carter. As such, they headed off the invasion, then already in its early stages.

According to the agreement, Haiti's military high command would step aside to allow the return of the duly elected president no later than October 15, 1994. A provision stipulated that some form of amnesty would be accorded those who had mounted the coup. The transition of power, and the general security of the country and its citizens following it, would be overseen by a force of some 15,000 to 20,000 U.S. troops at first, and some 2,000 to 6,000 UN peacekeeping troops thereafter, at least until mid-1996.

The elected president did indeed return on October 15, 1994, shortly after Lieutenant General Raoul Cédras fled to Panama. Aristide's return was marked by great fanfare and strict security. In his first speech—behind a barricade of Plexiglas placed on the palace steps, distant from all but the international celebrities, the president's closest advisers, and the retinue of security personnel—Aristide reiterated the pledge of reconciliation over vengeance and violence. He asked his people to exercise restraint. If you apprehend a criminal, he instructed, turn him over to the soldiers who are here to protect us. Human rights, he underscored, would now be protected and guaranteed.

Though the president's return instilled most Haitians with a feeling of euphoria and a sense of security and relief accompanied by hope, there were immediate signs that those whose rights had been so thoroughly abused over the previous three years would seek more than the president asked. Perhaps this sentiment was best expressed by a large banner unfurled in the midst of the crowd of thousands listening to the president's speech and stretching beyond the palace fence, filling up the Champs de Mars. It read: "No Reconciliation Without Justice." This phrase, as stripped down as the president's "no violence, no vengeance, yes reconciliation" mantra, framed the mood of most of Haiti's citizens upon the return of their president.

Aristide's return was a required element of a longer term and hopefully irreversible transition in Haiti, from authoritarian military rule to democratically elected civilian government. By itself, however, one man's restoration to democratically elected leadership is no guarantee that either democratic processes or an end to grave violations of human rights will be sustained. For this to happen, fundamental changes in social, economic, and political relationships in Haiti are required. Essentially, a contract for democratic governance between the state and the nation will have to be consummated, with the former becoming accountable to all the people of Haiti.

Both the Aristide government, as evidenced in its broad framework for the postcoup social and economic reconstruction of Haiti, and its successor government, headed by President Préval, recognized the need to forge new relations between those who govern and those who are governed, starting with fundamental reform of state institutions.[8] No single government, however, can do more than develop policies and initiate programs to begin to overcome the torturous past. Those who will ultimately shoulder the responsibility of implanting democratic processes and respect for human rights are the Haitian people.

Changing Relations Through Grassroots Organization

Alan Durning once observed: "Like all development efforts, self-help is inherently political: It is the struggle to control the future. Where governance is undemocratic, grassroots movements sometimes meet opposition and repression."[9] In Haiti, as elsewhere in the world and certainly in the Caribbean over roughly the past twenty-five years, the environment for democratic political evolution and development has been influenced tremendously by the emergence and growth of nongovernmental organizations (NGOs) and grassroots citizens' groups involved in efforts toward sustainable, community-based, self-help development. Forming a "latticework" of bottom-up action for change in Haiti, these new actors have spread within the national borders and spilled over them as organizations in one village, town, city, region, and/or country discover that they share characteristics, aims, and strategies with organizations elsewhere.

In the period before the 1991 coup d'état, Haiti's organized grass roots had begun to flourish into associations of groups, some of which were identified as peasant movements. Neighborhood associations in the cities joined more established small-farm family groups to fill in the latticework, so that practically every nook and cranny of Haiti could boast of some form of community-based organization or organizations. An estimated total national membership of at least 2 million ordinary Haitians by the time of the coup is not extreme.[10]

Catalyzing this movement of "people power," in Haiti as throughout the world, have been continuing and exacerbating crises of dehumanizing poverty, human rights abuse, collapsing ecological systems, and deeply stressed social structures.[11] Correspondingly, in Haiti as elsewhere, formal institutions of economic and political power—governments and state agencies, multilateral and bilateral donors, banks, and corporations—have failed to effectively confront these crises. Indeed, as has been increasingly and convincingly argued in analyses of global development, to a significant degree these established institutions are responsible for perpetuating, and for deepening, this profound global crisis.[12]

Haiti is among a handful of countries worldwide where grassroots organizing for change has been pervasive.[13] There the community-based groups of poor people that are at the root of emerging social, economic, and political action networks include small farmer associations, neighborhood committees, women's clubs, literacy groups, religious study groups, water use and management committees, and innumerable other organizational types. These grassroots units are usually guided by leadership that emerges from within the community, although that process is sometimes catalyzed and supported by nongovernmental organizations that are not from the community.[14] That leadership as well as those they lead tends to be practical and pragmatic, mobilizing to develop strategies and launch programs designed to achieve and sustain, through popular participation, three overarching goals designed to address the failures and continuing/exacerbating crises identified earlier:

- to improve members' economic status;
- to improve members' capacity to gain access to, use, and manage resources; and
- to enhance members' ability to have an effective voice in the debate and determination of public policies and programs that affect their lives.

State Against Nation

In Haiti, as nowhere else in the Caribbean, as grassroots organizations have gathered strength and made progress toward meeting these goals they have clashed with unrepresentative elites and powerful vested interests. Additionally, where elites and their allies have attempted to exert power through unrelenting control of a nondemocratic state, the clash between the newly emerging and consolidating actors of organized civil society and those representing established institutions affiliated with or in control of the state has been of seismic proportions. This conflict spilled beyond Haiti's borders, particularly after the 1991 coup d'état, compelling international agencies to respond to the waves of desperate, displaced people fleeing into hiding and onto boats, seeking respite and safe haven from a state at war with its people.[15]

This conflict between representatives of the state and the ordinary citizens of the nation as well as its impact on the human rights environment and its effect on democratic social, economic, and political change has not gone un-noticed by scholars. Several writers have placed Haiti's state/nation di-chotomy at the center of their analyses of the country's political culture and economic development. Michel-Rolph Trouillot, in an important compre-hensive study that examines the origin and legacy of the Duvaliers and Du-valierism, argues convincingly that today's state/nation tension stems from uneven human relationships embedded in Haiti's plantation colonial and postrevolutionary past that are vigorously maintained by a small group at the expense of the larger one.[16] Christian Girault affirms Trouillot's analysis, likening the nature of the relationship between state and nation to one that replicates that of total conjugal rupture—that is, a divorce.[17]

For Haiti's new actors to be able to achieve their goals and hence to play a constructive, significant, and sustained role in the desperately needed re-forms away from political authoritarianism and toward democratic political, social, and economic development and the respect for human rights, the ap-parent total alienation between these divorced partners will somehow have to be moderated, with some form of peaceful coexistence attained. Even with the presence of a government seeking to address past abuses, engage-ment between the state and the nation will not occur without some reserva-tions. Before we move to a discussion of this elusive goal, two vignettes are offered. They illustrate the magnitude and gravity of the rupture and result-ing confrontation in Haiti between a state monopolized by and serving the interests of the country's political and commercial elites and a nation com-posed of the rest of the country's citizens and increasingly organized in a plethora of citizens' groups.

The more benign vignette illustrates the insidious nature of the economic abuse of most ordinary Haitians. The vignette of outward aggression illus-trates the abuse of the human rights of that same significant group. Despite the apparent contrast, the forces illustrated in these vignettes function in tandem, contributing equally to the alienation and the violence of the state/nation division and equally responsible for the repression experienced by today's new Haitian actors for political evolution and development dur-ing the three-year period of military rule. As such, they contribute equally to the continued tragedy of irreconcilable relationships between two groups—one small and one large—occupying the same deteriorating space.

Vignette One: Economic Abuse

At the nineteenth conference of the Caribbean Studies Association (CSA) in Merida, Mexico, in May 1994, a panel explored a newly created regional en-tity, the Association of Caribbean States (ACS). After speakers from the Commonwealth Caribbean, Puerto Rico, Colombia, and Mexico discussed the pros and cons of this government-driven initiative, a Haitian NGO activist rose to speak. Pointedly, he recoiled against the concept of an association of *states*. Since states represent only the interests of those who control them, he asked, what will be the significance of the ACS for the rest of the region's population, those who are not of the state and who have at best only been minimally consulted during the process of putting together the regional entity? The Haitian commentator went on to urge nongovernmental organizations and citizens' groups in each of the region's countries to join forces in challenging the authority of states to take initiatives like the ACS without adequate consultation with and accountability toward their populations.

Implied from this Haitian perspective is a concern that a "statist" approach toward regional cooperation virtually guarantees, at least from a Haitian perspective, representation of the interests of the few at the expense of the many. Coming to the CSA meeting from a country where the state has been variously identified in recent times as "parasitic," "predatory," and "kleptocratic," this concern over state's ability to be accountable to citizens and to serve as a model for citizen participation, and the parallel skepticism toward the ACS expressed by the Haitian participant, is understandable. The speaker's coming to Merida from a state that has been forcing its people to flee or to go into hiding and thus is systematically seeking the dissolution of the organized nation doubly underscores his concern.

As mentioned earlier, Trouillot identifies the historical roots of the state/nation dichotomy, noting the significance of its longevity and depth. Since independence in 1804, he emphasizes, the Haitian state has been the virtually exclusive domain of urban "parasites" who have transformed themselves into a political "class" aligned with the country's dominant seacoast merchant elite. This alliance is organized in such a way as to ensure a monopoly over the state and its resources by the political class and to issue assurance that the state will not interfere with the exclusive control over wealth emanating from the country's productive economic resources by the merchant elite. By creating mechanisms that efficiently siphon wealth away from the nation's predominant working class—particularly the small-scale agricultural producers and their families who form the base of Haiti's economy—the parasites have guaranteed the inability of honest, hard-working producers to accumulate a surplus, thus ensuring their persistent poverty.

Widely held among Haiti's new actors organized for change, including its small agricultural producers, is the notion of state extraction as a squeeze and suck tandem. Called *pese-souse* in Creole, the tandem functions so that not just economic surpluses but also citizen rights are extracted by the predatory state.[18]

Haiti's state-connected extraction system encompasses a geography in which approximately 70 percent of the population lives in a rural milieu. As such, extraction reached into remote areas beyond small communities situated in a series of culs-de-sac. Rural settlements, including those at the end of culs-de-sac, served as collection points for resources from the surrounding countryside. The extractive flow from these communities built volume as it passed through other villages and towns located farther along the roads or at their intersections. Within Haiti the ultimate urban repository of resources has been the capital, Port-au-Prince, a city that holds some 20 percent of the country's people. Traditionally, Port-au-Prince has been allocated about 80 percent of the national budget, and it is the principal home of the parasitic class.

But not all resources have ended up in the hands, pockets, or domestic and foreign bank accounts of urban-based members of this group. At various points along the way, those at lower levels of the "pecking order" that maintains the system have been accorded the privilege of siphoning off some of them. Any corresponding return flow of resources from the urban milieu to rural milieux has been minimal—just enough to ensure the maintenance of the extraction infrastructure and the well-being of those who make it work.[19]

The reality of the Haitian state as a forced extraction enterprise is illustrated clearly in the fact that since the creation of the Haitian state after 1804 there have been only two entities of the state regularly present throughout the countryside where most Haitians live. They are the appropriately named Bureau des Contributions (Tax Office) and the Caserne or Avant Poste (Military Post). The first has served for the systematic extraction of resources and the second to ensure that the nation's citizens comply with extraction policies, paying arbitrarily levied taxes to state authorities for "literally dozens of means, including taxes of the declaration of a birth or natural death, funeral preparation, surveying, issuing warrants, animal licenses, construction, and authorization to cut trees."[20] Citizen perception of the state has clearly been influenced by this reality. In Creole, the only language spoken by most of those citizens, *leta*, the word for "state," also means "bully."[21]

State Control: An Army Against the People

Vignette Two: Aggressive Abuse of Human Rights and Reinforcement of Economic Exploitation

On Haiti's Armed Forces Day, November 18, 1992, Lieutenant General Cédras, then commander in chief of the Haitian Armed Forces (FADH), addressed his troops, calling for a truce (*trêve*) in Haiti. Because a truce calls for a cessation of hostilities between two or more warring parties, implicit in the general's statement is the fact that his army, in late 1992, was at war. Since no foreign government had declared war on Haiti and no forces were involved in aggressive action against the FADH at that time, it was not entirely clear with whom Cédras considered his army to be at war, and with what hostile entity he therefore called for a truce. An examination of the history and evolution of the FADH as it existed up to late September 1994 begins to clarify this matter.

When the U.S. Marine Corps initiated its nineteen-year occupation of Haiti in 1915, one of its first acts was to disband Haiti's army. In its place the U.S. occupation force created a professional military police, the Gendarmerie. The Gendarmerie was quickly tested as a fighting force when it was called upon by its mentors to help crush Haitian resistance to the occupation, which reached its peak in 1919 when up to 15,000 irregulars, called *cacos*, skirmished with occupation forces in what has become known as the Caco War. The U.S. forces and their local counterparts undertook combat actions against the Haitian insurgents, effectively crushing their offensive that same year with the capture and murder of Charlemagne Péralte, the primary caco leader. Subsequently, the population was disarmed.[22]

Thereafter the Gendarmerie—commanded, outfitted, and armed by foreigners—was unleashed against the nation to maintain order and in effect to serve as an indigenous occupation army. Thus this reformed, "professionalized" force, whose name later changed to the Garde d'Haiti and thereafter to the Forces Armées d'Haiti, became an instrument of state abuse of the nation from the first stage of its evolution. Haiti's army was obviously no match for an external, professional military force, but against a populace armed only with sticks, stones, and farmer's tools, it was formidable.[23]

"Souvenirs" from the U.S. occupation that were still used effectively by the FADH included some weapons and the physical infrastructure of occupation such as the still-intact command centers, pillboxes, guard houses, barracks, and prisons, all painted in the infamous orange-ocher that distinguishes all military structures. The command-and-control structure of an occupying military force was in the aftermath of the 1991 coup another still-used remnant of the past. As the FADH enhanced its weaponry over what it had inherited, the FADH artfully built upon the occupation's command-and-control structure to spread its vigilant presence to the most remote rural sites and throughout the most byzantine urban slums. It did this using both active-duty personnel and armed auxiliaries who were integrated into an omnipresent FADH structure.

A cursory examination of the functional formal *and* informal organizational framework of the FADH at the time of Cédras's speech clarifies to whom he was speaking when he issued his 1992 call for a truce. To best understand that framework, it is essential to keep in mind that the FADH was born fighting alongside an army whose goal was to occupy the entire country and maintain order therein. An image of Haiti's political geography is also useful. Geopolitically, Haiti is composed of nine departments. Each department is subdivided into districts and subdistricts. Each of these, in turn, is divided into the country's smallest geopolitical administrative unit, the rural section, of which there are 565 in Haiti.[24]

Until the start of the U.S.-led military intervention on September 19, 1994, the FADH's leadership at the General Headquarters in Port-au-Prince was served by twelve operational units.[25] Three of them—a mobile special forces light infantry called the Tactique; the Presidential Guard, providing security to the High Command; and the Port-au-Prince police, a separate corps within the FADH—were based primarily in Port-au-Prince and had a lesser or an occasional presence in Haiti's secondary cities. These units functioned in tandem with nine army corps assigned to each of the country's geopolitical departments to ensure the all-encompassing blanket of country-wide occupation.

The Departmental Corps's hierarchy of command and control originated from a headquarters in the department's major urban area and flowed to subunits assigned to the districts and subdistricts of the department. An army regular, with the title of *chef seksyon* (section chief) and accountable to a district or subdistrict commander, was assigned to each rural section, completing the formal chain of FADH command and control. The *chefs seksyon*, also known as the rural police, in effect have served as official gatekeepers of the usually compact geopolitical unit they oversee. Their power has been enormous. A section chief fulfilled the role of police *and* served as judge, jury, executioner, and extortionist of his realm. In other words, he exercised the power to arrest, fine, sentence, imprison, tax, and liberate those within his jurisdiction. To each section's citizens, the *chef*, therefore, has been *leta*—in both senses of the word.

As pervasive and critical to the army's maintenance of its stranglehold over the nation as its official hierarchy was its unofficial structure: paramilitary auxiliaries, active in both rural and urban locales. Providing an insight into both their link with the FADH and their approach to their work were two articles published in the *Washington Times* on July 18, 1994: "Cédras Keeps Order with Thugs at Grass Roots" and "Haitians Tell of Rapes, Beatings— Refugees Say Army-Backed Thugs Terrorize Countryside." They also provided further indication of the full extent of the audience to which the commander in chief directed his November 1992 speech and with whom he considered his forces at war.

Haiti's paramilitary auxiliaries have been active in both urban and rural Haiti. In urban areas they were known generically as *attachés*. In essence, *attachés* were guns-for-hire, providing cover for and doing the dirty work of military and police officials. In their midst were "double-dippers"—army and police regulars who, when out of uniform, were active *attachés*. Mafia-like characters, these armed thugs in civilian clothing were free to sow terror. Although they did kill, more typically they terrorized through false arrest, theft, shakedowns, and other forms of economic extortion and physical abuse, including the use of arson and rape as tools of political terror.[26] They were urban thugs at work among the grass roots, the lowest level of a violent, extortive food chain.

Urban *attachés* tended to be grouped into gangs loyal to specific military officers and police personnel. In some instances, they were called upon by state officials supported by the military. The neo-Duvalierist extremist group that made its debut in mid-1993, the Front for the Advancement and Progress of Haiti (Front pour l'Avancement et le Progrès d'Haiti, FRAPH), appears to have coalesced from a combination of this latter group, a second generation of hard-line supporters of François Duvalier, and street thugs loyal to the Port-au-Prince police. FRAPH's leadership has acknowledged its ties with the military and police.[27]

Haiti's rural auxiliaries usually had a link with the section chief and, through him, the military chain of command. According to FADH regulations, each *chef seksyon* was allowed two unpaid assistants, or *sous chef seksyon*. In fact, however, section chiefs expanded that prerogative to have under their command units of unpaid paramilitary troops numbering as many as 150 men per section. Estimates of the total number of Haiti's rural auxiliaries have ranged from 25,000 to more than 60,000. These assistants to the chief, variously called *secrétaire-maréchal, adjoint, police,* and *souket lawouze* ("those who collect the dew"), assisted him in exerting his unrestrained powers of arrest, imprisonment, punishment, taxation, and virtually unmitigated extortion from the rural residents under his authority. Like urban *attachés,* the minimally salaried section chief and his unsalaried assistants lived off of shakedowns, providing kickbacks to the military officials who gave them their privileged position.

This, then, was the overall configuration of uniformed and nonuniformed personnel overseen until recently by Lieutenant General Cédras and his colleagues of the FADH High Command. As historical function and contemporary form suggest, the opponent confronting this military and paramilitary configuration in late 1992 was not a bona fide military force but rather the people of Haiti, whom the FADH had been organized to fight, and with whom it had been at war since its modern-day creation until late 1994.

The general's call for a truce in 1992 was more a matter of words than action. Following that speech, up to the days immediately following the arrival of the first U.S.-led international intervention force in Haiti, the state-sponsored military and paramilitary campaign against the Haitian nation was unrelenting, particularly as the people grouped themselves in various organizations and associations to become active players in the country's political evolution and development. Following the coup d'état one source characterized the campaign as follows: "The army's campaign . . . has been systematic and ruthless. . . . [T]argets of this violence include pro-Aristide elected officials, rural development and peasant organizations, neighborhood and community associations, trade unions, and literacy, pro-democracy, students' and women's groups. Soldiers and section chiefs have hunted down, arrested, beaten and killed leaders and members of these groups."[28]

Rethinking Conventional Wisdom on Democracy and Human Rights

Since the 1970s, an emerging universe of nongovernmental, grassroots, and community-based organizations, viewed as presenting an alternative for achieving urgently needed political evolution and development, can be viewed as attempting to "de-dichotomize" Haiti's state/nation polarity. The efforts of these new actors are aimed partly at moving their members from a status of marginalized players on the periphery of the state to one of demarginalization whereby they have a "voice" in state affairs, hence achieving greater state accountability for the nation. The political, social, and economic evolution and development that began to solidify during the democratic moments before the 1991 coup d'état show that those goals were being achieved. The price paid for their incipient progress, however, was exceedingly high.

Conventional wisdom following a military coup holds that its primary victims are members of the ousted government, and this applies fully to the September 1991 military coup. The government of President Jean-Bertrand Aristide was swept from office—and largely from the country and into prolonged exile—with the violent coup. In this case, however, conventional wisdom must be revised to include the coup's other set of primary victims: those vast numbers of Haitian citizens who voted to elect the ousted government. It must include, therefore, the array of civil-society/grassroots organizations of which so many of those voters were members and that had rallied around the Aristide candidacy and later the Aristide government as partners in the struggle for sustained political, social, and economic change. Even before the coup, one hypothesis offered was that Aristide's grassroots support was mobilized to a significant extent by community-based and other nongovernmental organizations, including church-affiliated ones.[29] As a result, Haiti's grassroots organizations were far from peripheral casualties of coup-linked violence; they were as much its target as the elected leaders.[30]

The experience of the September 1991 coup suggests that another element of conventional wisdom pertaining to a military coup in Haiti—and this may apply more broadly in the hemisphere and the post–Cold War world—needs to be rethought: the suggestion that, like it or not, a military coup will succeed in consolidating itself, at least over the short term, and in receiving international recognition. Before the end of the Cold War, a shortcut for recognition by Western powers, even if the coup ousted an elected government, was a declaration by the military of its own anticommunist credentials.

After three years of both its attempt to reverse the tide of change in Haiti and its repeated attempts to become viewed as legitimate, the Cédras-led military and its de facto government were unable either to consolidate power or to gain recognition. Certainly, in the context of Haiti, the length and nature of this limbo-like situation was unusual, if not unprecedented. Two factors, clearly interrelated, no doubt contributed to this situation. In terms of recognition and legitimacy, the rejection of the coup by the international community—led by the UN, the OAS, the United States, and the "Friends of Haiti"—was unswerving. Though the commitment of these agents to their own policies aimed at reversing the coup and the effectiveness of those policies have been questioned, the fact remains that even three years after the violent removal of the democratically elected government the nations of the world firmly withheld the recognition desperately sought by the usurpers.[31]

In terms of the internal consolidation of power, the military and its allies, in spite of their relentless intimidation and use of force against the population, were unable to beat it into submission. From within the country, and more significantly from within organized civil society, a stubborn unwillingness to acquiesce to those attempting to turn back the clock emerged. As such, resistance, albeit passive for the most part, became the modus operandi. The army's constant need to resort to gruesome violence against Haitians was a tragic indication of the continuation of that resistance.[32]

Regardless of the ineffectiveness of international measures for reversing the coup—sanctions and embargoes—and regardless of how much these actually benefited those against whom they were levied and injured those whom they were supposed to benefit, Haitians supporting change and rejecting the coup expressed continuing support for sanctions and the international actors that put them in place, as long as the de facto government held sway. Though frustration and dissatisfaction with those policies increased from within Haiti, particularly after the failure of the Governor's Island Agreement of July 1993 to restore President Aristide and his government in October 1993, it remained the view of those supporting the thwarted democratic process that any withdrawal of or radical shift in those policies without the application of other, more effective measures against the military and its allies, would be tantamount to providing the coup leaders with the recognition they sought.[33]

The inability of those leading and supporting the coup to consolidate power after three determined years, as well as the maintenance of the international rejection of the coup, was to a significant extent the result of a very important conclusion drawn by Haiti's new actors from the grass roots—and this conclusion is at the essence of the critical role these actors play in contemporary processes of political evolution and development: Once these previously marginalized actors became mobilized, declared themselves, and entered onto the playing field of a democratic process of change, they *could not*, and indeed, *do not*, retreat to the sidelines when the change for which they became mobilized is threatened or reversed.

The determination and resilience of Haiti's latticework of nongovernmental organizations and community-based and grassroots groups in this regard has been apparent in the framework of their ability to draw upon the time-tested Haitian strategy of *mawonaj* (elusiveness) to frustrate or defeat a stronger foe. Unable to undertake such normal organizational activities as holding membership meetings and continuing such programs as civic education and credit unions, Haiti's new actors devised other methods of maintaining organizational cohesion. Members came together to engage in "safe" group activities, for example, the maintenance of the physical infrastructure, such as roads. In other instances, where repression and surveillance were so great that organizations were unable to function in any capacity in their communities, members and leaders—particularly the latter, who tended to be more openly hunted down by military and paramilitary operatives—successfully reconstituted themselves elsewhere, mostly in the relative anonymity of the city, awaiting the time when they could recommence the work cut short by the coup.[34]

From day one of the coup, the apparent strategy of those seeking to reverse the push toward social, economic, and political reform was to stall for time in order to outlast Aristide's five-year term of office. As the February 6, 1996, end of Aristide's term approached with each passing day, the army and its allies saw their total victory draw nearer. If indeed this was their attitude, they missed the fundamental factor making Haiti today vastly different from the Haiti of just twenty-five or fewer years ago and making this coup d'état significantly different from its predecessors. Jean-Bertrand Aristide, even by his own admission, is merely a messenger.[35] However, the message he carries is profound, undeniable, and compelling. The nation of Haiti, as represented by people organized in the growing array of nongovernmental civil-society organizations, requires that the state be accountable to them. It requires that the state/nation dichotomy, in which the former lives off the latter, become a relic of the past. It requires an end to the unlawful violence and abuse by state authorities against citizens. It requires reforms of state institutions and agencies that will compel them to function within the law of the land and to the service of a body politic that includes all the nation's citizens. A strategy of simply waiting out Aristide's term was to ignore the reality and the lessons of the past twenty-five years of organization and action for change by the new actors who pursued political evolution and development.

Postcoup Progress Toward
Reordered Relationships

During his 1991 inaugural speech, President Aristide, in alluding to a new relationship of mutual respect—a marriage—between the army and the people, noted that as Haiti redefines itself as a country, the relationship between the state and the nation will have to change. Unfortunately, that proposed marriage never took place, as one party had little interest in respecting the integrity of the other. Following three years of repressive military rule, most Haitians, as evidenced by a public opinion poll conducted in March 1995, do not seek reconciliation with the army. Rather, they support its complete elimination.[36]

Even without an army, Haiti still faces the considerable challenge of finding workable equations for moderating the entrenched alienation within its dichotomized society and between those accustomed to exercising power—its "haves"—and those historically the victims of power—the "have nots." Otherwise, the country faces the likelihood that sustained political evolution and democratic development simply will not occur.

As the Préval government began its five-year mandate in February 1996, with considerable material and financial support from international sources, it was undoubtedly seeking to implement sustainable policies and programs aimed at reforming the state and making it accountable to the nation. Faithful to President Aristide's stated goal of "moving Haiti from misery to poverty with dignity," Préval government initiatives seek both to improve the social, economic, and political status of Haitians historically preyed upon by those with power and to strengthen the economy as a whole.[37]

Some government efforts, such as abolishing separate birth certificates for *paysans* (peasants) and *citadens* (citizens), have immediate symbolic or psychological significance and help to de-dichotomize the society. By acknowledging the equal status of all Haitians, their significance is also long term, as they help to level the playing field through respect for human rights and equal access to the law. Other postcoup initiatives, such as the abolition of the section chief system and the creation of a new, professionally trained police force under the jurisdiction of the Ministry of Justice, have had a tangible impact. Apart from improving the environment for the respect of human rights, this change also improves the economic situation of those people previously subject to extralegal taxation and extortion.[38]

Still other programs, such as the creation of a joint private/public-sector Presidential Commission for Economic Growth and Modernization, and the support of initiatives that aim to privatize poorly run state enterprises while concurrently democratizing Haiti's economic assets, hold the promise of fostering both economic growth and improved relationships among social and economic sectors. Finally, the 1995 municipal and parliamentary elections stand to democratize participation in government through the election of local leaders who can solidify democratic gains at the village level while helping to ensure that all elected officials take heed of their constituents' concerns and expectations.

Those people involved in any degree of social, economic, and political change and democratic development in postcoup Haiti must confront the challenges of finding, enacting, and sustaining a workable equation to de-dichotomize the country. Responsibilities lie on each side of the equation. Whatever specifics emerge, there would appear to be certain prerequisites for its construction. The necessity of ending the occupation of the country by its own hostile force—be it formally organized or loosely knit in gangs—is one of them. Linked to this is the need for those Haitians long accustomed to regarding the majority of their fellow citizens as little more than draft animals for use in the creation and continuation of their own well-being to recognize the legitimate aspirations of those people to improve their lives and the prospects of their children.

Finally, Haitians, particularly those accustomed to living within the protection of the predatory state, will have to somehow find ways of overcoming their fear of each other and of living together. They will have to recognize that improvements in the status of the majority can and should be beneficial to the minority as well. Those marginalized for so long will have to demonstrate openly and with unceasing determination their intentions to engage in change constructively, not destructively. In sum, if Haiti is to overcome its abysmal human rights record and make lasting progress in the quest of the majority of its citizens for political, social, and economic evolution and development, those controlling the established—and in many respects the failed—institutions will have to accommodate, indeed to welcome, the new actors intent on pursuing change.

Notes

1. As found in Paule Marshall, *The Chosen Place, The Timeless People* (New York: Random House, 1969).

2. See Robert Maguire, "Bootstrap Politics: Elections and Haiti's New Public Officials," Hopkins-Georgetown Haiti Project, Briefing Paper No. 2, February 1996.

3. UN Security Council, "Report of the Secretary-General on the United Nations Mission in Haiti," June 5, 1996.

4. See, for example, *Haiti: A Human Rights Nightmare* (New York: Lawyers Committee for Human Rights, 1992).

5. The status of the judiciary and the press in Haiti has been analyzed in several publications, including *Haiti: A Human Rights Nightmare*; Human Rights Watch/Americas and National Coalition for Haitian Refugees, *Silencing A People: The Destruction of Civil Society in Haiti*, February 1993; and Inter-American Commission on Human Rights, *Report on the Situation of Human Rights in Haiti*

(February 1994). Literacy in Creole in Haiti has increased significantly in the past decade. Though no reliable data on Creole literacy are available, empirical data indicate that among Haitians involved in community-based civic organizations, such literacy has become widespread.

6. In addition to the reports cited earlier, other representative reports documenting the severe violence and violation of human rights in Haiti since the coup are Human Rights Watch/Americas and National Coalition for Haitian refugees, *Terror Prevails in Haiti: Human Rights and Failed Diplomacy*, New York, April 1994; and testimony by Ian Martin from the Carnegie Endowment for International Peace in U.S. Senate, Committee on Foreign Relations, *The Human Rights Situation and Its Implications*, Hearings, Subcommittee on Western Hemisphere and Peace Corps Affairs, 103d Cong., 2d Sess., June 28, 1994.

7. The most thorough account published thus far on this period is that of James Ridgeway, *The Haiti Files: Decoding the Crisis* (Washington, DC: Essential Books, 1994). The final section of the book provides a detailed chronology of events leading up to and following the 1991 coup.

8. See Government of Haiti, "Strategy of Social and Economic Reconstruction," August 22, 1994.

9. Alan Durning, "People, Power, and Development," *Foreign Policy*, vol. 76 (Fall 1989):79.

10. See Robert E. Maguire, "The Grassroots Movements," in *Haitian Frustrations: Dilemmas for U.S. Policy*, ed. Georges Fauriol (Washington, DC: Center for Strategic and International Studies, 1995).

11. See David C. Korsten, *Getting to the Twenty-first Century: Voluntary Action and the Global Agenda* (West Hartford, CT: Kumarian Press, 1990).

12. See, for example, Korsten, *Getting to the Twenty-first Century*; Stephen Hellinger, Douglas Hellinger, and Fred M. O'Regan, *Aid for Just Development: Report on the Future of Foreign Assistance* (Boulder: Lynne Rienner, 1988); Lakshman S. Yapa, "Ecological Relations of Production and Poverty" (paper presented at the annual meeting of the Association of American Geographers, Baltimore, MD, 1989); and Stuart Corbridge, *Capitalist World Development* (London: Macmillan, 1986).

13. In Alan Durning's article, "People, Power, and Development," he identifies Haiti as one of seven countries worldwide where by 1988 significant national political developments demonstrated "evidence of grassroots groups' increasing political importance." Other countries identified are Mexico, Brazil, the Philippines, Guatemala, India, and Peru.

14. Since the term *nongovernmental organization* is used more often in an all-encompassing manner, covering a multitude of organization types, distinctions among NGO types becomes necessary. Many writers now make a distinction between community-based membership organizations (MOs or CBOs) and organizations that render services to these grassroots organizations. For the latter, some terms increasingly used are grassroots support organizations (GSOs) and organizations promoting development (OPDs). Private voluntary organization (PVO) is still commonly used to identify noncommunity organizations but refers more generally to international organizations with programs *in* a given country; GSOs and OPDs are more commonly organizations *of* a given country.

15. Human Rights Watch/Americas and National Coalition for Haitian Refugees, *Silencing a People: No Port in a Storm: Misguided Use of In-Country Refugee Processing in Haiti*, September 1993; and *Terror Prevails in Haiti: Human Rights Violations and Failed Diplomacy*, April 1994.

16. Michel-Rolph Trouillot, *Haiti: State Against Nation: The Origins and Legacy of Duvalierism* (New York: Monthly Review Press, 1990).

17. Christian Girault, "Society and Politics in Haiti: The Divorce Between the State and the Nation," in *Society and Politics in the Caribbean*, ed. Colin Clarke (London: Macmillan, 1991), pp. 185–206.

18. Robert E. Maguire, "Standing Tall: Balanced Development in Haiti," *Grassroots Development*, vol. 10, no. 2 (1986):8–11.

19. Robert E. Maguire, *Bottom-up Development*, Paper No. 1, Inter-American Foundation, 1981.

20. Mark Weisbrot et al., *Restoring Democracy to Haiti: A Question of Economic and Ecological Survival*, Institute of Policy Studies Special Report, July 1994.

21. Michel-Rolph Trouillot, "Haiti's Nightmare and the Lessons of History," *NACLA Report on the Americas*, vol. 27 (January-February 1994):46–51.

22. Robert E. Maguire, "Haiti: A Military and Its Auxiliaries" (paper presented at the annual meeting of the International Studies Association, Washington, DC, 1994).

23. In mid-July 1994, when tensions were mounting toward a possible U.S.-led military intervention in Haiti, military analysts agreed that the FADH would be easily overcome by an intervening force. See, for example, "Cedras' Military Poses No Threat," *Washington Times*, July 15, 1994. All agreed, however, that the FADH—and armed auxiliaries linked to it—were effective in terrorizing the Haitian population. See, for example, "Cedras Keeps Order with the Thugs at Grass Roots," *Washington Times*, July 18, 1994. That order was being kept with a combination of both old and new weaponry. The former included World War II vintage M-1 rifles and carbines, and the latter included Uzi machine guns and Galil assault rifles.

24. This is the number of rural sections most commonly seen, though the number has been placed as low as 535, and a recent source places it at 562. Apparently fluctuation in the number has occurred in the past as the boundaries of the sections are occasionally reconfigured by state authorities.

25. The abolition of the Haitian army took place rather quickly. Shortly after the intervention began, the heavy weapons unit of the FADH was disbanded. Subsequently, enlisted men and low-ranking officers were either recruited into an interim police force or decommissioned into a jobs training program. In February 1995 Aristide further whittled away the army with the forced retirement of its top officers, and by June 1995 the Haitian army had in fact been pared down to a fifty-man presidential brass band.

26. See "Political Repression by Rape Increases in Haiti," *Washington Post*, July 22, 1994, and a report on the same subject released in early July by the National Coalition on Haitian Refugees and Human Rights Watch.

27. Statements made by one of FRAPH's primary leaders in an interview with television journalists and broadcast on the U.S. television program *Sixty Minutes* on April 17, 1994, verify this link.

28. Human Rights Watch/Americas, *Silencing a People*, p. 4.

29. Robert E. Maguire, "The Peasantry and Political Change in Haiti," *Caribbean Affairs,* vol. 4 (April-June 1991):1–18.

30. Human Rights Watch/Americas, *Silencing a People*, p. 4.

31. The only state that officially recognized the de facto military government of Haiti was the Vatican. The "Friends of Haiti" were the United States, Canada, France, and Venezuela, although other nations, Argentina in particular, were sometimes included within the group. Caribbean Community (CARICOM) states, particularly Jamaica, supported the positions of Haiti's "friends." In terms of the post–Cold War dimensions of the international response to the 1991 coup, it should be noted that in addition to the fact that the Aristide government was declared duly elected in free and fair elections by official international observer missions representing those key international actors, the coup came shortly after the Santiago declaration of the OAS, which was a pledge not to accept military coups in the hemisphere.

32. Marx V. Aristide and Laurie Richardson, "Haiti's Popular Resistance," *NACLA Report on the Americas,* vol. 27 (January-February 1994):30–36.

33. See, for example, "Haitian Embargo Fails: Restore Aristide," letter to the editor written by Rep. Corrine Brown (D–Fla.), *Wall Street Journal,* July 11, 1994, for the opinion that the long-supported embargo policy had succeed. See Peter Selvin and Yves Colon, "The Rich in Haiti are Feeling, and Fearing, the Winds of Change," *Miami Herald,* July 4, 1994, for a report on the difficulties that heightened sanctions had begun to impose on the elites. For an overview of popular support for sanctions, see Aristide and Richardson, "Haiti's Popular Resistance."

34. The resistance to the coup and the strategy of *mawonaj* were enacted beyond Haiti's shores as well, particularly among the Haitian diaspora in North America—a group with an important role, though beyond the scope of this chapter. That grassroots and civil society leaders reengaged the democratic process after the restoration of legitimate authorities is seen through their participation as candidates for elected office in 1995. See Maguire, "Bootstrap Politics."

35. Jean-Bertrand Aristide, with Christopher Wargny, *Aristide: An Autobiography* (Maryknoll, NY: Orbis Books, 1993).

36. A poll conducted under the auspices of the Arias Foundation for Peace and Human Progress from March 17 to 24, 1995, found that 72 percent of those surveyed approved Aristide's purge of the army. Sixty-two percent of the sample favored disbanding the army. Though President Aristide, with overwhelming public support, took steps to practically eliminate the army, an amendment to Haiti's constitution is required to formally abolish it.

37. The policies of the Préval government, headed by Prime Minister Rosny Smarth, emphasize the development of Haiti's productive capacity, focusing on agriculture, while seeking enhanced revenue through the regularization of tax collection and the capitalization of state enterprises.

38. After the presentation of its social and economic reconstruction plan to donors in early 1995, the Aristide government received pledges of US$1.2 billion in assistance over a twelve-to-sixteen-month period. U.S. officials called Haiti's support, which came from more than two dozen different countries and international financial institutions, remarkable evidence of international burden sharing. See "Statement of the Honorable Strobe Talbott, Deputy Secretary of State, Before the House International Relations Committee, February 24, 1995."

11

Globalization, Structural Adjustment, and Democracy in Jamaica

Dorith Grant-Wisdom

Liberal democracy has thrived, at least at the conceptual level, on the premise of a global society of sovereign nation-states, each having its own regime of governance whose supreme authority over its jurisdiction is recognized and respected by other states and by external nonstate actors. Attempts to intervene in another state's jurisdiction are generally considered illegitimate, and entities external to the nation-state are usually accorded little or no recognition by the international community in questions concerning internal rule. It has therefore been taken for granted in analyses of and debates on liberal democracy that the sovereign nation-state had control over its own fate.[1]

Of course when such assumptions and analyses are applied to developing states, it becomes obvious that the effective power that sovereignty bestows is largely dependent on the economic power and resources that a given state can command. In other words, the exercise of sovereignty is historically linked to the accumulation and expansion of capital and the concomitant structure of power relations. Notwithstanding this qualification, the general assumption of the sovereign state has been central to democratic ideas associated with the process of the emergence of nation-states. Thus even for a country such as Jamaica, de jure sovereignty, at the very least, was of critical importance to the nationalist forces that championed political independence in terms of sovereignty and autonomy during the struggle for freedom from colonialism.

Obviously the global scene today departs considerably from the traditional picture of sovereign nation-states interacting with each other only at the margins of their existence. Hence any analysis of the liberal democratic state in general and that of Jamaica in particular must take into consideration the intense patterns of interconnectedness that are reaching beyond the control of any one state. In other words, we now have to question the status of the nation-state as the unit within which issues of democracy can be resolved. Qualitative changes in the global political economy are now challenging the view that the sovereign democratic state presupposes a national community that governs itself and determines its own fate.[2] As the contours of the sovereign nation-state shift according to global forces, democracy as a national form of political and economic organization becomes problematic.

The task here, then, is to identify what David Held calls the "internal and external disjunctures" between the "formal domain of political authority" that the nation-state claims for itself and the "actual practices and structures of the state and economic system at the national, regional, and global levels."[3] This affords the identification of the forces that are rendering the boundaries of domestic and international politics obsolete, altering the institutional, organizational, and legal context of national politics, and obscuring the lines of responsibility and accountability of the nation-state.[4] Through this approach one can illustrate the extent to which the general tendencies of globalization and the specific requirements of structural adjustment that complement it have compromised the national system of accountability and control, thereby reducing the options available to the state, as well as its ability to effectively empower the citizens of Jamaica.

Globalization and Nation-State Sovereignty

It is important to recognize that globalization is an ongoing historical process linked to the requirements and conditions necessary for capital accumulation and expansion. However, the present phase of this process has qualitatively distinct characteristics that are reordering both time and space. The new imperatives include: the restructuring of production that is replacing national systems of production founded on the logic of nationally defined social agreements; the constant need for technological innovation and increased competitiveness; and the intensification of communication and the accompanying worldwide spread of culture. All of these are a reflection of the configuration of capital with the ascendancy of transnational finance capital.[5] Finance capital does not know or respect national borders. In this scenario the state is forced to redefine the national within the global, thereby eroding the scope for autonomous action and the capacity to carry out some of its most traditional functions, such as the management of the domestic economy.

Transnational flows in their various forms are nullifying national policies and undermining national and cultural identification. The system of national economies linked by government-regulated trade and exchange rates is being transformed beyond the reach of national regulation. The fact is that governments have traditionally defined trade in terms of territoriality. Hence control over trade was a major element of sovereign authority. However, the new factors of production, such as information, and the global in-trading of components are defying the logic of trade as understood in the traditional nation-state system. Thus the flow of information and information products rooted in ever-expanding technological innovation is not bounded by territory and geography. Satellites, for example, transmit information from space to the globe as a whole, regardless of borders, governments, and so on. The salient point is that these new developments result in the diversion of power away from the state. Information and its products get to individuals, corporations, and other private forces without going through customs and other forms of government regulatory mechanisms, thereby reducing the assertion of sovereignty.

Nowhere is this reality more obvious than in the area of finance. The dimensional changes in communications and information technology have brought out the invisible and flexible qualities of money. Money as an information product can now move around the globe at tremendous speed, enabling the shift toward the "end of geography."[6] The increasing flows of money have been a powerful force driving the relationship between economics and economic policy. In fact, these flows are the main determinant of exchange rates, rendering fruitless the controls put in place by central banks. In South Korea, Japan, Argentina, and several other countries, private forces now exercise relatively greater powers than do governments, because capital accounts are determining the state of current accounts rather than the other way around. In addition, countries like Jamaica have experienced cutbacks in investment and the flight of capital, which have resulted from attempts to control capital movements and foreign exchange.[7] In essence, the global electronic market driven by private traders has made it very difficult for governments to stabilize national currencies and to control national credit policies, budgets, and taxes. These are just a few signs that the national state is no longer in a position to effectively define and implement financial policies to secure domestic public policy goals.

Neoliberalism and Democracy

Because of the dynamics of capital accumulation historically, globalization and restructuring required what Henk Overbeek and Kees van der Pijl term "comprehensive concepts of control," which structure class formation and class conflict and are expressions of capitalist hegemony that "reflect a historically specific hierarchy of classes and class fractions."[8] From this perspective hegemony occurs if and when the acceptance of the key principles and political ideas of a leading class or collectivity of interests becomes widespread. "When this happens, according to Stephen Gill, "the policies which embody these principles will appear to be more natural and legitimate to broader elements within civil and political society. What is critical to this argument, however, is that such a nucleus of ideas is not simply a form of direct ideological domination, but rather a structural force which conditions and constrains class and other social forces."[9] Thus if the hegemonic capitalist class has a transnational outlook and orientation, then its key principles would focus on the market, free trade, and capital mobility.

Because the national component of capitalist production began to erode with the crisis in world capitalism of the 1970s, the need to restructure economic, political, and social conditions required a new offensive. Neoliberalism is the new hegemonic concept of politics and control guiding the new forms of technological production on a global scale. As the "fundamental expression of the outlook of transnational circulating capital," neoliberalism has become the dominant ideology legitimating the privatization of the state-controlled economy and the substitution of the market for the social provision of basic welfare.[10] Interestingly, the state has to be the mechanism for laying this framework and lowering the social costs of production. The need to compete thus becomes the key feature in both discourse and practice, and it is transmitted to policy in the guise of reducing the scope of government and promoting the pursuit of self-sufficiency and less reliance on government.

State regulation in a system of representative democracy is perceived as undermining economic growth.[11] The logic is that economic growth will occur when businesses are left alone and relatively unencumbered by state intervention, for intervention only distorts the market, increases the cost of production, and reduces flexibility. Emphasis is placed on efficiency, the market, and the need for capital to retain substantial profits that can be reinvested in new technology and productive capacity. This potential for reinvestment is undermined by the welfare state because of high levels of taxation, redistribution, and assertive labor power, which are usually attained under democratic conditions. From this perspective democracy could become a deterrent to economic growth, for it leads to conflictual demands and situations and interferes with the operation of the market.

For the liberal democratic state this means the further separation of the economic from the political. The primacy of privatization, deregulation, and the free market means insulating the economic sphere from immediate popular control. As the exercise of state power becomes recast in the process of global changes, the ability of the state to operate as a sovereign unit and as a mechanism for representing interests on a national basis is grossly impaired. However, we must not immediately conclude that the idea of a nation-state with a national economy and corresponding economic management has been totally superseded. In the hierarchy of nation-states, the erosion of national authority has not been uniform since some states are better situated to attempt to interpose some kind of insulation.[12] It is within this context that we examine the nature of the weak and dependent liberal democratic state of Jamaica.

Structural Adjustment and the Practice of Democracy in Jamaica

The neoliberal offensive was launched under the auspices of the Ronald Reagan/Margaret Thatcher alliance and enveloped the "heartland of world capitalism" and its "outposts."[13] Hegemonic control in terms of the transnational fraction of capital in general and the United States as a global and regional power in particular meant that the Caribbean would in some way be a part of this process. The Caribbean political economies were drawn into the process of globalization and restructuring not as integral players but as sites for markets and cheap labor—as capital saw fit.[14] Structural adjustment conditionalities provided the means to transport the neoliberal strategy to the Caribbean.

By the 1970s the postwar economic growth in Jamaica began to wane, revealing the colonial legacy of a structurally weak and dependent economy. The acute debt crisis that ensued provided the means by which the International Monetary Fund (IMF), the World Bank, and increasingly the Interamerican Development Bank (IADB) came to play a fundamental role in the scope and direction of policy. The extent to which the views of these multilateral institutions coincided with those of transnational finance capital rests with the "congruence of material and institutional forces" and the common outlook of the key intellectuals involved.[15] Stephen Gill cites the key intellectuals as the "leaders of transnational financial corporations, key financial institutions such as the International Monetary Fund, central banks and economics and finance ministries, especially the United States Treasury and Federal Reserve."[16] The capacity to theorize the conditions of existence for capitalist hegemony is linked to the relative closeness of these intellectuals to the forces of production and exchange and to their positions in bureaucracies that serve to maintain these conditions.

The main focus of the multilateral institutions was to set the Jamaican political and intellectual framework for policy and decisionmaking within parameters befitting the requirements of the hegemonic neoliberal strategy. This automatically meant changing the concept and role of the state from a nationalist and pro-interventionist orientation to one that accommodates a fraction of capital favoring openness and liberalization. Jamaica is a good example of dichotomous ways of viewing the power of transnational forces, for it is one of the most "structurally adjusted" countries both in terms of degree and timing. Hence by 1990 Jamaica had undergone thirteen years of "a succession of International Monetary Fund . . . Agreements and World Bank structural adjustment loans, sector adjustment loans and programs loans, with the recent addition of IADB adjustment loans, and USAID conditionalities."[17] The degree of intrusion into the sovereign autonomy of the Jamaican state has been immense. A brief examination of the situation helps to explain this.

After World War II (and up to the introduction of structural adjustment) the Jamaican government acquired legitimacy as "benefactor" to all classes and class interests.[18] Coexisting with a capitalist economy, the fledgling democratic institutions supported a pattern of minority ethnic ownership while placating the demands of the majority through paternalistic ties to the state via a system of patronage. In the absence of a strong local capitalist class tied to production, attempts by the state to industrialize through import substitution, as well as the need to address social problems, led to an increasing state role in the economy. Public expenditures increased as government became the largest employer and provider of social services. The number of public enterprises proliferated along with an increase in government subsidies.

This structure was further consolidated under the democratic socialism advocated by the Michael Manley government in 1974. The notions of egalitarianism and social inclusion raised the level of national consciousness and state activism in accordance with growing expectations. The struggle over the weak liberal democratic state's priorities took on a particular logic relative to the level of class conflicts and how they were manifested. The democratic component tilted toward social and economic equality and participation, often giving the appearance of being unconstrained by its liberal counterpart. However, in reality, this egalitarian strain was more at the level of populist discourse than concrete popular control.

An interesting factor that is pertinent to this analysis is the role and position of the Manley government in the demand for a New International Economic Order (NIEO) by Third World countries in the United Nations (UN) and the Non-Aligned Movement (NAM). Similar to that of others within the NAM, the Jamaican economy was primarily subordinate to foreign capital, but the nature of the governments' predisposition to it meant that the avenue for addressing this subordinate status was through multilateralism and Third World ideological and political solidarity. Regulation of foreign capital was the key strategy. This meant emphasizing the rights inherent in national sovereignty that could be exercised by voting equality in forums such as the General Assembly of the UN.

The attempts to bridge the gap between de jure and de facto sovereignty using the NIEO demands represented a move toward democratizing the nation-state system. This movement was highly contradictory, however, because the need to retain state power for local capital to realize itself "narrowly circumscribed the possibilities for domestic democratization."[19] It is this contradiction in connection with the need for capital to address the growing crisis of capitalism that resulted in a backlash. The regulatory requirements of the NIEO movement, despite its inherent weakness, threatened capital, at least in capital's bid to reverse the tendencies of falling profit margins.

The internationalization of state sovereignty within the UN General Assembly was therefore incompatible with the free movement and "sovereignty" of capital, especially finance capital. The counteroffensive had to be launched, and the restructuring of production that could circumvent national scrutiny was necessary. Ironically, this offensive gained ascendancy through the UN system as well, but in the economic institutions of the IMF and the World Bank, where democratic principles of sovereign state equality do not apply. The acquiescence to transnational capital would thus be realized through the neoliberal offensive.

The options available to the Jamaican government and its actions vis-à-vis the national political economy have been restricted. The structural adjustment conditionalities have focused the orientation and direction of state policies toward the market. Competing on the world market through exports is the name of the game. In addition, the government must endeavor to attract foreign investment by liberalizing the foreign exchange system and by promoting the private sector and market efficiency. This has required the state to virtually dismantle itself, privatize, deregulate the economy, and rationalize its budget and cut subsidies. In short, the policies of the state toward the market, labor capital relations, and the general welfare of the national populace are recast in a framework to be in consonance with global forces.

This recasting of state policies took place through the transformation of the conditions of political decisionmaking and the changing institutional framework and administrative practices. The imposition and influence over the levers of government policy mandated the maximum and immediate attention of top policymakers and government officials.[20] In addition to requiring local expertise to function in relation to an externally driven economy, the institutional framework and administration of the state had to be changed. For example, increased weight is given to certain government agencies, notably the finance, investment, and commerce ministries, as well as the office of the prime minister. Significantly, ministries that are linked to labor, employment, and welfare are downgraded as the state competes for foreign capital and markets. In sum, national resources and development are diverted from domestic needs to export markets, as the free-market economy is considered to be the only acceptable model of development. This shift, incidentally, has occurred in Guyana and elsewhere in the Caribbean as well.[21]

Another significant point regarding the intrusion of the multilateral institutions on the national authority of the state lies in the nature and style of negotiations. The term implies a level of mutuality and a degree of bargaining in discussions; one would therefore assume a certain amount of give-and-take on either side of the negotiating table. But the real world of IMF/Word Bank negotiations, especially with countries like Jamaica, is in no way democratic in style or content. These negotiations are inherently unequal, with directives invariably given in a unilateral manner regardless of their harsh consequences.

Future negotiations often rest on the ability and capacity of a state to meet specified standards and performance appraisals. The prefabricated prescriptions built on the outlook of global forces are laid out in technocratic and economistic terms that give the appearance of neutrality and objectivity but are really wrought with external biases. These negotiations are also highly secretive and far removed from public debate and consultation. The general public knows about institutions such as the IMF and the World Bank, but only in terms of the impact of structural adjustment conditionalities applied by them. The Jamaican people have to live with the consequences, but they are totally ignored in the negotiating and decisionmaking process.

The concerns that are now brought to the fore center on questions of consent, participation, representation, and accountability, which are integral components of democracy.

The practice of political democracy that is territorially linked to the nation-state operates on achieving political equality through the ballot box. A government that is elected by the people is supposed to represent their interests, and the legitimacy of government actions and decisions lies in the underlying principle that the exercise of state power is based on the consent of the governed. Accountability is thus achieved (to a certain degree) in the people's ability to change representatives whose performance does not reflect the interests of the governed. This level of democratic stability and change has worked in the Jamaican context since 1944, but the cracks that are now showing are in part related to the intrusion of forces from above. For one thing, participation in elections has traditionally been high in terms of voter turnout rates. The relevant factor here is that the state along with the two major parties were able to achieve a level of national consensus that masked the use of state power in the interests of the dispossessed classes.

A generalized consensus was built around the notion of a state that pulled various groups together along patron-clientalist lines. Leadership in the state was legitimized through popular acceptance and popular appeal. Change was perceived by the poor majority more in terms of benevolent leaders rather than of their own class struggles. Disaffection with one party translated into a transfer of loyalties to the other party. Stability amid poverty was achieved in part by the fact that the two major political parties drew disproportionately hard-core party support from the poorest—the bottom 40 percent of income earners.

According to Carl Stone, "the working class's . . . lack of organizational capacity, combined with their deep sense of alienation in a social system in which power is controlled by a few and only the privileged and the middle class have access to the levers of decision making, creates a political vacuum that has been filled by the major political parties since the early 1940s. . . . How well they have filled that vacuum remains to be evaluated."[22] What is relevant here is that political parties have been the main channel for the very poor and powerless to gain access to decisionmaking centers: "[P]olitical parties guarantee political stability and a minimal level of support for the middle class professionals who control these parties and their leadership. . . . [They] help to bridge the class gap in a class-stratified society and provide a direct channel of communication that sensitizes these leaders to the expectations, aspirations, and world view of the very poor."[23]

The state's ability to maintain this stability and level of democratic consensus was reinforced by its use of welfare politics as a means of allocating benefits to the party faithful. This was achievable to the extent that the state had the political space and authority (as well as the fiscal means) to increase spending and engage in redistributive gestures in line with the intensity of class struggle and discontent. Acting in the interests of global forces now undermines this political space and authority, which is organized along national lines. Democratic procedures and practices as they developed within the Jamaican national political culture had no mechanisms to relate directly to external forces. Hence the state is in crisis in terms of its ability to mold the various groups and classes around a national consensus and thereby build allegiance to the nation-state.

The widening disjuncture manifests itself in decreasing rates of political participation and growing disaffection with political leaders and institutions. Voter turnout rates have been dropping since the 1980s, and the 1993 election witnessed a lower turnout than that of 1944. In fact, one survey conducted in 1994 indicated that 51 percent of those polled would not have voted if an election had been called. This does not reflect well on a political system that once had turnout rates of 80–85 percent. The poll also indicated that 62 percent of the people were disillusioned by the political process.

There has also been a decline in the number of votes attracted by candidates' personal appeal, indicating that charisma and highly personalized means of gaining support are waning in their effectiveness. In addition, the political party as the main vehicle of mass support is beginning to lose its efficacy as a channel for democratic stability. Loyal party voting declined from 90 percent in the 1950s and 1960s, to 80 percent in the 1970s, to 48 percent toward the 1990s.[24] Correspondingly, "issue voting" has increased from 10 percent to 52 percent since the 1940s.

One could infer that with the drop in loyal party support people are becoming increasingly concerned about issues other than allegiance to a particular party, reflecting the declining ability of the parties to act as effectively as they did previously. During the 1950s and 1960s 65 percent of the electorate voted consistently for one party, and 35 percent shifted from one party to another. Now the latter group has grown to 80 percent. It is significant that political discourse directed to the populace is still carried out with a level of rhetoric that assumes national authority and control. This partly accounts for the growing gap between what is promised and what is actually delivered. The simple fact is that the state does not command the authority and maneuverability enjoyed in the earlier years. Moreover, the fiscal constraints and reduced options imposed by external forces have incapacitated the patronage system. Political rhetoric alone cannot maintain this kind of system.

The crisis of the state comprises two problems. First, the state is losing its already tenuous ability to shape and direct national development. Second, it is losing the capacity to determine and shape the limits of political activity directed toward maintaining a social and legitimizing base. The reality is that democratic consciousness is confined within the narrow limits of neoliberalism. As people see themselves less as part of a collectivity and more as individuals with specific interests, they become depoliticized relative to traditional institutions of the state and to political parties.

The economic compulsion of structural adjustment and transnational capital create a situation in which it is better to "do your own thing" and "hustle" in order to survive than to engage in politics. This only creates disillusionment. After all, do the multilateral institutions operate in a manner that respects the participation and acceptability of the populace? To whom are they accountable? Do they need the consent of the governed? There is no basis or mechanism whereby citizens can give consent to these external forces except through the government. But the government colludes with the multilateral institutions in a way that undermines democratic principles and procedures.

It is critical at this point to highlight the fact that there are people within and outside of government whose interests happen to coincide with structural adjustment and who therefore benefit from it. Hence there is a degree of willing compliance with the external forces. However, there is also the problem of the national politician's lack of an understanding of the causality of political and economic events and phenomena. As Ghita Ionescu asserts, there is an undercomprehension of science, and as knowledge increases it is becoming less and less accessible to the average human mind, resulting in a cognitive incompetence.[25] The cognition of the political reality of globalization depends on gaining knowledge and being able to exercise judgment accordingly. The awareness of leaders, local capitalists, and citizens of the global changes propelled by science and technology and their implications is a serious matter.

There is the difficulty of the average political leader trying to explain to constituents what he or she understands so little of. It is no wonder that many remain at the level of national rhetoric and tribal politics, trapped by the overwhelming forces from above and the increasing levels of disenchantment from below. Their discourse is therefore filled with neoliberal notions of excessive government and the need to build efficiency and entrepreneurship. This narrow view of development serves to restrict the ability of the subordinate classes to analyze the nature of the political economy and to construct comprehensive alternatives. Instead, the populace becomes increasingly removed and disengaged from political life and the government gets labeled as the "enemy." In essence, the very process of governance becomes problematic in the face of forces that supersede the nation-state from above and disengagement from below.

The Diminishing Role of the Jamaican State and the Quality of Democracy

Neoliberalism through structural adjustment has fundamentally reduced the quality of democracy in Jamaica by imposing the principle of the unregulated free market. As implied earlier, it is possible for liberal democracy to exist in a number of different forms, depending on the tension between the democratic logic of equality and the liberal logic of liberty. How democratic a society chooses to be is dependent on how it is structured, the nature and intensity of the class struggle, and the corresponding response of the state. The quality of democracy is therefore determined by the role that the state plays in mediating class differences and in maintaining political and social stability. The ability of the state to intervene in order to carry out its mediating functions is of necessity linked to the degree of national space accorded to it. By advocating a minimal role for the state, neoliberalism limits the jurisdiction and space for the possible expansion of democratic rights for citizens.

The new framework of structural adjustment has redefined the rights, powers, and capacity of the Jamaican state. Privatization and deregulation have served to transfer real power from the public sector to the private sector, effectively placing issues of national development objectives and national welfare beyond public debate. This has limited the ability of the government to intervene in the economy and to pursue social and economic policies. The power to impose restrictions on the activities of capital has been impaired. Property rights and rights of corporations take precedence over the rights of citizens.

One of the most important factors that determine the quality of economic—and political—democracy is the level of protection for the rights of labor. The assumptions of neoliberalism presuppose greater freedom for capital to utilize labor only as the new techniques dictate. In applying these assumptions, subsistence minimum wage, market flexibility, and trade have become the central principles guiding policymaking in Jamaica.

This set of principles has operated to the detriment of labor in a number of ways. The creation of employment under structural adjustment has been linked to the internal restructuring of the system of production. This restructuring has entailed the promotion of some industries, such as tourism and those of the export processing zones, and the neglect and elimination of industries linked to the manufacturing and agricultural sectors, with a corresponding decline in job creation. In fact, there was a 6.2 percent decline in the goods-producing sectors (agriculture, fishing, mining, manufacturing) between 1990 and 1994, resulting in a 9.1 percent reduction in these sectors' share of total employment.[26] To be more specific, despite improved labor productivity, the agricultural sector witnessed a loss of 29,200 jobs between 1992 and 1994, due in part to the divestment of government-owned agricultural entities such as Victoria Bananas.

The relatively high levels of employment creation achieved during the 1960s fell dramatically between 1977 and 1980 and subsequently recovered at the end of the 1980s.[27] As such, the failure to produce sufficient employment opportunities did not mean that new jobs were not created. What is interesting about the expansion of job creation in the 1980s is that most new jobs came with no worker protection or benefits, offered low wages, and required low skills. As Patricia Anderson and Michael Witter indicate, these jobs were in the service sector, in areas such as tourism, retail, trading, free trade zones, and the informal sector.[28] In addition, job sectors with good pay, security, and high skill have not generated much employment. Though there are better-paying jobs in services, for example, consultancy work, the service sector is mostly a low-paying one.

Under structural adjustment, there is the trend toward poor quality employment with low skill levels and the generalized movement toward self-employment as workers become disengaged from the formal economy. The quality of employment is thus the key factor. The public sector that was originally a major employer of labor has continued to downsize as a result of cutbacks in public spending. In fact, public sector employment contracted by 11 percent over the period of 1990 to 1994, while that of the private sector (the largest employer of labor) increased by 10.1 percent.[29] In leaving the employment of an ever-increasing workforce to the vagaries of the market, structural adjustment has reduced employment at the formal level and polarized labor according to skill and pay.

A further stratification of the workforce has also occurred along gender lines. Women are the single most important supply of low-wage labor. They are concentrated in low-paying jobs that are perceived as predominantly women's work—textiles, tourism, and personal services. In fact, women make up more than 90 percent of the free trade workers. Despite the fact that women have entered the workforce in record numbers, the average wage for women in the service sector is lower than that of men.[30] The wages of men are double those of women in the female-dominated areas of garments and electronics. In addition, although more women have been absorbed into the high-paying category over the years, the men still dominate this area. Thus despite the increased job creation for women, the quality of employment has been relatively poor, and women still face a higher unemployment rate than men. The unemployment level for women in 1994 was still double that of males. The harsh conditions faced by women is reflected in the fact that in 1994 households headed by women were worse off than in 1993: Among women who head households, 3,500 fewer were employed.

Exacerbating the situation, especially for women, is that structural adjustment has had a downward pressure on wages, making it extremely difficult to make ends meet. In fact, the pressures of structural adjustment programs and devaluations have affected minimum wages to the extent that the earnings of garment workers (predominantly female) have dropped below those of Haiti, Guatemala, Honduras, and the Dominican Republic.[31] As a comparison with other sectors, the minimum hourly wage of garment workers in 1988 was US$0.41, compared to US$0.52 in manufacturing, and US$3.00 for long-haul drivers in the bauxite industry.[32] The minimum wage for garment workers in 1995 is about US$0.75 per hour. The key point is that despite the rise in labor output, increases in real wages have not matched productivity, creating superexploitation of labor generally, and of female labor particularly.

The distribution of income is also another major indicator of the structural inequality of status as free citizens in a democratic society. Income inequality has been a historical phenomenon in Jamaica, but it has been exacerbated under the pressures of structural adjustment. Attempts that were begun in the mid-1970s to implement some measure of income redistribution have been abandoned. For one thing, the increased openness of the economy was a determining factor in the transfer of an additional 7 percent of the gross domestic product to foreigners between 1977 and 1989, thereby reducing the amount of national income for Jamaicans.[33] In addition, the compensation of employees as a share of national income dropped 16 percent between 1977 and 1989. Consequently, the economic dependence of wage earners has been heightened by the dramatic loss in the share of the national income.

Reduced economic democracy is even more readily apparent when one focuses on what Ernest Mandel calls "the sovereign capacity of consumers." Structural adjustment has been successful in lowering general consumption as a share of the gross domestic product (a major component of its overall strategy). However, the decline turns out to be largely a result of cuts in expenditure by the public sector and by people who earn wages and salaries.[34] Yet consumption has increased for those who earn nonwage income. This rise in consumption—often in luxurious and ostentatious ways—has occurred with a concomitant decline in consumption among the poorer segments of society. Hence under structural adjustment the ability of the wage earner to be "sovereign" in his or her capacity to enjoy a certain level of consumption has been negligible. Consumer sovereignty has been limited in two basic ways. First, on the supply side, by insufficient goods and services; and second, on the side of effective demand, by the lack of purchasing power to gain access to available goods and services.

A critical aspect of structural adjustment is that wages have seriously lost the battle with persistent inflation. Prices have continued to skyrocket amid the dominance of market forces and the absence of regulations by the state. After an encouraging drop in the mid-to-late 1980s, inflation escalated, peaking at 80.2 percent in 1991 and then slowly declining to 26.9 percent in 1994. The average consumer has been left trying to play "catch-up," with food and other basic necessities occupying an increasingly large share of household expenditures. One study found that the purchasing power for workers was cut to almost 50 percent between 1977 and 1989. The researchers derived a measure of employment adequacy by comparing individual earnings to the cost of maintaining a family of five on a low-income budget and came up with some dramatic results. The major finding was a massive deterioration in relative earnings between 1977 and 1985 as well as large increases in the numbers of workers whose income did not constitute a family wage.[35]

In addition, in 1977, 35 percent of the employed workers who reported incomes earned no more than half of the minimum family income. This figure rose to 61 percent in 1985. The reality was even more grim when these figures are broken down according to gender. The number of low-earner female household heads increased by 116 percent between 1977 and 1985. Yet the proportion who earned less than half of the required income moved from 40 percent in 1977 to almost 70 percent in 1985. By 1989 "women who headed households were a third more likely than their male counterparts to find that their earnings could not purchase more than a half of minimum family requirements."[36]

The deterioration of the purchasing power of the working consumer is further illustrated when one looks at the housing situation. Housing costs have surpassed the purchasing ability of most workers. Here again there is the twofold problem of supply and effective demand. Low-income housing has been in a sharp decline to the point where there is an acute shortage of housing. Government has traditionally been the provider of low-income housing, but it has given way to allowing the private sector to be in full control. In 1976 the public sector was providing up to 7,852 housing units. This number fell to a low of 1,821 in 1985 and has barely risen to little over 2,700 in 1994. Private-sector investment has taken place but has not seriously addressed the concerns of the poor and needy.

In the era of the free market, there has been the tendency for businesses naturally to orient their ventures toward prospects with the highest returns by speculating and profiteering. Housing is one of those areas in which, in the absence of price controls, the private sector has gravitated toward the provision of houses that generate higher-than-average profits. As a result, the rise in construction reflects the taste and pockets of sellers and buyers who are in the highest income brackets. The average wage earner is therefore left "out in the cold" with inadequate housing and the inability to purchase what the market makes available.

The need for some kind of "social insurance" against the loss of the earning power of labor was central to the welfare state model. Because the purchasing power of workers was critical along with their labor power, a central task of the state was to ensure the general reproduction of labor; social services such as health care assisted in reducing workers' dependence on wage labor as the sole means of subsistence. In this context, the importance of the social wage (amid patron-clientelism) to maintaining a reasonable standard of living for the average Jamaican was essential. As part of the larger neoliberal project structural adjustment has curtailed the role of the state in the distribution of the social product and the alleviation of the cost of survival. The social dimension has been virtually removed from state policy as social progress becomes incompatible with the demands of the worldwide expansion of capital. The state's role in providing welfare diminishes as social justice comes to be subordinated to the market.

The quality and quantity of social services have been impaired by reduced public-sector spending and cutbacks in subsidies for foods, education, health, and so on. The contraction in the government's role as the main health care provider has led to a decline in the quality and efficiency of health care delivery. There has been a shortage of health care personnel, overcrowding in facilities, closures of hospitals and hospital wards, inadequate drug supply, escalating drug prices, and an increase in sexually transmitted diseases, including AIDS, and in stress illnesses and psychiatric disorders.

A similar situation is found in education. There has been a general decline in enrollment, overcrowding in classrooms, and an increase in the functional illiteracy rates under structural adjustment policies. This of course does not bode well for a nation trying to compete in a global marketplace in which the value of labor is based on knowledge and skill. The state's inability to cope with the educational needs of the populace is reflected not only in less public expenditure but also in the policy of cost-sharing at the secondary and tertiary levels that the government introduced in September 1994.

The main principle behind this policy is that government has the responsibility for the payment of teachers' salaries and related expenses, but operating expenses must be met by schools from tuition. The harsh reality is that this new policy is adding to the burden of the average Jamaican, who has been facing higher costs of living and increased taxation. In fact, in April 1995 the government raised the General Consumption Tax from 12.5 percent to 15 percent. This in turn will increase the costs of the majority of goods and services, including transportation and electricity. Thus parents will be facing not only higher costs in general but also the new costs derived of the operating expenses of schools. One can only conclude from all this that in the struggle for who pays for the social wage, the dominant class forces have indeed asserted themselves powerfully.

The goal of the new paradigm is to expand the protection of investor and intellectual property rights while weakening the rights and duties of the community. The focus on private property rights and individualism reduces the capacity of the government to protect and promote the social dimensions of democracy and underscores the rights of those who are unable to take care of themselves, such as the elderly, children, the disabled, and poor single parents who are in dire need of assistance. This in turn leaves very little room for groups that exist between the individual and the state—groups such as families, associations, unions, and the like—for individualism reduces notions of collective rights, rights of peoples, and group rights.

It has become increasingly difficult to protect labor rights and standards that were usually protected through national legislation. In addition to the lowering of wages and the gradual loss of some degree of control over living conditions previously gained by the labor movement, there is the generalized trend toward the conversion of labor power to a complete subordination to the interests of capital. The strictest possible control over workers for the purposes of maximum extraction of surplus labor is the central factor in the absence of state intervention and regulation.

Unions and their advocacy for workers' rights have been major targets of attack under neoliberalism, as they are perceived as impediments to progress and a deterrent to foreign investment. The tolerance for trade unionism has therefore diminished as unions lose the capacity to effectively capture a share of profits that could be redistributed to workers. They have not been able to counterbalance global trends and the conditionalities of structural adjustment. In fact, the state now operates to protect the nonunion status of workers such as that of the free trade zones. Moreover, the growth of the informal sector (and the free trade zones) is rendering "an increasing proportion of the labor force non-unionized and perhaps, non-unionizable with traditional methods."[37]

The irony of the situation is that the number of work stoppages recorded in 1994 (two-thirds related to wages and conditions of employment), was the highest since 1982, and about 38 percent higher than in 1993. However, these figures reflect the frustrations of labor under structural adjustment rather than any serious attempt to organize as an autonomous force vis-à-vis capital. The wave of industrial unrest is not necessarily a sign of strength, for it is inevitable that in an open economy there will be conflict between capital and labor. But strikes such as these do not have a major impact on wage growth as a whole. The creation of the Jamaica Confederation of Trade Unions is a step in the right direction, but it now has to develop new ways of addressing the global realities that have seriously polarized and marginalized the labor force and diminished the national space for achieving certain fundamental rights that are critical to any democratic society.

Conclusion

The new global environment has redefined the national agenda to fit the requirements of transnational forces. The focus on economic growth may increase material wealth, but without the democratic content, the likelihood that all members of the community will receive an adequate share of resources for full human development is vastly reduced. Freedom for the market and its beneficiaries automatically implies restriction on other peoples' freedom. Reliance on economic efficiency as structural adjustment takes its course has led to a rise in poverty, erosion of labor rights, and social exclusion in Jamaica. There are those who have benefited from structural adjustment, but they constitute a minority who have gained lavishly at the expense of the vast majority of Jamaicans.

The feeling of alienation that comes with these exclusionary policies heightens as democracy manifests itself only in elections, the results of which seldom have sufficient clarity or sense of direction. In attacking the strong state, the neoliberal project also challenges citizenship in terms of economic equality as a key feature of human rights. Citizenship is not only a national concept; it is related to the problem of unequal distribution of resources in society, and so it involves human rights. Democracy cannot therefore be confined to individual rights. The term *human rights* has very little meaning for people who, for reasons beyond their control, are unable to exercise the rights in question. The core of civil rights has to be supported by a secondary set of rights that increases social participation and integration rather than to produce exclusion. Otherwise the price that society will have to pay will be exceedingly high. As the nation-state becomes increasingly less a locus of authority, people will resort to other areas, which, in the Jamaican context, usually include gangs, drugs, and crime—forms of social decay that the country cannot afford.

Notes

1. David Held, *Political Theory and the Modern State: Essays on State, Power, and Democracy* (Stanford: Stanford University Press, 1989), chapter 8.

2. David Held, "Democracy, the Nation-State, and the Global System," in *Political Theory Today*, ed. David Held (Stanford: Stanford University Press, 1991), p. 202.

3. Ibid., p. 212.

4. Ibid.

5. Henk Overbeek and Kees van der Pijl, "Restructuring Capital and Restructuring Hegemony: Neo-liberalism and the Unmaking of the Post-war Order," in *Restructuring Hegemony in the Global Political Economy: The Rise of Transnational Neoliberalism in the 1980s*, ed. Henk Overbeek (New York: Routledge, 1993), pp. 4–5.

6. Richard O'Brien, *Global Financial Integration: The End of Geography* (New York: Council on Foreign Relations, 1992), chapter 1.

7. See Anthony Payne, "Liberal Economics Versus Electoral Politics," in *Modern Caribbean Politics*, ed. Anthony Payne and Paul Sutton (Baltimore: Johns Hopkins University Press, 1993), pp. 28–53.

8. Overbeek and van der Pijl, "Restructuring Capital and Restructuring Hegemony," p. 3.

9. Stephen Gill, "Neo-Liberalism and the Shift Towards a US-Centered Transnational Hegemony," in *Restructuring Hegemony in the Global Political Economy*, ed. Overbeek, p. 267.

10. Ibid., pp. 261–263.

11. See, for example, Mancur Olson, *The Rise and Decline of Nations* (New Haven: Yale University Press, 1982).

12. See Held, *Political Theory and the Modern State*, and Overbeek, *Restructuring Hegemony in the Global Political Economy*.

13. Overbeek and van der Pijl, "Restructuring Capital and Restructuring Hegemony," p. 12.

14. See Dorith Grant-Wisdom, "Constraints on the Caribbean State: The Global and Policy Context," *Twenty-First Century Policy Review*, vol. 2, nos. 1–2 (1994), pp. 155–157.

15. Gill, "Neo-Liberalism," p. 266.

16. Ibid.

17. Patricia Anderson and Michael Witter, "Crisis, Adjustment, and Social Change: A Case Study of Jamaica," in *Consequences of Structural Adjustment: A Review of the Jamaican Experience*, ed. Elsie Le Franc (Kingston, Jamaica: Canoe Press, 1994), pp. 1–2.

18. For more on this subject, see Carl Stone, *Class, State, and Democracy in Jamaica* (New York: Praeger, 1986); and Carlene Edie, *Democracy by Default: Dependency and Clientelism in Jamaica* (Boulder: Lynne Rienner, 1991).

19. Kees van der Pijl, "The Sovereignty of Capital Impaired: Social Forces and Codes of Conduct for Multinational Corporations," in *Restructuring Hegemony in the Global Political Economy*, ed. Overbeek and van der Pijl, pp. 37–38.

20. Grant-Wisdom, "Constraints," pp. 158–159.

21. See Ramesh F. Ramsaran, "Domestic Policy, the External Environment, and the Economic Crisis in the Caribbean," in *Modern Caribbean Politics*, ed. Payne and Sutton, pp. 238–258.

22. Stone, *Class, State, and Democracy in Jamaica*, pp. 50–51.

23. Ibid.

24. Carl Stone, "The Jamaican Party System and Political Culture," in *Jamaica: Preparing for the Twenty-First Century*, ed. Patsy Lewis (Kingston, Jamaica: Ian Randle, 1994), p. 143.

25. Ghita Ionescu, "The Impact of the Information Revolution on Parliamentary Sovereignties," *Government and Opposition*, vol. 28, no. 2 (Spring 1993):224–225.

26. Planning Institute of Jamaica, *Economic and Social Survey* (Kingston, Jamaica, 1994), p. 18.4.

27. Anderson and Witter, "Crisis, Adjustment, and Social Change," p. 24.

28. Ibid., p. 23.

29. *Economic and Social Survey*, pp. 18.3–18.4.

30. Anderson and Witter, "Crisis, Adjustment, and Social Change," p. 26.

31. Cecilia Green, "Historical and Contemporary Restructuring and Women in Production in the Caribbean," in *The Caribbean in the Global Political Economy*, ed. Hilbourne A. Watson (Boulder: Lynne Rienner, 1994), p. 170.

32. Ibid.

33. Anderson and Witter, "Crisis, Adjustment, and Social Change," p. 21.

34. Ibid., p. 16.

35. Ibid., pp. 32–39.

36. Ibid., p. 36.

37. Trevor Munroe, "The Industrial Relations Culture: Perspectives and Change," in *Jamaica: Preparing for the Twenty-First Century*, ed. Lewis, p. 130.

12

Democracy and Human Rights in Suriname

Betty N. Sedoc-Dahlberg

> *That the system of representative democracy is fundamental for the establishment of a political society wherein human rights can be fully realized, and that one of the fundamental components of that system is the effective subordination of the military apparatus to civilian power.*
>
> —Twentieth General Assembly of the OAS

After military rule in Suriname during the 1980s, political and civil rights have been reinstated despite the inefficacy of ordinary law enforcement. Under civilian rule in the 1990s progress has been made in the restoration of human rights, but social and economic rights continue to suffer because of the stagnation of the country's economy. Electoral democracy and the replacement of the highest-ranking military officers was a necessary condition but not a sufficient one for a successful transition from a military-authoritarian system to a democratic society in which human rights—civil/political and social/economic—are protected but not guaranteed.[1]

In this chapter the question of whether a balance between civil/political and economic/social rights can be worked out to prevent repeated authoritarian interruptions is explored through an assessment of the connections among political instability, economic stagnation, and decrease of state security in Suriname. Regime change is examined, with attention devoted to the role played by political parties and the army, and an assessment is made of the impact of Dutch policies on developments in Suriname.

On Human Rights and Democracy

Like most Caribbean countries, Suriname recognized the Universal Declaration of Human Rights and the Human Rights Covenants at the time of its

212

independence in 1975. In 1986 Suriname ratified the Organization of American States (OAS) Inter-American Convention on Human Rights, and Suriname accepted the compulsory jurisdiction of the Inter-American Court of Human Rights. In context and scope both civil and political as well as social and economic rights are incorporated in the constitution of Suriname. In philosophical outlook, given the country's constitution, laws, and regulations as well as statements by political actors and representatives of nongovernmental organizations (NGOs), human rights in Suriname reflect the liberal and communal-oriented perspective.[2]

The view is taken by this author that political stability is obtained in a democratic-pluralist regime if political and civil rights and economic and social rights are equally protected and implemented. This view is in line with the findings in Zehra Arat's study on human rights and democracy in developing countries confirming the argument that the stability of democratic systems is threatened if the elected government cannot reinforce social/economic rights at levels comparable to those of civil/political rights.[3]

The concept of democracy applied here is not one that is limited to periodic electoral contests by political parties for representation in legislative bodies but rather one that has in addition four defining characteristics.[4] The first is citizens' political participation at micro-, meso-, and macrolevels. Continuous testing and monitoring of government's objectives and goals, and policy implementation by citizens, are as important as participation in elections. Mechanisms to participate in policymaking are required. Second, individual rights should include political and civil rights as well as social and economic rights. Third, interest representation should be characterized by voluntaristic autonomous group representation. The state should be neither in control of nor able to abolish these interest groups even if their goals are competitive with those of the government. NGOs thus become political instruments for change. Finally, there should exist in the society as well as among political decisionmakers a centrist and reformist ideological orientation that seeks to accommodate the interests of the underclasses through social and economic policies that guarantee adequate economic space for private-sector accumulation.

Political instability might occur when the gap between social/economic and political/civil rights becomes wider and politicized masses, aware of the discrepancy, agitate for improved living conditions and social provisions. Political instability can develop into a crisis if political actors do not implement adequate and appropriate policies to mitigate antagonistic contradictions between social policy and capital accumulation. Such political crises in a democratic-pluralistic system can also be induced by supporters of the far left or the extreme right. Developments in this direction are usually reinforced in periods of sharp economic decline.

According to Carl Stone, Third World countries can prevent a shift to authoritarian or statist-populist regimes "if their strategic elites who control political power are firmly attached to middle-of-the-road policies and reformist ideological positions."[5] It may occur, though, that financial resources are insufficient for the implementation of reformist policies such as substantial redistribution of wealth. Moreover, in a political democracy conflict management requires open communication channels to secure people's participation. A serious gap between public interest and government's decisions and priorities can be bridged by effective communication and information about constraints on the execution of policies and national objectives; government responsiveness does not necessarily require the fulfillment of all needs. An infrastructure to address public demands is of crucial importance in securing interactive dialogue between government and citizens. A lack of citizens' communication, including micro- and mesolevel communication, can quickly reverse voter support for the regime and induce (further) political instability, a climate that can easily lead to a regime change and even a loss of or sharp decline in human rights.

Reporting on Human Rights

In one short generation, between 1980 and 1996, regime change between democratic-pluralism and military-authoritarianism occurred twice in Suriname. This turbulent period was marked by a dramatic increase in violence and other abuses of human rights. Approximately 30,000 people (7.5 percent of the country's population) fled their homes fearing threats to their lives or property. Thousands of Surinamese refugees were accommodated in neighboring French Guiana and in the Netherlands, and around 15,000 displaced persons from the Surinamese countryside sought refuge in Paramaribo, the country's capital.[6]

In 1982 fifteen civilian opponents of the regime who urged restoration of democracy, including labor union leaders, faculty of the university, journalists, and lawyers, were arrested in Paramaribo and executed by the National Army.[7] Inexperienced with foreign relations and international court systems, the military rulers and their immature political actors did not anticipate the negative reactions other nations would have to their human rights abuses or to their inconsistent and untrue explanations. In his response to queries concerning the massacre, the acting minister for foreign affairs, Glenn B. Sankatsing, wrote to the OAS Inter-American Commission on Human Rights (IACHR) on January 11, 1983: "Concerning reports of executions in Suriname I wish to inform you that those reports do not reflect the truth of the matter. In an official statement of the military authority it is stated that on 8 December 1983 a number of persons detained for their involvement in activities to overthrow the government through violent means were killed in an unfortunate accident as a result of their attempt to escape custody. The national army and the government will see to it that such occurrences be prevented in the future."[8]

In another example of the unhealthy political situation, after 1982 more violations of human rights followed when the military was confronted with armed forces claiming to restore democracy in Suriname. A guerrilla war, started in 1986, became internationally known because of the National Army's massacres of civilians. That year, Mooi Wana, a Maroon village suspected of collaboration with the Jungle Commando, was flattened by air bombing, and its inhabitants—by that time mainly the elderly and women and children—were killed by the military. Many more killings by the National Army followed, including several that took place under civilian rule.[9] This was evidence that restoration of (electoral) democracy in 1987 did not prevent human rights abuses. Quite correctly, the IACHR observed that President Ramsewak Shankar's civil government "was a crude illustration of the power reality in the country, one in which raw military force lurked behind a facade of constitutional democracy."[10]

Indeed, restricted access to state power was characteristic of the first civilian government (1988–1990) after military rule. A lack of state security became obvious when in 1988 a repatriated refugee from Holland "died" the day after his arrival in Suriname in a cell at the airport, where he was detained by the military. This case, known as *Gangaram Panday v Suriname,* and the infamous *Aloeboetoe et al. v Suriname* case dealing with the brutal killing of six Maroon citizens by the National Army on December 31, 1987, are good examples of the inefficacy of law enforcement and the ineptitude of the Surinamese government. In the *Aloeboetoe* case the government accepted responsibility for the killings.[11]

In the case of Suriname, assistance by external actors to end authoritarian rule and reinstate human rights has been decisive. The establishment of the Institute for Human Rights in Suriname (IHRS) by the junta in 1986 and the signing of the OAS document on compulsory jurisdiction of the Inter-American Court on Human Rights the same year cannot be separated from the impact of external reporting on human rights violations by the OAS, the United Nations Commission on Human Rights (UNCHR), the United States Committee for Refugees (USCR), Amnesty International, and Americas Watch. Untrue and hypocritical statements by the IHRS about human rights conditions in Suriname were systematically unveiled by Mooi Wana '86, a local human rights nongovernmental organization. The founder of the organization, Stanley Rensch, a Maroon academic, survived several physical attacks because of effective protection by external supporters.

Before 1980 Suriname's record on human rights had not been marked by atrocities or other serious violations. Civil/political and social/economic rights were well developed and protected. With independence in 1975 welfare benefits included pensions, medical coverage, child allowances and support to the lowest income groups, subsidized food supply, housing, utilities, and a good education system.[12] The economy was heavily dependent, however, on foreign (Dutch) capital injections. Thus external monitoring of domestic politics took place through the mechanism of development planning. An analysis of Suriname's twentieth-century political history reveals that the rise and fall of governments has been linked to support or suspension of development aid.[13] However, prior to 1980, changes of government were achieved without violence, by electoral means. Suriname was thought of until the end of the 1970s as a peaceful country with well-developed individual rights, and it was referred to by tourists as a tropical paradise. What was it that caused the shift of regime to military authoritarianism in 1980 and the traumatic events that followed?

Shifts of Regime: Role of Political Parties, the Dutch Government, and the National Army

The period from 1975 to 1996 may be divided into shorter periods that mark regime changes and their impact on human rights. During the first period, from 1975 to 1980, Suriname had a democratic-pluralist regime in which social and economic rights were protected and guaranteed. During the second period, from 1980 to 1987, the country was under military-authoritarian rule in which civil and political rights were lost and social and economic rights declined. Since then, from 1987 to 1996, Suriname has again had democratic-pluralist regimes under which civil and political rights have been reinstated but under which a dramatic decline of social and economic rights has occurred. (For the purposes of this chapter the short interim period of military rule from December 1990 through September 1991 is not distinguished separately.) Each of these periods is taken up in turn in the following sections.

1975–1980: Democratic-Pluralist Regime

Upon gaining independence in November 1975, the Republic of Suriname adopted its first constitution, drafted in the spirit of the Dutch conception of democracy, which was based on a house of parliament (composed of elected candidates of political parties), a cabinet, an independent judiciary, and a national defense force.[14] Human rights were enshrined in the constitution. Through dissolution of parliament new elections could be held before the scheduled period of four years had passed. According to the constitution, elections were the only legitimate instrument for removing undesired rulers.

The traditional political parties had emerged in the 1940s. These parties were predominantly organized along ethnic lines, corresponding with the three largest ethnic groups: Hindustani, Creole, and Javanese.[15] In multiethnic Suriname, as in Guyana, the newly emerging political elites secured their support through "strategic activation"[16] of racial identity. However, physical oppression or violence were absent. In contrast to the Unified Reform Party (VHP) of the Hindustani and the Party of Peasants from Indonesia (KTPI) of the Javanese, the ethnically more heterogeneous National Party of Suriname (NPS) consisted, apart from Creoles, of the smaller ethnic groups of Jews, Chinese, Dutch, Indians, Lebanese, and Syrians.

Significant ideological differences did not exist between the large parties. The NPS, identified from the start with reformist ideals and revolutionary rhetoric, could fit easily within a centrist social-democratic ideological orientation, and the VHP, dominated by the interests of its influential private sector members, could be ranked as more liberal, occupying a slightly right-of-center position. The KTPI evolved from a politicized repatriation movement (back to Java) to a centrist Surinamese political party. Microparties in the 1950s, 1960s, and 1970s (first the split-offs from the ethnic-based traditional parties and later the emergence of the Party of the National Republic [PNR], a democratic-socialist party, followed by the founding of tiny Marxist-Leninist parties) never seriously challenged the leading parties, and all the microparties of the 1950s disappeared.

The leaders of the tiny parties of the 1960s and 1970s represented several leftist-to-radical ideological streams of thought in the academic world in the Netherlands and emerged from Surinamese political student movements.[17] These parties aimed to strengthen social and economic rights. The first and most important has been the PNR, which, in coalition with the NPS, was in opposition only from 1973 to 1977. As will be illustrated later, the 1980 coup d'état served for a number of these competing radical leftist parties as an opportunity to obtain control over the state. Surinamese politics were basically ethnic, and the state became an instrument for political patronage.

With independence the Suriname Defense Forces (SKM) of 600 men was founded overnight. The issue of a national army received attention only during the independence negotiations in 1974 and 1975. Some advisers thought it better to extend the police force, bearing in mind that Suriname was located in South America and therefore could easily catch the "Latin American disease" of successive coups. Finally the military's role was anchored in the Charter of the Army as a defensive and developmental force. However, conflicting ideological orientations between commissioned officers and leftist-oriented noncommissioned officers (NCOs) and disagreements on promotion policies and salaries split these two groups. The relationship between the army high command and the government was even worse, because of disagreements on the supply of materiel and increases in salaries. Relations between the army's Lieutenant Colonel Hans Elstak and Dutch Lieutenant Colonel Henk Valk, chief of the Dutch military mission to Suriname and adviser to the country's army, were poor, and therefore Valk was in no position to play the role of mediator.

During the infamous conflict with the NCOs the government was shown to be highly inefficient and incapable of mediating between conflicting groups. Apart from its struggle with the army, the government was also confronted with a growing conflict with the Netherlands, which had committed itself according to the Development Cooperation Treaty of 1975 to provide financial aid to the amount of US$1.5 billion over a ten-to-fifteen-year period, 1975–1990. The Dutch government has "traditionally" interfered in domestic politics in Suriname by providing or suspending development aid: Through development planning, the Netherlands set priorities by approving or disapproving projects. As the capital budget was largely financed by Dutch aid, the influence of Holland on Suriname's development goals and policies was stronger than that of the nation's parliament. The result was inconsistencies between goals formulated in government declarations on the one hand and policies based on the Annual Plan presented to parliament on the other. Thus project planning and Annual Plans were more strongly influenced by the Dutch than by parliament.[18] Friction between the two governments grew in the years prior to the coup d'état as the government of Henck Arron disagreed with the Dutch about allocation of development aid resources and return migration policies.

During the periods of civilian rule in Suriname the efficiency and legitimacy of governments were widely discussed in the country. Some of the critical areas were: (1) the electoral system, which precluded representation of important segments in parliament and contributed to the manipulation of microparties; (2) limited participation in political life because of the parties' authoritarian nature and the strong position of political brokers in these organizations; and (3) the paternalistic administration, inherited from the colonial past, which served as a main instrument for patronage politics. In addition, the year prior to the coup d'état was marked by dissatisfaction in the broader society on issues such as low-income housing, health insurance, and minimum loans.

In sum, a high degree of financial dependence on the Netherlands, a poorly professionalized army, and weakly developed democratic and civil institutions (accompanied by political patronage effectuated through the use of external—i.e., Dutch—financial resources) characterized democratic-pluralist regimes in Suriname prior to 1980. These conditions facilitated the coup d'état by the NCOs, to the success of which a misguided Dutch military adviser (Colonel Valk), several radical labor unions, and the mass media also contributed substantially.[19]

1980–1987: Military-Authoritarian Rule

On February 25, 1980, the NCOs took over power from the civilian government. For the first time in the country's history a regime change was achieved by nonpeaceful and nonelectoral means. The junta announced for Suriname the socialist route to development and declared that "international treaties and human rights [would] be respected, [although] a period was needed to develop a new constitution before elections could come."[20] Political parties were banned and parliament was dissolved. The junta ruled by decree from August 1980 until December 1987.

This new regime pledged to end corruption, ethnic politics, and political patronage. The civilians, inexperienced with these armed forces, saw the military as a body that would represent order, discipline, and efficiency. In the broader society the loss of political and civil rights was overshadowed by a development optimism and high expectations. At the beginning (1980–1982) various important interest groups, including labor unions and the Committee of Christian Churches (CCC), cooperated with the junta. By 1982 labor became more fragmented as the dominant political actors as well as the army and leftist forces struggled to control factions of organized labor.

The left—in collaboration with the junta—proved to have no capacity to set the tone for the socioeconomic reconstruction of Surinamese society. Disappointment and frustration emerged when after nearly two years no viable social and economic structures had been created to bring about "an authentic Surinamese-socialist" society with improvements in social and economic rights. On the occasion of Maurice Bishop's visit from Grenada in October 1982 the mass media (press and broadcasting stations) disregarded censorship and criticized the performance of the military government. The authoritarian nature of the regime, combined with violations of human rights, the arrogance and patronizing attitude of the leftist intelligentsia in its dominant role in the state apparatus, and the lack of evidence of corruption on which the old political leaders could be sentenced all contributed by the end of 1982 to the disillusionment of the people and the reversal of their original attitude toward the junta.

The government of the Netherlands contributed to the consolidation of the junta's power from 1980 until 1982 with diligent financial support through the so-called Urgent Projects Program: an influx of unconditional development aid in the amount of US$222 million. Between 1981 and 1983, Cuba lent military support by training of the military forces and the people's militia, supplying equipment and personnel, and providing advisers on internal security. By 1984, however, these backers of the junta—first the Dutch and later the Cubans—had lost their influence on the social, economic, and political direction of the Surinamese "revolution." Increasing control by the army over the affairs of the state and society was accompanied by the rapid erosion of popular support manifest eighteen months after the coup. The junta had not been able to progress in developing legitimacy and efficiency.

Between 1984 and 1987 the junta maintained its grip on the state through the effective control of the "revolutionary bodies" it created: people's militia, anti-intervention committees, and district councils. The loss of popular support, expressed by public criticism, sabotage, and ridiculing of the army and the military elites, drew from the regime increased oppression and extended human rights violations. It became evident that this regime was not able to regain support to galvanize the lower, middle, and working classes. Beneficiaries of the army—cooperative elements of all strata—became socially isolated and more dependent on the military elites, and hence the balance of power between the classes did not change. As Tony Thorndike observed, "socialism, at least of the Surinamese military variety, represented violence, killing, and repression of human rights."[21]

The failure to implement a socialist system in Suriname cannot be explained merely by factors such as lack of know-how, weak organization and leadership, competition among the Marxist-Leninist intelligentsia, and a weak connection between the intelligentsia and the working class. In Suriname under military rule the citizens rejected violation of human rights and indicated that such immaterial properties as freedom of speech and movement are more important than material goods.

As a result of effective external pressure for democratization of the Surinamese society by Venezuela, the United States, France, and the Netherlands, in 1986 the military invited the leaders of the traditionally ethnic parties to participate in the "Topberaad" (the highest ranking military council), by then the highest-level decisionmaking body. In 1986 and 1987 preparations were made for transition from military-authoritarian rule to a democratic-pluralist regime. The last two years of military rule, however, were marked by a violent civil war with the Jungle Commando (JC), led by Ronnie Brunswijk, a Maroon and a former bodyguard of the junta leader. Support from the rural population and the Dutch and French contributed to the army's inability to defeat the JC.

The loss of political and civil rights in 1980 was followed by a severe deterioration of the economy, resulting in the decline of the quality of social and economic rights. Domestic monetary and budget policies, the suspension of Dutch development aid, and a drop in bauxite prices contributed to further stagnation of the economy. Moreover, in 1987 the internationally isolated junta had been accused of drug trafficking. Rumors circulating since 1985 were proven when in 1986 in Miami the U.S. Drug Enforcement Administration arrested Captain Etienne Boerenveen, the National Army's second-in-command. He was convicted on drug trafficking charges and imprisoned in the United States from 1986 until 1989. A few years later, in 1992, citizens in Suriname were confronted with the country's drug problem when a peace conference in Paramaribo, in which the highest-ranking military officers and the JC participated, was abruptly ended because of a conflict between Lieutenant Colonel Desi Bouterse and JC leader Ronnie Brunswijk over drug trafficking. Brunswijk announced at the meeting that a plane loaded with drugs had landed around Moengo, "his" territory. Later the U.S. ambassador, witnessing the destruction of the cocaine, publicly lauded Brunswijk for contributing to the fight against drugs.[22] Along with the negative effects on international relations of the many human rights abuses, the military's involvement in drug trafficking contributed to the further isolation of the junta.

In sum, by 1987 the National Army had been confronted with four major problems: its legitimation; its grip on the populace; the deteriorating economic situation; and the civil war. To address these problems the junta finally agreed to hold a referendum for a new constitution, drafted by the military-appointed members of the National Assembly, and it scheduled elections. These moves would serve to meet requirements imposed by The Hague for a reinstatement of Dutch development aid.

1987–1996: Democratic-Pluralist Regimes

The junta had preconditioned the holding of elections on acceptance of its constitution, in which the vanguard role of the army was included.[23] The constitution was adopted in the referendum and elections were held, both in 1987. The outcome of the elections brought an overwhelming victory for the Front for Democracy and Development (FRONT), a federation of traditional, previously competing, ethnic political parties. Antimilitary and democratic forces regained ruling power over the country in 1988. The fragile civilian government of President Ramsewak Shankar, however, could not handle the three most urgent issues, for which there was domestic as well as external pressure: replacement of the highest-ranking military officers; changes of the status and position of the army in the constitution; and peace in the country.

Policies of accommodation of the military in accordance with the constitution of 1987 prevented the Shankar government from responding to the demands of the major interest groups to reduce the role of the military in the country's affairs. A pact with the military elites could not be worked out since, on the one hand, the majority interest groups urged for complete subordination of the army to the civilian government, and on the other, the government's accommodation policies were doomed to failure because the military's object was to regain political power. To destabilize the government the army took advantage of dissatisfaction with the economic situation in the broader society and stimulated public disorder. As part of its takeover strategy, the military called elections before the scheduled time. The civilian political actors understood too late the military's strategy and the role played by crisis initiation groups, subversive armed collaborators of the army.

In 1990 the military again took over power from the civilian government, and an interim cabinet consisting of the junta's appointees ruled for nine months. The military handed over power for the second time in 1991 after elections. Some significant differences can be observed in the composition of the participating political parties in the elections of 1987 and 1991. A new, right-of-center, multiethnic party emerged, Democratic Alternative 1991 (DA'91), which was in favor of closer economic and political ties with the Netherlands. A ruling coalition formed as well, the NEW FRONT (NF), consisting of the FRONT parties plus the Suriname Labor Party (SPA).

The outcome of the 1991 elections reflected a growth in the strength of the National Democratic Party (NDP), the political arm of the military, as well as a substantial number of seats for the new DA'91 and a modest victory for the NF.[24] The growth of the NDP was due in part to the army's policies during the military-appointed interim cabinet of 1990/91: massive patronage politics, including donations of material goods to supporters, importation of subsidized Dutch herring and salted meat, and redistribution to favorites of land that had been expropriated. This largesse appealed in particular to the numerous unemployed young people, as they saw it as the creation of the "welfare state" and the "easy life." Decisive for the number of seats in parliament of the NDP and DA'91, however, was the further worsening of the economy as well as the civil government's inability to mobilize strategic actors in and outside Suriname for political and financial support.

Policies of appeasement and accommodation of the military, characteristic of the previous civilian government of President Shankar, were abandoned. The government of President Runaldo Venetiaan, installed in 1991, managed in 1992 to nominate a new military leader, have the vanguard role of the army expunged from the constitution, and ratify a peace treaty with the JC to end the civil war. Consequences for the economic downfall were evident, however, in the social and economic areas. In the 1990s pensions and some social welfare benefits were adjusted to compensate for the reduced purchasing power caused by inflation. The effects of the International Monetary Fund (IMF) Structural Adjustment Program (SAP) policies resulted in a further worsening of the standard of living.[25] The social welfare system, though still responding to a variety of needs, has come close to collapse. Given the outcome of the policies, it is evident that President Venetiaan's elected government could not reinforce social and economic rights at levels comparable to those of civil and political rights. Yet compared with the civilian government of President Shankar (1988–1990), considerable progress has been made in the recovery of the economy as well as in the sphere of human rights. One illustration of the latter, for example, is the decision of the National Assembly in December 1995 to request an investigation of the massacre of December 1982.

The outcome of the 1996 elections showed trends similar to those of the previous elections. The NDP gained four seats, increasing its total to sixteen, and the NF lost six seats, reducing its hold to twenty-four. DA'91 lost half of its seats, leaving it with only four. The remaining seven seats went to two new coalitions: Three went to the Progressive Development Alliance (Alliantie), composed of two groups that splintered from the NDP and the VHP. The other four seats went to the Pendawa Lima, a splinter from the KTPI. The Party for Liberation and Development (ABOP), a new party founded by former JC leader Ronnie Brunswijk, did not win any seats.

The 1996 elections, surprisingly, resulted in a victory for the NDP presidential candidate, Jules Wijdenbosch. The KTPI and five of the nine VHP cabinet members left the NF coalition and jointed the NDP, while the Alliantie advised its voters to support the NDP presidential candidate. The factors leading to the outcome of the election merit closer scrutiny than can be provided here, but a partial list of claims, circumstances, and viewpoints worth exploring would include:

- claims within KTPI and VHP circles of an "undemocratic" and "racist" attitude on the part of President Venetiaan;
- the consequences of the absence of democratic decisionmaking structures in the VHP;
- allegations within NDP circles that the financial interests of wealthy VHP members were well protected and that they had strong connections with drug trafficking;
- apparently successful voter intimidation and bribery by the NDP before the May general elections and the September presidential election;
- the KTPI's shift to the NDP, and whether bribery and threats to (re)open corruption probes contributed to the realignment.

Within the Javanese group the impact of personal conflicts between the leaders of the KTPI and the Pendawa Lima has been overlooked. Notably, both were victims of human rights abuses during the period of military rule.

How do we interpret Dutch policies toward Suriname? Between 1982 and 1995 the Dutch persistently added new elements to the list of preconditions for reinstatement of development aid: From 1982 until 1986, the holding of elections was most prominent among Dutch demands; in 1987, investigations of human rights violations; in 1988, replacement of the highest-ranking military officers; in 1989, constitutional changes; in 1991, adoption by parliament of a Structural Adjustment Program/Multi-Annual Development Plan; in 1992, acceptance by the government of IMF monitoring. The elected civilian government fulfilled most of the requirements prior to 1991, but it opposed the Dutch demand for IMF austerity measures.

Bearing in mind the distributive impact of economic policies for the fate of democracy in developing countries and this government's inability to provide citizens with relative economic security as consumer prices increase or to offer compensation for inequalities by providing better accessible services through a comprehensive viable welfare and health care system, one might wonder why the Dutch government did not contribute to the consolidation of power of the democratically elected civilian government by promoting policies to balance both categories of human rights. Their developmental policies have clearly contributed to, and perhaps induced, political instability in Suriname.

Prior to the elections of 1996, Dutch policies shifted in favor of President Venetiaan. The question remains, however, of whether this change was caused mainly by the threat of Bouterse's returning to power. Nevertheless, the recovery of the economy was acknowledged by the IMF and cannot be neglected by the Netherlands. Dutch aid, however, was not fully reinstated under President Venetiaan, despite Holland's acceptance of him in the 1992 extension of the 1975 cooperation development treaty. Because of the NDP's links with former junta leader Bouterse, the cabinet of President Wijdenbosch is now confronted with threats of further suspension of Dutch development aid.

Conclusion

Because of their inability to change the socioeconomic system inherited from the colonial past, successive governments in Suriname as elsewhere have been incapable of meeting the substantive mass welfare aspirations associated with political democracy. Optimism after the military takeover declined rapidly when it became evident that the junta had failed to change the socioeconomic system—to meet expectations concerning social policies to the benefit of the underclasses and a favorable climate for the development of the private sector. The army was confronted with increasing discontent about growing military oppressiveness, human rights abuses, and economic decline. The imbalance in favor of social and economic rights, to which the huge influx of Dutch financial aid contributed, during the first period after the coup d'état was essentially annulled by economic decline, and it became evident that no compensation was available or replacement possible for the loss of civil and political rights.

With the restoration of electoral democracy in Suriname and the implementation of the SAP a shift toward the opposite occurred, and the regime came to be characterized by an imbalance in favor of political and civil rights. This writer disagrees, however, with Arat's pessimistic view that "[such a] regime reflects the characteristic of a democracy doomed to decline."[26] Expectations of the performance of the welfare state could be revised to more realistic levels if a social-political infrastructure existed for communication— taking the form of interactive dialogues—and for citizens' participation, which would mean further democratization of the Surinamese society and a strengthening of its weak democratic institutions. Arat is correct in noting that elections, apart from the other components of democracy, do not manifest any particular pattern of progress through time.[27]

The case of Suriname shows that elections were a necessary condition but not at all a sufficient one for political stability and the consolidation of power by a civil regime. There was limited access to state power (along with an inability to control the armed forces), communal fragmentation of the ruling political elites unified in a grand coalition, a lack of communication with and participation of the citizens, and a further sharp decline in the economy, all of which contributed to ineffective government performance. Once more a case study of democracy shows that procedural and substantive issues cannot be examined without investigating the political mechanisms through which social conflicts are processed.

Economic development and electoral democracy should not be treated as the single determinants of democratic development. Another determinant, emphasized in this study, is the lack of communication with and participation of citizens at all levels—micro, meso, and macro—in policymaking and decisionmaking. The absence of access in Suriname contributed to disputes about the system's legitimacy. To improve the quality of all individuals' rights and reduce political instability, further democratization of the society is as important as economic development and elections. Furthermore, complete access to state power is required. This process may take time, and opposition groups will continue with antigovernment mobilization; for the civilian government, however, it is primarily a matter of survival.

The pivotal question is whether democracy and human rights can be strengthened in the absence of support from the external environment. The impact of Dutch controlling and monitoring mechanisms has been crucial in the contemporary history of independent Suriname. Strong interconnections between domestic and Dutch policies explain in part regime changes as well as progress and stagnation in social and economic development. In 1993 the central issue for the Dutch was the IMF's monitoring of the adjustment program as a prerequisite to releasing the treaty funds. Between 1991 and 1995 Dutch policies included "divide-and-rule" tactics and support for antigovernment circles, specifically favoring a number of NGOs, some controlled by nondemocratic Marxist-Leninist forces, as well as support for DA'91, a political party in favor of the reestablishment of close economic and political ties with the Netherlands. Although DA'91 gained eight seats in 1991, it lost four of them in 1996, which suggests that the Dutch policies of "recolonization" are not approved by the majority of the country's citizenry; Suriname is unlikely to be maneuvered into a neocolonial arrangement.

Dutch support for President Venetiaan's government became manifest during the latter half of 1995. Two crucial factors contributed to this support. The first was Holland's growing disapproval of the apparently increasing number of supporters, many of them young, for the NDP, led by former Lieutenant Colonel Bouterse. Opinion polls had even predicted a "landslide" victory for the NDP in the May 1996 elections. The second factor influencing Holland's position was the positive commentary emanating from the international financial institutions such as the Inter-American Development Bank (IDB) and the World Bank on the recovery of Suriname's economy, indicating the government's success with the SAP. It was impossible to disregard the virtual disappearance of the black market (with an exchange rate that had peaked at US$1 to Sf750 by December 1994) and the stabilization of the Suriname guilder to the level of US$1 to Sf450 in 1995.

The impact of the Dutch mass media (newspapers as well as "Radio Nederland," a Dutch short-wave broadcast to Suriname and the rest of the Caribbean) on voters should not be underestimated. Prior to the elections, twice daily, the Surinamese population was able to receive information on the violation of human rights and on drug trafficking, crimes of the 1980s during Bouterse's regime. These reports prompted responses by the National Assembly, such as its decision to request an investigation into human right abuses, resulting in the appointment by President Venetiaan of a committee to investigate human rights violations in Suriname. Reports in the Dutch press concerning charges by a Dutch Juridical Court against Bouterse for his alleged involvement in drug trafficking also contributed to lengthy discussions in parliament and during election campaigns. However, no firm action on the part of the government materialized toward undertaking such an investigation.

As it turned out, the Surinamese population did not vote overwhelmingly for the NDP. Rather, the NF garnered 41.75 percent of the votes cast, and the NDP only 26.21 percent. Given the country's electoral system, such a significant margin of popular support was not reflected in parliamentary seats because the number of seats does not properly reflect the nationwide proportional support in percentages for the distinct parties or party coalitions. The NF gained twenty-four seats but was followed closely by the NDP, with sixteen seats. The remaining seats were shared among the DA'91, which won 13.08 percent of the vote and four seats; the Pendawa Lima, with 9.25 percent and four seats; and the Alliantie, with 8.36 percent and three seats.

Attempts by the NF to govern by extension of the coalition with DA'91 and the Pendawa Lima did not materialize because a substantial number of VHP members in parliament and the KTPI abandoned the NF to join the NDP. As noted earlier, this resulted in a victory for the NDP candidate, Jules Wijdenbosch. In sum, we can observe that at the September 1996 presidential election, nondemocratic forces, which received 25 percent of the electoral vote, now acting in a democratic framework, managed to return to power, albeit in a coalition with other parties.

With the creation of the Association of Caribbean States (ACS) in 1994, Suriname became a member of that body, and in 1995 its membership in the Caribbean Community (CARICOM) was approved. Optimistic democratic circles hope for regional integration and a political climate favorable to democracy and human rights. The question must be raised as to whether Suriname will be able to strengthen civil society and speed up the recovery of its economy in order to break out of the vicious circle of economic stagnation, political unrest, and declining social and economic human rights. The further democratization of society and diversification of its economy and international relations may be decisive for the nature of human rights in Suriname.

Notes

The author wishes to thank Edward Dew for his helpful comments on an earlier version of this chapter.

1. For a review of Suriname's contemporary political history, see Edward Dew, *The Trouble in Suriname: 1975–1983* (Westport, CT: Praeger, 1994).

2. See, for example, Government Declarations (RVs) of 1974, 1977, 1988, and 1992. See also speeches made by Mrs. Ilse Labadie, Chairperson of the Organization for Peace and Justice (OGV), 1986, 1987, and 1988, all published in local Suriname newspapers.

3. See Zehra F. Arat, *Democracy and Human Rights in Developing Countries* (Boulder: Lynne Rienner, 1991), p. 29.

4. See Carl Stone's main attributes of regime types in *Power in the Caribbean Basin: A Comparative Study of Political Economy* (Philadelphia: Institute for the Study of Human Issues, 1986), p. 15. The distinctive characteristics presented in this chapter are not identical to Stone's main attributes. The typology presented here is ideal-typical with regard to human rights, and individual rights include freedom to dissent.

5. Ibid., p. 13.

6. In 1982 a few hundred Surinamese refugees fled to the Netherlands Antilles, mainly to Curaçao, and to the United States. Repatriation and resettlement of refugees from French Guiana and displaced persons from Paramaribo is in progress. The vast majority of the Maroons of Surinamese origin left the camps in the area of St. Laurent, and according to the United Nations Commission on Human Rights (UNCHR), the case is closed. Most refugees who sought asylum in the Netherlands did not repatriate. See also Humphrey Lamur and Betty N. Sedoc-Dahlberg,

"Refugees and Displaced Persons from Suriname: Case Closed," in *Under Threat: An Atlas of Refugees and Forced Displacement,* ed. Lubomir Luciuk and Martin S. Kenzer (forthcoming).

7. The victims were organized in the Association for Restoration of Democracy in Suriname. The National Army accused them of collaboration with external forces to end military rule. This event resulted in the first flow of refugees to the Netherlands. See also the report by Amos Wako of the United Nations Commission on Human Rights.

8. *Report on the Situation of Human Rights in Suriname,* CIDH.OAS/Ser.L/ II.61.Doc. 6, rev. 1, October 5, 1983, pp. 2 and 6.

9. See the annual reports of the Inter-American Commission on Human Rights for 1982–1992.

10. *Annual Report of the Inter-American Commission on Human Rights, 1990–1991,* CIDH.OEA/Ser.L.V.II.79 rev.1.Doc. 12, February 22, 1991, p. 499.

11. Prior to his departure, Gangaram Panday had expressed to Dutch agencies concerns about his security in Suriname. Upon his arrival he was detained and died after being tortured. His case and that of *Aloeboetoe et al. v Suriname* were brought to the IACHR. The court decided that evidence was lacking of government's responsibility for the death of Panday. In *Aloeboetoe,* however, the court was convinced of the government's responsibility for the killing of the six Maroons. See *Aloeboetoe et al.,* Reparations (Art. 63[1] of the American Convention on Human Rights) Judgment of September 1993. See also David J. Padilla, "Reparations in *Aloeboetoe v Suriname,*" *Human Rights Quarterly,* vol. 17, no. 3 (May 1995):541–555. As for the December 1982 massacre in which fifteen opponents of the regime were killed, nothing has been done thus far to investigate and punish army officers responsible. However, the government has started to implement the IACHR's recommendations with regard to financial compensation of victims.

12. See *Republic of Suriname: Rehabilitation, Growth, and Structural Adjustment: The Social Program* (Warwick, England: Warwick Research Institute, University of Warwick, 1992).

13. See Betty N. Sedoc-Dahlberg, "Suriname 1975–1989: Domestic and Foreign Policies Under Civilian and Military Rule," in *The Dutch Caribbean: Prospects for Democracy,* ed. Betty N. Sedoc-Dahlberg (New York: Gordon and Breach, 1990), pp. 17–24.

14. The Suriname Defense Forces (SKM) was founded in 1975 with 600 men. After the coup in 1980 it changed its name to the National Army (NL). By 1986 there were 3,000 members in the army, including paramilitary forces of some 1,000. The navy and the air force account for 10 percent of the armed forces.

15. See Edward Dew, *The Difficult Flowering of Suriname: Ethnicity and Politics in a Plural Society* (The Hague: Martinus Nijhoff, 1976). This outstanding study provides the best overview of Suriname's contemporary political history.

16. See Percy C. Hintzen, "Trinidad and Tobago: Democracy, Nationalism, and the Construction of Racial Identity," in *Democracy in the Caribbean,* ed. Carlene J. Edie (Westport, CT: Praeger, 1994).

17. See Betty N. Sedoc-Dahlberg, "Suriname Students in the Netherlands" (Ph.D. diss., University of Amsterdam, 1971), and "Academicians as Political Actors:

The Case of Suriname" (unpublished Latin American Studies Association paper, 1994).

18. See also Betty N. Sedoc-Dahlberg, "The Surinamese Society in Transition: A Test-Case on Consistencies in Values and Goals in a Caribbean Society," in *Politics, Public Administration, and Rural Development in the Caribbean,* ed. Hans Illy (Munich: Weltforum Verlag, 1983).

19. See Emmy Verhey and Gerhard van Westerloo, *Het Legergroene Suriname* (The Inexperienced Army of Suriname) (Amsterdam: Vrij Nederlands Weekblad Pers B.V., 1983).

20. Press briefing on March 18, 1991, at Hotel Torarica in Paramaribo, Suriname. See also Tony Thorndike, "Suriname and the Military," in *The Dutch Caribbean,* ed. Sedoc-Dahlberg, pp. 35–62.

21. Thorndike, "Suriname and the Military," p. 61.

22. According to Radio Netherlands Holland, Suriname contributed 50 percent of the drugs imported to the Netherlands during 1987.

23. According to the Constitution of Suriname, 1987, Articles 177 and 178(2).

24. Of the fifty-one seats in the National Assembly, in 1987 FRONT had forty-two and the opposition held nine, of which three went to the NDP. In 1991 NEW FRONT had thirty seats, NDP, twelve, and DA'91, nine.

25. See *Republic of Suriname*, p. 3. See also Jean-Charles Ameels, *Development Cooperation with the Government of Suriname: Quarterly Report* (Paramaribo: Warwick Research Institute, 1994), pp. 2, 3, and 11, concerning the need for implementation of a Social Urgency Program (SUP).

26. See Arat, *Democracy and Human Rights in Developing Countries*, p. 7.

27. Ibid., p. 53.

13

Human Rights and State Security in Trinidad and Tobago

Clifford E. Griffin

Has the Westminster-derived system of government planted roots of systemic stability in the Republic of Trinidad and Tobago? In this chapter this question is examined by probing the extent to which the democratic system of government guarantees the flourishing of human rights while preserving the integrity and security of the state. The focus here on the relationship between human rights and state security as barometers of democratic stability in Trinidad and Tobago is driven largely by two seemingly contradictory sets of factors. One is that the rule of law anchors political and civil society in Trinidad and Tobago, where regularly held free and fair elections legitimize the civilian-run governments that control the police and defense forces and ensure the maintenance of human rights, especially political rights and civil liberties. The other is that despite this, since the country's independence from Britain in 1962, three nonconstitutional attempts have been made to unseat governments.

The first attempt took place in the course of the unrest and army mutiny that erupted during the 1970 Black Power Revolt. Three years later, urban guerrillas belonging to the National Union of Freedom Fighters were killed in their abortive coup attempt. As a result of these two events, citizens of Trinidad and Tobago became all too familiar with the ideas and implications of coups, guerrilla uprisings, revolution and counterrevolution, repression, and political trials.

Nevertheless, by 1990 the conventional wisdom was that the country had abandoned such concerns and that the democratic process flourished because the political system consistently allows citizens the freedom to dissent and publicly challenge the arguments of the country's highest officials. Moreover, the general impression was that significant progress had been made in avoiding the sort of circumstances that spark armed uprisings. When such discontent did occur, it was usually addressed in a humane and legal/juridical manner. The eruption of gunfire on July 27, 1990, the sight of armed individuals in the streets, and the rampaging and looting of the capital city's commercial district therefore surprised more than a few people. This third and latest illegal attempt to change the government again calls into question the viability of the democratic system in that country.

More than anything else, however, the 1990 coup attempt suggests that a democratic political culture is firmly rooted in Trinidad and Tobago and that the various manifestations of political instability do not amount to democratic instability. It also suggests that since economic and social issues have been central to each of these extralegal attempts at governmental change, political and civil rights may be necessary but not sufficient to guarantee stability and security. That is, severe economic downturns may lead to social and political unrest and thereby threaten the country's security. The state's responses to such threats may result in the infringement of certain categories of human rights precisely because of the overlapping relationship between development, human rights, democracy, and state security.

Informed by the democracy/human rights/development debate, this analysis tests a few propositions. The first is that poor economic performance is a major precipitant of political instability in Trinidad and Tobago, which has profound implications for human rights and state security there given the republic's strongly negative growth rates during the 1980s. Moreover, prolonged economic decline and a concomitant rise in narcotics activities are linked to the rapid growth in the number of serious crimes in the country. Compounding this is the widening perception that the Police Service is corrupt, inefficient, and incapable of protecting citizens from criminals.[1]

The second proposition is that the judicial system is woefully inefficient in prosecuting and securing sentences for criminals, whose activities consistently violate the basic rights of citizens. Of the 327,307 crimes reported to the police between 1982 and 1991, an average of 25 percent were prosecuted, and about 20 percent of these resulted in convictions. This inefficiency has resulted in a high degree of citizen dissatisfaction with the criminal justice system.[2] These factors threaten the security of the state, serve to undermine the democratic system, and highlight human rights concerns. Among those concerns is a very high degree of citizen support for retaining the death penalty, high degrees of support for the death penalty for crimes such as rape and drug trafficking, and very high degrees of support for corporal punishment for crimes such as burglary, vehicle theft, and grievous bodily harm.

The third proposition is that despite this rapid increase in criminal behavior and three illegal attempts at governmental change, the democratic system in Trinidad and Tobago appears inherently stable. This is especially evidenced by the defense and preservation of the political and civil rights of the perpetrators of the 1990 coup. However, questions about human rights violations, due process, and the integrity of the democratic process itself are raised by the willingness of the government to dispense with institutions like the Privy Council, its attempt to pass the Corporal Punishment (Amendment) Bill, and the vocal and practical support for corporal punishment by a jealously independent judiciary.[3]

One key argument here is that economic and social decline need not lead to democratic instability, nor should it undermine the integrity of the state unless serious abrogations of human rights accompany it. Where economic decline leads to an upward spiral in criminal activity, as has occurred in Trinidad and Tobago, it can lead to political instability and indirectly increase the potential for democratic instability. This is because the state may find it prudent and even necessary to infringe upon certain categories of human rights by sentencing criminals to hanging and/or to corporal punishment, including public floggings, in order to restore stability and public confidence. Under these conditions the impact of economic and social decline on social and political behavior and the response of the state's security apparatus to such behavior become central to understanding the relationship among human rights, development, and democratic stability in Trinidad and Tobago.

Democracy and Economics

The conventional wisdom is that the emergence and maintenance of democratic regimes is far more likely in societies that are economically developed than in those that are not. The argument holds that economic development leads to democracy because it changes the way people think about politics. With increased intellectual and material resources to growing numbers of citizens come growing expectations of shared decisionmaking as well as a disposition toward democratic ideas and institutions.

Economic development, however, does not sufficiently explain the emergence of a democratic polity. There have been numerous examples of developed yet undemocratic countries. The Soviet Union and Eastern bloc countries are frequently cited, as is Germany under Nazi rule. South Africa, until recent political changes, and Taiwan today are also examples. Other countries, such as Trinidad and Tobago and others in the anglophone Caribbean, have maintained democracy at relatively low-to-moderate levels of development.[4] How might this discrepancy be explained? The answer, of course, depends on the definition of democracy applied.

In this analysis democracy is defined as "a set of institutions that permits the entire adult population to act as citizens by choosing their leading decision makers in competitive, fair, and regularly scheduled elections, which are held in the context of the rule of law, guarantees for political freedom, and limited military prerogatives."[5] This multidimensional concept incorporates several items: (1) debate and dispute over policy and political competition for office; (2) active citizen participation through partisan, associational, and other forms of collective action; (3) representative government grounded in the rule of law under which leaders are held accountable to citizens; and (4) a military that is controlled by civilian authority.[6] From this perspective, the problems generally associated with relying almost exclusively on elections and/or the ideal of a polity reflecting economic and social equality are avoided. It is also from this perspective that the relationship between democracy and state security can meaningfully be probed.

Democracy and Security

A secure nation is relatively invulnerable to threats to its development and national sovereignty. These threats may be territorial, political, and/or economic, and they may take on a military character.[7] Political security concerns may involve external pressures for policy change, destabilization and subversion, extraterritorial jurisdiction, and the undermining of social and cultural identity. Economic security matters tend to reflect a country's inability to improve its economic conditions.[8]

As in most states in the Caribbean, security concerns in Trinidad and Tobago are related to geopolitics, resource base, and country size.[9] And, like other Caribbean countries, Trinidad and Tobago has entered the 1990s with some of its gravest security threats rooted largely in economic matters.[10] The country continues to suffer from the stresses of very high levels of citizen expectation, unacceptable levels of unemployment, and an ongoing wave of criminal activity that calls into question the ability of the state to protect its citizens. This is due partly to the fact that after two and a half decades of state capitalism, Trinidad and Tobago has had to undergo a painful transition from a nation that enjoyed huge economic surpluses during the 1970s to one with huge deficits from the early 1980s to the present.

As Trinidad and Tobago has attempted to adjust to new global economic arrangements, and in the face of its own economic downturn, internal security problems have been generated. During the latter part of the 1980s the country lost millions of dollars in a wave of strikes, public demonstrations, riots, arson, and vandalism against private and public property that were driven largely by economic issues. Thus, although it is reasonable to view security in traditional military terms, a broader view that encompasses the political and economic dimensions of security is most useful in understanding the relationship between human rights and state security in Trinidad and Tobago.

Development Strategy

Like other developing countries that underwent decolonization during the 1950s and 1960s, Trinidad and Tobago embarked on a quest for rapid economic development. Economic strategies and political direction were chosen with an awareness of the conventional wisdom that short-term and medium-term sacrifices of human rights are necessary for such development. Unlike those of many developing countries, however, particularly in Latin America and Africa, Trinidad and Tobago's development strategy entailed a growth-with-equity approach to improve many of the failings of the colonial administrations. The successes (and failures) of this approach are attributable largely to the vision and leadership of Dr. Eric Williams, leader of the Peoples' National Movement (PNM), which first secured political power in 1956.

Under Williams's guidance, the PNM sought to establish a democratic system of government undergirded by a mixed economy. Foreign private investment was welcomed, but the state was also expected to play an important role in economic development in order to (1) spur economic growth and development; (2) shift the center of economic decisionmaking affecting enterprises in Trinidad and Tobago from the corporate boardrooms of multinationals to local planning units; (3) increase revenues from profitable economic activities; (4) minimize domestic unemployment; and (5) ensure broad-based, local participation in the operation and management of high technology. In addition, racial and cultural integration were to be enhanced and Caribbean integration advanced.[11] These objectives were to be attained through a series of five-year plans.

Using the Arthur Lewis model of development as a guide,[12] the PNM pursued a mixed economic strategy of import substitution and export promotion activities. Under this strategy the state's role was to provide the necessary infrastructure and fiscal incentives that would facilitate a climate in which both local and foreign private capital would thrive. Employment creation in a diversified economy was expected to improve income distribution. Over time the role of the state as entrepreneur increased as it undertook to provide basic health care and education in addition to the necessary infrastructure to promote economic opportunities. By the third five-year-plan (1969–1973), however, the private sector had not adequately responded to its challenge to reform the economy. Further, the Black Power riots of 1970 signaled the government's failure at income redistribution. This outbreak of political unrest compelled the state to expand its role by becoming even more directly involved in productive activities.[13]

The economic situation improved between 1974 and 1982 as the Arab oil crisis produced huge revenue windfalls for the economy. This bonus was used to further expand the state's entrepreneurial activities in order to maintain its growth-with-equity strategy. However, after 1982 revenues and economic activity declined steadily, as did the huge reserves amassed during the oil bonanza of the 1970s. By the late 1980s, when reserves had virtually dried up, the government faced the politically expedient but economically undesirable choice of purchasing the Texaco oil refinery that had threatened to close operations and furlough approximately 4,000 employees due to financial losses.

Having become accustomed to a government that not only provided large numbers of jobs but also subsidized, regardless of need, their loftiest expectations in health care, education, employment, and other social/cultural areas, citizens of Trinidad and Tobago were totally unprepared for the recession of the 1980s that dramatically reduced their quality of life. Though Trinidad and Tobago, unlike many of its Caribbean neighbors, was able to escape its dependency on sugar and other agricultural products, it managed only to replace it with an almost exclusive dependency on petroleum.

Oil is, of course, subject to the vicissitudes of the global market, and because it was now Trinidad and Tobago's major revenue earner, fluctuations in its price affected development objectives and social, economic, and political conditions in the country. Whereas oil revenues contributed 42 percent of gross domestic product (GDP) in 1980, the proportion plummeted to 27.8 percent in 1989, with the worldwide recession of the 1980s contributing significantly to economic and social decline between 1980 and 1989. For example, per capita gross national product (GNP) declined by 7.3 percent during this period, private consumption by 11.3 percent, and gross domestic investment by almost 20 percent. (See Table 13.1.) This dramatic

TABLE 13.1   Trinidad and Tobago Growth Profile (annual growth rates, in percent)

	Period	*Growth*
GNP	1980–1989	−5.6
GNP per capita	1987–1989	−7.3
GDP	1980–1987	−6.1
Agriculture	1980–1988	−4.5
Industry	1980–1988	−8.6
Manufacturing	1980–1988	−9.5
Services	1980–1988	−3.4
Energy production	1980–1988	−3.4
Energy consumption	1980–1988	0.2
Exports	1980–1988	−6.0
Imports	1980–1988	−15.0
General government consumption	1980–1988	−3.1
Private consumption	1980–1988	−11.3
Gross domestic investment	1980–1988	−19.1

Source: George Kurian, *Encyclopedia of the Third World,* vol. 3, 1990.

decline in oil revenues forced the government to withdraw its subsidies, a decision that disproportionately affected the poor—those who most needed the subsidies. The hardships produced by that policy shift, combined with rampant corruption, crime, drugs, and the perception that the Police Service was part of the problem, created a politically unstable climate by the end of the 1980s. These developments produced worrisome implications for human rights and state security in Trinidad and Tobago.

Human Rights and State Security

Political rights and civil liberties in Trinidad and Tobago, a parliamentary democracy, are constitutionally provided for and generally respected in practice. Over the 1973–1992 period, for example, Trinidad and Tobago averaged scores of 1.5 and 1.8 for political rights and civil liberties, respectively, according Freedom House's annual survey.[14] The general impression (endorsed by the U.S. Department of State) is that respect for human rights in Trinidad and Tobago is such that political killings, disappearances, torture and other cruel, inhuman, or degrading treatment or punishment, arbitrary arrest, detention or exile, denial of fair public trial, presence of political prisoners, arbitrary interference with privacy, family, home, or correspondence are not the norm.[15] The citizens of Trinidad and Tobago have exercised a wide range of freedoms and individual rights and have maintained this democratic tradition—and continue to do so—since independence in 1962.

Although these rights have been violated from time to time, the violations have been neither of the nature nor of the intensity to have been able seriously to call into question the state's legitimacy. During the recent past, however, credible allegations of police brutality, extrajudicial killings, widespread drug-related criminal activity, a growing feeling among citizens that crime is escalating out of control, and a gnawing suspicion that the Police Service is part of the problem, bespeak a growing concern for personal safety and political security in the country. The emergence into political salience of this crime wave and the consequent concern for personal safety seem to correlate with the economic downturn of the 1980s. It therefore appears to be these developments that contribute to political instability and continue to test the resilience of the democratic process in Trinidad and Tobago.

A growing number of incidents contributed to suspicion of corruption within the police high command and led to an erosion of the public's confidence in the state's security forces. In 1987, for example, Police Constable Bernadette James was shot to death during a training exercise in which only blank ammunition was to have been used. The victim's mother alleges that her daughter witnessed a shadowy transaction involving two government ministers and a high-ranking officer the day before the training exercise.[16] In

1991 a man was killed by a police officer, who was then charged with manslaughter rather than murder. In late September of the same year, another man was severely beaten by police and died in prison several days later. The police commissioner's office attributed the death to "natural causes."

During the first nine months of 1992 there were at least seventeen police shootings, nine of which resulted in deaths. One highly publicized case of police brutality occurred in June of that year, when nineteen-year-old Kenton Sylvester claimed he was severely beaten by police in the aftermath of a carjacking incident in which Sylvester himself was taken hostage. His injuries included numerous broken bones, torn muscles, a punctured lung, a ruptured liver, and massive internal bleeding. At the hospital, police stated that his injuries resulted from an auto accident. While preparing to sue the attorney general, Sylvester was indicted on manslaughter charges related to an earlier incident in which he had been previously all but cleared.[17] The death of another young man in July 1992 prompted the minister of national security to demand an immediate investigation into charges that a police officer had shot him dead at close range as the man, kneeling, pleaded for his life.

Increasing numbers of incidents of police brutality and allegations of corruption prompted Prime Minister Patrick Manning (who is now also minister of national security) in 1992 to invite a team from Scotland Yard to investigate allegations of a drug cartel operating within the police force. Although the team found no evidence of a drug cartel, it cited a number of instances of police misbehavior, including allegations of involvement with the drug trade, and concluded that there was evidence of corruption and the abuse of power. The inaction of the Police Service Commission in implementing some of the recommendations made by the Scotland Yard team has eroded the level of public trust in the police. According to the *Trinidad Express* newspaper, "the very institution charged with maintaining law and order in the country is accused of being a law unto itself and nothing is done about it."[18]

Further, alarmed over the spate of criminal activity believed to be "both directly and indirectly linked to the dubious state of the Trinidad and Tobago Police Service,"[19] the Trinidad and Tobago Chamber of Industry and Commerce took the lead in calling for a special prosecutor to bring some probity to the service and restore the public's trust. In that regard, the *Trinidad Express* opined, "We are already faced with a very difficult problem of discipline among a whole generation of young people who seem to take a special delight in breaking the law. But that problem can only be made worse in a situation in which the Police Service itself is suspect."[20] Echoing this sentiment, the *Trinidad Guardian* stated that "crime remains a major threat to the well-being of our country, both in terms of the safety of citizens and our economic progress. . . . We will never be able to deal effectively with the scourge of crime in the country at large, particularly the flourishing drug trade, until we deal ruthlessly with the crime that exists at every level of the Police Service itself."[21]

Action by the Chamber of Commerce and other groups, demanding that this "appalling threat to law and order be halted in its tracks," has resulted in the implementation of some of the recommendations made by Scotland Yard. In an announcement on February 1, 1994, the national security minister at the time, Russell Huggins, informed the nation that "the original power of discipline in respect of officers in all ranks is to be vested in the Commissioner of Police, who will have power to delegate to other senior ranks to deal with minor offenses."[22] This was welcome news for Police Commissioner Jules Bernard, who once described himself as a "toothless bulldog." Among these reforms are a Police Management Board invested with the authority to undertake disciplinary action "in respect to any officer falling under its purview" and a Police Appeals Board to hear appeals on all disciplinary matters.

Other reforms include a planned increase in the number of Senior Superintendents and Sergeants; retaining one Deputy Commissioner of Police and six Assistant Commissioners of Police, who will advise the Commissioner on policy; the creation of seven new Senior Superintendent posts; a US$2.4 million investment in the computerization of the Police Service; a radio communication system; the establishment of an Organized Crime and Narcotics Unit; an Office for Strategic Services; and the restructuring of the Police Service. Within the Ministry of Security itself, a civilian post of Inspector of Police Service is to be established. Among its duties are inspection of the efficiency and management of the Police Service, regular inspections of police divisional offices and stations, and recommendations to maintain levels of efficiency. Further, the Police Management Board and the Police Service Appeals Board are required to report to Parliament by March 31 annually and will be accountable to a parliamentary committee.

These developments have produced two seemingly contradictory outcomes. On the one hand, the individual's right to due process through the legal systems is steadfastly upheld (though probably often delayed). On the other hand, there is the perception and reality that the individual's right to the enjoyment of his property has been seriously threatened by the notable increase in violent crimes against person and property. For example, citizens are alarmed over the significant growth in violent crimes—just under 19,000 officially listed for 1993, a 9 percent increase over 1992—and as many as 9,067 as of June 30, 1994. (See Tables 13.2, 13.3, 13.4, and 13.5.) Related to these developments is a significant decline in levels of citizen confidence in the police. Moreover, the instruments needed to protect individuals and property are poorly maintained. For example, the police and defense forces have inadequate fleets of patrol vehicles, and police stations and army dormitories are in disrepair.[23] A senior police officer recently bemoaned the fact

TABLE 13.2   Crime Reports to Police, by Type, 1982–1991

Year	Reports to the Police Serious Crimes	Minor Crimes	Number of Prosecutions Serious Crimes	Minor Crimes	Number of Convictions Serious Crimes	Minor Crimes
1982	10,697	8,442	1,867	2.452	196	1,062
1983	11,369	11,709	2,215	3,007	446	1,173
1984	11,725	11,689	2,311	3,004	396	1,085
1985	13,979	15,756	2,856	3,553	549	1,437
1986	14,361	17,018	2,909	3,859	721	1,972
1987	15,232	20,539	3,494	5,315	588	2,288
1988	19,385	24,297	4,970	6,340	983	2,680
1989	17,759	22,499	4,782	6,763	885	3,059
1990	16,202	21,918	4,857	6,532	756	2,255
1991	16,157	22,574	4,610	6,600	982	2,846

Reports to the Police 1982–1991 Serious Crimes	Minor Crimes	Percentage of Prosecutions 1982–1991 Serious Crimes	Minor Crimes	Percentage of Convictions 1982–1991 Serious Crimes	Minor Crimes
146,866	176,441	23.5	26.8	18.6	41.8

Source: Trinidad and Tobago Annual Statistical Digest 1991, 1993.

TABLE 13.3   Persons Committed to Prison and Sentenced to Death, by Age and Previous Conviction, 1982–1991

Year	Total	Age 16–21	22–25	26–50	Convictions One	Two+	Death
1982	727	138	243	331	154	172	3
1983	901	164	280	440	158	199	1
1984	1,041	162	343	502	210	254	3
1985	1,650	201	497	859	340	386	4
1986	2,169	244	626	1,240	415	532	7
1987	2,508	131	626	1,662	514	693	7
1988	2,855	149	679	2,027	611	785	41
1989	2,767	145	610	1,932	555	957	27
1990	3,193	332	627	2,160	696	992	10
1991	3,169	281	725	2,097	720	1,088	12

Source: Trinidad and Tobago Annual Statistical Digest 1991, 1993.

TABLE 13.4   Serious Crimes in Trinidad and Tobago, 1990–1992

Division	1990	1991	1992
Northern	3,222	3,477	4,346
Port-of-Spain	3,092	2,893	2,825
Southern	2,689	2,843	2,647
North Eastern	1,784	1,725	1,860
Western	1,729	1,519	1,872
Central	1,387	1,317	1,539
South Western	953	1,076	1,179
Eastern	862	835	907
Tobago	484	472	505
Total	16,202	16,157	17,680

Source: Report of crime research and assessment team to crime, race and related circumstances in Trinidad and Tobago, 1993.

TABLE 13.5   Snapshot of Crime in Trinidad and Tobago, 1992–1994

Categories	1994[a]	1993	1992
Murders	95	108	109
Woundings	275	614	423
Rapes	128	283	274
Break-ins	3,837	8,321	7,941
Robberies	2,475	4,692	3,783
Larceny:			
General	1,436	2,710	2,543
Dwelling house	176	344	388
White collar crimes[b]	188	325	417
Narcotics	457	1,075	967
Total	9,067	18,472	16,845

[a] Up to June 1994.
[b] Fraud, forgery, embezzlement, etc.
Source: Police Public Affairs Unit, published in *Trinidad Guardian,* July 15, 1994.

that this shortage of vehicles hampers the investigation of important cases—and that the only vehicle used by the San Fernando Criminal Investigations Department (CID) has not been in working order since May 1994.

Due to this shortage of reliable vehicles, nontraveling officers are now required to use their own vehicles to respond to reports. In many instances, depending on the nature of the incident, civilians are asked to transport the officers to and from the crime scene.[24] Consequently police officers often seem to lack the motivation to follow up leads regarding criminal activities.

Thus limited intervention by the police, combined with the perception of corruption at all levels, has contributed to an increasing state of lawlessness.

The level of crime rates and the lack of confidence in the police have forced citizens to form neighborhood watch groups. In Chaguanas, for example, the absence of police patrols plus the slow rate of response by the police to calls for help have driven these groups to take aggressive measures to protect their neighborhoods. One strategy has been the imposition of curfews. Any nonresident entering the neighborhood after nine o'clock at night is subject to inquiry and must state his/her destination. Persons failing to comply are often detained until the arrival of the police. In some instances, neighborhood watch groups have resorted to vigilantism. In one 1992 incident in St. Augustine a car thief was caught by one of these groups and beaten to death. Mishandling of the evidence by the police and the absence from the country of the state's key witness at the time of the trial resulted in an acquittal.

This trend toward vigilantism has led to the call for a national neighborhood crime watch group. This organization would superintend and coordinate the activities of the various neighborhood watch groups around the country, conduct workshops to educate citizens in crime-spotting techniques and ways to assist the police in their fight against crime. These groups would take note of strangers in the neighborhood and inform the police about the location of abandoned buildings (potential drug houses and "shooting galleries") and areas that need better street lighting.

In general the failure of the state to deliver the economic and social goods to match the expectations of its citizens is creating conditions for political instability in the country. The security threat, therefore, seems to emerge from an ongoing pattern of economic decline. This in turn has led to vigilantism, increased support for the death penalty for a variety of crimes, and support for corporal punishment. These attitudes have profound implications for human rights observation in Trinidad and Tobago.

Human Rights and the Rule of Law

Calls for hanging and caning as justifiable forms of punishment for criminal activity in Trinidad and Tobago transcend race, religion, income group, educational level, and residential area.[25] This outcry correlates with the high levels of citizen dissatisfaction with the workings of the criminal justice system in the country. As Tables 13.6 and 13.7 indicate, the overwhelming majority of citizens support harsher sentences for criminals.

Despite this, the execution of Glen Ashby on July 14, 1994, who had been convicted of murder five years previously, produced mixed reactions, including allegations of illegality and circumvention of due process by the state. Many felt that Ashby's hanging reflected the government's reaction to

TABLE 13.6   Attitudes Toward the Death Penalty (percentage of citizens supporting)

Issue	Support
Retention of the death penalty	96
The death penalty for drug traffickers	60
The death penalty for rapists	60
The hanging of Glen Ashby	90

Source: Trinidad Guardian, July 28, 1994.

TABLE 13.7   Attitudes Toward Corporal Punishment (percentage of citizens supporting)

Issue	Support
Flogging in school	70
Flogging for rape	96
Flogging for grievous bodily harm	91
Flogging for burglary/robbery	80
Flogging for vehicle theft	72

Source: Trinidad Guardian, July 28, 1994.

public outrage against the volume and nature of violent crimes affecting the country. Critics voiced concern that in its attempt to allay citizens' fears, the government violated some of the legal norms in which the country's democratic system is anchored.

Caribbean Rights, a regional human rights organization, expressed dismay over the resumption of hangings in Trinidad and Tobago and was especially critical of what it considers "an abuse of power by the state." The group contended that the state proceeded with Ashby's execution while the condemned prisoner's appeals before the United Nations Commission on Human Rights as well as before the Privy Council in England were pending. The issue under appeal was the defense's contention that five years on death row was cruel and inhuman and that the death sentence should be commuted to life imprisonment. Under the circumstances, argued Caribbean Rights, the state's action constituted a breach of the constitutional right to due process. Though acknowledging the prevailing mood in the country where the incidence of violent crimes and execution-style murders has generated widespread fear among the population, the organization argued that "it would be better to pursue an educational course to defuse tension and provide the public in Trinidad and Tobago the opportunity to express their views on the burning death penalty issue."[26]

The opposition leader at the time, Basdeo Panday, opined that "until such time as the law is changed, it must be enforced. If, therefore, the present law is [to have] hanging as capital punishment, then the law must be enforced [because] a society degenerates into anarchy whenever the rule of law breaks down. We must therefore maintain the rule of law. We must comply with the laws and we must comply not as a matter of convenience, but as a matter of duty."[27] Former attorney general Anthony Smart commented that he would have been satisfied if Ashby had been "legitimately and properly hanged within the rule of law." In his opinion, however, Ashby was executed on the instructions of the political directorate and in defiance of the legitimate order of the courts. In that case, "if it is right for the State to hang Ashby in defiance of the rule of law, then it must also be right for the State to immediately capture and hang Abu Bakr, who committed treason on the television in the presence of all."[28] Ironically, it is that very legal system that triumphed in the wake of one of the country's worst political crises as it protected the rights of Yasin Abu Bakr and the Jamaat-al-Muslimeen, the perpetrators of the 1990 attempted coup.

Democratic Stability

Due largely to the persistent erosion of economic and social conditions, especially between 1986 and 1990, the government, the citizens of Trinidad and Tobago, and their political traditions were held hostage for five grueling days beginning July 27, 1990. Yasin Abu Bakr and 113 members of his Jamaat-al-Muslimeen group attempted an armed seizure of the reins of government, in contravention of the established political tradition. By the time the guns fell silent and the smoke and dust had cleared, twenty-five people had been reported killed, a number of buildings burned, and the capital, Port-of-Spain, pillaged. The estimated cost of destruction was between US$300 million and US$500 million as well as the loss of about 4,000 jobs.[29] Abu Bakr had incorrectly calculated that due to the level of economic and social decline, the army and the poor would rally behind his movement in support of this action. The masses, however, were apparently prepared to adhere to the political process and use their vote to change the government.

The negotiations to end the state of siege entailed a "concordat" involving the resignation of the prime minister, his replacement by Winston Dookeran, the formation of a caretaker government, elections in ninety days, and an amnesty for the Jamaat-al-Muslimeen.[30] Other particulars included a provision for fifteen Muslimeen militants to carry weapons, legally conceding to the Muslimeen the lands that they occupied at Mucurapo, and the inclusion of the Muslimeen on the committee that would select the caretaker government.[31] The agreement having been reached, the coup makers surrendered to the security forces and were placed in preventive detention. While incarcerated, this group sued, claiming that their detention was illegal and that the criminal charges leveled against them by the government were unconstitutional because they had been granted an amnesty prior to their surrender.

In accord with the constitution, the case was argued before the Privy Council in London in November 1991. The court determined that the amnesty issue must be settled before proceeding with the civil and criminal cases. In a landmark ruling in June 1992, Trinidad and Tobago Justice Clebert Brooks declared valid the amnesty document that had secured the safe release of the hostages and brought an end to the July 1990 coup. A subsequent ruling ordered the immediate release of the 114 detainees and found them entitled to damages for illegal detention plus recovery of court costs. The state subsequently appealed these decisions, which were upheld in 1993. Although most citizens were appalled at this outcome, the instructive element is that the democratic process in Trinidad and Tobago, which is guided by the rule of law, triumphed. Ironically, the constitutional process against which this group lashed out guarantees a legal/judicial system to which these outlaws appealed and prevailed, despite their highly seditious activities. Thus one of the most revealing elements of the democratic process in Trinidad and Tobago is a profound belief in the legal/judicial and constitutional processes.

Conclusion

In sum, though neither this latest coup attempt nor the economic decline seems to have shaken the people's faith in the political system, the government's inability to create an environment conducive to the flourishing of job opportunities, improvement in economic and social well-being, and personal safety continue to create worrisome security concerns for citizens of Trinidad and Tobago. Nevertheless, the inescapable conclusion is that democracy has indeed planted deep roots in Trinidad and Tobago. This is further evidenced by the fact that the Jamaat-al-Muslimeen, under the leadership of Yasin Abu Bakr, has formed a political party and now is attempting to bring about political change within the guidelines of the constitution.

Notes

The author wishes to acknowledge the assistance of June Alleyne in the completion of this work.

1. Among other matters discussed later, citizen perception of corruption increased as a result of the disappearance of rock cocaine that had been seized from drug dealers and held as evidence. The police subsequently claimed that the evidence had been eaten by rats.

2. In a survey conducted during the first two weeks of July 1994, 72 percent of the citizens of Trinidad and Tobago expressed dissatisfaction with the performance of

the police, compared with 26 percent who were satisfied; 33 percent of the respondents were very unsatisfied with the way the police performed their duties. Also, 78 percent expressed their dissatisfaction with the country's criminal justice system, compared with 19 percent who were satisfied. Of those surveyed, 33 percent were very unsatisfied (*The Guardian*, July 28, 1994).

3. See Lennox Grant, "Age of Licks in the Square," *Sunday Express*, July 3, 1994, p. 8.

4. Trinidad and Tobago is listed by the World Bank among the middle-income countries of the world. See *World Development Report* (New York: Oxford University Press, 1991).

5. See Terry Lynn Karl, "Dilemmas of Democratization in Latin America," *Comparative Politics*, vol. 23, no. 1 (October 1990):2.

6. Ibid.

7. See Clifford E. Griffin, "Postinvasion Political Security in the Eastern Caribbean," in *Strategy and Security in the Caribbean*, ed. Ivelaw L. Griffith (New York: Praeger, 1991), pp. 76–97.

8. See Andrew Axline, *The International Crisis in the Caribbean* (Baltimore: Johns Hopkins University Press, 1984), p. 146.

9. See "Dialogue on Economic Reality and Policy Options," in *Latin America, the Caribbean, and the OECD* (Paris: Center for the Organization of Economic Cooperation and Development, 1986); Griffin, "Postinvasion Political Security"; and Ivelaw L. Griffith, *The Quest for Security in the Caribbean: Problems and Promises in Subordinate States* (New York: M. E. Sharpe, 1993), pp. 3–15.

10. See Ivelaw L. Griffith, "Security Perceptions of English-Caribbean Elites," in *Strategy and Security in the Caribbean*, pp. 3–26.

11. See June Alleyne, "Defining a New Role for the State: Trinidad and Tobago from State Capitalism to Privatization" (master's thesis, American University, 1991).

12. Initially, Lewis saw industrialization as the best development strategy for the Caribbean. By the early 1950s he recommended a mixture of import substitution and export promotion. In this policy the state would provide the necessary climate within which the private sector (both local and foreign) would operate. (See W. A. Lewis, "The Industrialization of the British West Indies," *Caribbean Economic Review*, May 1950). When the PNM government came to power in 1956, it pursued a variation of the Lewis model that neglected the development of an export manufacturing sector and concentrated on import substitution.

13. Some critics attribute the abandonment of the five-year plan during the ten-year period of 1973–1982 to the oil profit windfalls that the government enjoyed as a result of the Arab oil crisis of 1972–1973. However, Williams had already stated in 1969 that should long-range planning fail to produce the desired results, it would be abandoned in favor of more direct measures. Consequently, Williams substituted the state for the private sector as the prime mover of the economy after concluding during the 1969–1973 period that the local private sector was far more entrepreneurial than the foreign corporate sector, which was largely unamenable to the country's development needs.

14. See Clifford E. Griffin, "Democracy in the Commonwealth Caribbean," *Journal of Democracy*, vol. 4, no. 2 (1993):84–94. On a scale of 1 to 7, with 1 as the highest, these scores indicate that Trinidad and Tobago is a free country and that its

citizens enjoy levels of human rights protection that are among the highest in the world.

15. Trinidad and Tobago's constitution was drafted in 1972 when there was no parliamentary opposition. It would appear that the drafters wanted to ensure that the rights and freedoms of all citizens were provided for. In that regard, they might have gone a bit overboard. Nevertheless, among those rights and freedoms are: (1) respect for civil liberties, including freedom of speech and press, freedom of peaceful assembly and association, freedom of religion, and freedom of movement, within the country as well as for foreign travel, emigration, and repatriation; (2) respect for political rights, including the right of citizens to change their government; (3) freedom from discrimination based on race, sex, religion, language, or social status; (4) worker rights, including the right of association, the right to bargain collectively, prohibition of forced or compulsory labor, and minimum age for employment of children; and (5) respect for human rights, entailing respect for the integrity of the person, including freedom from political and extrajudicial killing, as well as interdictions on disappearances and torture or other cruel, inhuman, or degrading treatment or punishment.

16. See *Country Reports on Human Rights Practices for 1992*, Report Submitted to the Committee on Foreign Relations, U.S. Senate, and the Committee on Foreign Affairs, House of Representatives by the Department of State (Washington, DC: U.S. Government Printing Office, February 1993).

17. *Country Reports on Human Rights Practices for 1992.*

18. "Stop the Slide to Anarchy," *Trinidad Express*, January 7, 1994, p. 8.

19. Ibid.

20. Ibid.

21. See "After the 'Yardies,'" *Trinidad Guardian*, January 7, 1994, p. 8.

22. See "Full Power to Bernard: Commissioner Gets Authority to Discipline," *Trinidad and Tobago Guardian*, February 1, 1994, pp. 1, 11.

23. The entire police fleet consists of 300 vehicles, 50 percent of which is serviceable while the other half is parked due to a general lack of maintenance and/or lack of basic parts like batteries or tires.

24. See Yvonne Webb, "Cop Car Shortage in South: Investigations Hampered," *Trinidad Guardian*, Saturday, July 9, 1994, p. 3.

25. In a recent survey sample comprising 45 percent Africans, 38 percent East Indians, 2 percent Whites, 13 percent Mixed, and 2 percent "Other," 96 percent favored the retention of the death penalty in Trinidad and Tobago. (*Sunday Guardian*, July 24, 1994.)

26. See "Group Criticizes 'Abuse of Power,'" *Trinidad Guardian*, July 15, 1994, p. 6.

27. See "Nation's Law Must Be Enforced—Panday," *Trinidad Guardian*, July 15, 1994, p. 6.

28. Ibid.

29. See "A Time for Healing," in *Trinidad Under Siege* (Port-of-Spain: Trinidad Express Newspapers Limited, 1990).

30. Although opinions differ, columnist Selwyn Ryan claims to have been informed that Selwyn Richardson, in his capacity as minister of justice and national security, advised the acting president to grant the amnesty. See Selwyn Ryan, "What Was the Deal at the Red House?" in *Trinidad Under Siege*, pp. 69–72.

31. Ibid.

14

Conclusion: Democracy and Human Rights at the Century's End

Ivelaw L. Griffith and
Betty N. Sedoc-Dahlberg

We are now close to the end of an exciting and historic decade as well as century. It is therefore an opportune time for scholars and statesmen, in the Caribbean and elsewhere, to engage in stock-taking—to reflect on the course of prior events, assess conduct, recognize shortcomings, and acknowledge successes. Since the end of one decade and century marks the birth of new periods, it is reasonable to expect a little more than retrospection, though; prospective thinking is also in order. This book has engaged in both, although more of the former than the latter.

A central argument of this volume has been the need for attention to both the civil and political and the economic and social parts of the democracy and human rights equations. The scales of achievement lean more to the civil and political side. For example, most Caribbean countries, as indicated in Table 14.1, have high scores for political and civil liberties, and except for Cuba, they are ranked either as free or partly free. However, the situation on the economic and social side is not as salutary.

Particularly troubling is the large number of countries with high food import dependency, especially considering the region's huge debt burden. Also problematic are the high proportions of urban populations. Growing urbanization places a heavy toll on the already taxed social infrastructure and social services. And given economic conditions in the region and the implications of the debt and structural adjustment programs for any appreciable improvement of the situation in the near and medium terms, the urbanization figures point to serious future challenges. The chapter in this volume by Dorith

TABLE 14.1   Caribbean Political and Economic Quality of Life Indicators

Country	Political Rights[a]	Civil Liberties[a]	Freedom Rating[a]	Human Development Index Ranks[b]	Urban Population Percentage[c]	Food Import Dependency Ratio (%)[c]
Antigua-Barbuda	4	3	Partly Free	55	36	83
Bahamas	1	2	Free	26	85	64
Barbados	1	1	Free	25	46	72
Belize	1	1	Free	29	47	40
Cuba	7	7	Not Free	72	75	NA
Dominica	2	1	Free	69	57	64
Dominican Republic	4	3	Partly Free	96	62	38
Grenada	1	2	Free	67	NA	78
Guyana	2	2	Free	105	35	23
Haiti	5	5	Partly Free	148	30	26
Jamaica	2	3	Free	88	52	64
St. Kitts-Nevis	2	2	Free	37	41	86
St. Lucia	1	2	Free	84	47	76
St. Vincent & the Grenadines	2	1	Free	79	43	113
Suriname	3	3	Partly Free	77	49	40
Trinidad & Tobago	1	2	Free	39	70	81

[a] Data for 1995. The Political Rights and Civil Liberties rankings are on a 1–7 scale, with 1 the most free and 7 the least free.
[b] Data for 1992. The Human Development Index Ranks run from 1 to 173, where 1 is the highest.
[c] Data for 1989/90.
NA = Not Available.
Sources: United Nations Development Program, *Human Development Report 1994* (New York: Oxford University Press, 1994); United Nations Development Program, *Human Development Report 1995* (New York: Oxford University Press, 1995); and *Freedom Review* (January-February 1996).

Grant-Wisdom (Chapter 11) provides clear evidence of the impact of structural adjustment on the socioeconomic sphere in Jamaica, but much of her analysis is applicable to other countries in the region as well. Yet structural adjustment is not the sole impediment to socioeconomic advancement, as several other chapters have shown.

The Caribbean countries have generally adopted one of two competing development models—the market-consumerist model and the basic-needs model—in order to advance their political economies. Some countries, such as Grenada and Nicaragua, have shifted over time from one to the other, depending on regime changes. However, with the exception of Cuba,

Caribbean countries are typified by democratic-pluralist regimes and the market-consumerist model. Because the choice of model is linked with the type of political regime and therefore with democracy and human rights, some attention to development models is useful.

In the market-consumerist model, which is allied with democratic-pluralist regimes, civil and political rights are protected by law and enforced by constitutional guarantees and are supported by norms and international conventions on the misuse of power and on human rights and other violations. In this model the emphasis is on individual rights, and the government's responsibility for the quality of life is executed through implementation of social policies. Governments undertake to provide facilities for increased individual and family consumption, and property is held in high regard by the citizenry. Labor unions and other interest groups serve as protectors and initiators of social and economic rights, and the legitimacy of governments is often evaluated by their responsiveness to issues concerning civil and political as well as economic and social rights.

As several chapters in this volume have shown, there have been evident changes in levels of welfare protection in most Caribbean countries since the 1960s. Dramatic decreases in foreign exchange earnings during the 1980s and 1990s have contributed to severe gaps between tiny overconsuming middle classes and the majority of citizens. One of the consequences has been the implementation of structural adjustment programs and the pursuit of earnings from drug operations.

A major characteristic of the basic-needs model is the allocation of resources to meet the survival needs of the population. The highest priorities are the production and distribution of food, shelter, clothing, health care services, education, and community services. In this system individual consumer goods are marginalized in order to accommodate the pursuit of communal and collective facilities and resources. Unity and order are promoted as central social and political values, and the political elites reject dissent on their decisionmaking. Group interests are absorbed into a vanguard party. In this system, in which the dynamics of marketplace consumerism are absent, civil and political rights rather than social and economic rights are pursued. In the Caribbean context, only Cuba now follows this model, but Cuba's economic and political delinking from its former allies and backers partly explains the dramatic decline in the level of social and economic provisions there since the late 1980s. Thus it seems that the sharp distinction between the two competing models of development in the region has been eroded.

The severe economic deprivation in many countries since the mid-1980s has contributed substantially to further imbalances between civil and political rights and economic and social rights. How should the outcome be evaluated? According to Zehra Arat, the imbalance may cause political instability.[1] In struggling with socioeconomic crises and in implementing structural adjustment programs, will governments survive austerity measures? How to prevent a return to or a movement toward authoritarianism? In the case of Suriname military authoritarianism is seen to have collapsed because of inept, corrupt, excessively repressive abuses of power. No longer valid is the view taken by progressive elements during the 1960s that the only viable alternative to creating a state system capable of articulating the interests of workers and peasants is the populist-statist regime.

The Caribbean has been a bastion of electoral democracy, and the situation has improved over recent years with political adaptations in Guyana, Haiti, and Suriname, as the case studies on those countries in this volume demonstrated. On the human rights front, in comparison with other regions, the Caribbean's profile is remarkable, and in the anglophone Caribbean, all the more so. The point has been made that "Freedom House's *Comparative Survey of Freedom,* an annual assessment of political rights and civil liberties worldwide, shows that democracy in this subregion has proved to be more effective and durable than in any other in the developing world."[2] This fact should not engender complacency among Caribbean human rights activists, governments, and nongovernmental organizations (NGOs), nor should it mask the reality of numerous outlandish practices and situations in the region, including retention of the death penalty and its increasing use since 1993 in the English-speaking subregion and police brutality in the Dominican Republic, Haiti, Jamaica, and other places.

Looking forward, it seems that given the present reality in the Caribbean, efforts to strengthen democracy and human rights need to take account of initiatives at the national and international levels, by state and nonstate actors, both within and outside the realm of politics. Attention needs to be paid to at least four areas of operation: regime politics, institutions, NGOs, and international regimes.

Central to the maintenance of democracy and the respect for human rights, in all their dimensions, is the climate and character of the political environment. An environment in which political elites act as though they are indispensable to the survival of the state or the nation is not conducive to a healthy climate for democracy or human rights, as the experiences of Cuba, the Dominican Republic, Guyana, and Haiti reveal. This attitude not only leads to electoral malpractice to retain power, where there is a pretense of having electoral democracy, but it also has resulted in the co-optation of the military or their direct intervention into politics. Moreover, such a situation leads to gross violations of the civil and political rights of opponents of the regime specifically and of members of the body politic generally. Hence transparency and accountability in political rule are critical, not only for elections but for decisionmaking generally.

Political stability is not a guarantee of democracy and the observance of human rights. But it is clear from this study and from cases outside the

Caribbean that there are strong links between stability and democracy and between stability and human rights. Stability itself is a function of at least four factors: political legitimacy, political authority, political equality, and political participation. Legitimacy requires that the governing elites be representative and that their governance be based on a popular mandate. Authority obtains in a reciprocal relationship between government and people in which the political elites exercise power and the citizens consent to its use. Equality implies the possession of rights by citizens to participate actively in the political process without regard to distinctions such as race, ideology, gender, social geography, and social class. Participation, finally, involves the ability of citizens to influence the system of political rule through institutions such as political parties, unions, the courts, and the media. It is the absence of some or all of these that creates political instability.[3]

The factor of ethnicity cannot be overlooked in addressing issues of political stability, particularly in countries such as Guyana, Suriname, the Dominican Republic, and Trinidad and Tobago. In the contemporary political histories of these countries, the absence of consociational power-sharing between the major ethnic groups and/or political parties has led to social turbulence and political conflict. As others have shown, token consociationalism—political pacting of major ethnic parties with one or more splinter parties or other major ethnic groups—does not create political stability. However, a more or less proportional representation in the legislature reduces chances for polarization in parliament.[4] The cases of Guyana and Suriname show that multiethnic pacting does not guarantee political stability or democracy and human rights. For a government to survive socioeconomic crises and successfully implement austerity measures, a stronger, less vulnerable system is required to deal with citizens protesting against social and economic discrepancies based on both social strata and ethnic division. The absence of power sharing by major ethnic parties may become disastrous for a country. The challenge therefore lies in (re)constructing democracy on the basis of an appropriate political model that is not blocked or interrupted by ethnic politics.

It is obvious from the chapters on Guyana, Haiti, and Suriname that although electoral democracy and the stability to which it is conducive are both necessary, they are not sufficient for the maintenance of democracy and the enjoyment of human rights. One writer makes the important point that "ending civil conflict, holding relatively free elections, and installing elected civilian regimes [are] not, in and of themselves, sufficient to create democratic systems."[5] This brings us to the second of the four factors identified earlier: institutions.

In his chapter on human rights in the Eastern Caribbean (Chapter 8), Francis Alexis highlights an institution whose importance goes beyond the Eastern Caribbean and extends beyond human rights. That institution is the judiciary. The critical role of the judiciary to democracy generally and to human rights specifically needs no elaboration. What does need emphasis, however, is the need to strengthen the judiciary in the Caribbean. In most Caribbean countries the expression "justice delayed is justice denied" comes to life in case backlogs, absence of sufficient judiciary personnel, and inadequate facilities, among other things. The observation on Jamaica by one legal scholar has regionwide relevance: "Excessive or inordinate delays between the time of arrest and the final disposition of the case has frequently . . . extended into several years, and it is not unusual for cases to be finally determined after four or five years."[6] Indeed, the chapter on Guyana revealed that cases there have taken as long as ten years from the time of arrest to that of final disposition.

In assessing the functioning of the judiciary in drug-related cases—a regionwide dilemma with implications for democracy, as detailed in Chapter 5—one report on the Dominican Republic noted: "The judicial system is outdated, ineffective, and corrupt. Dominican law enforcement attempts to convict traffickers and seize assets are often undermined by long delays, poor preparation by prosecutors, and release of suspects."[7] Needless to say, the relevance of this statement is not limited to the counternarcotics area, nor does it reflect the reality only in the Dominican Republic.

Yet the judiciary is not the only institution in need of repair and sustenance. Though courts need to be independent in order to serve as effective arbiters of justice, they cannot operate in isolation; the nature and operation of police forces and prisons and other criminal justice agencies affect not only the work of the courts but also the quality of justice in general. Beyond the judiciary and these criminal justice institutions, the media, educational institutions, political parties, and labor unions are important pillars of functional democracy and human rights observance.

Thus far the factors we have addressed are state-related. It is clear, though, that state entities alone lack the resources to be effective guarantors of democracy and human rights, especially in the economic and social areas. Partnerships therefore become necessary, and NGOs become important to the partnerships. As Robert Maguire explains in Chapter 10, NGOs have been indispensable to the pursuit of democracy and development in Haiti, where the emergence and growth of such organizations have tremendously influenced the environment for democratic development. It must be emphasized, though, that NGOs are not only critical to situations such as that of Haiti, where democracy is being (re)constructed; they are also invaluable in places where democracy is already thriving and where human rights are very much respected, such as Barbados.

Our focus thus far has been on the domestic or national arena. But as we argued in Chapter 1, and as is made clear in the chapters by Anselm Francis, David Padilla and Elizabeth Houppert, W. Marvin Will, Ivelaw Griffith,

Robert Maguire, and Betty Sedoc-Dahlberg (Chapters 2, 3, 4, 9, 10, and 12), the pursuit, establishment, and sustenance of democracy and human rights in the Caribbean are not a function solely of domestic level action. International support for democracy is now generally seen as both necessary and acceptable. Thus there is every expectation that the United Nations, the Organization of American States, the Carter Center, the Commonwealth Secretariat, the European Union, the United States, Britain, the Netherlands, France, Venezuela, Spain, and other actors outside the Caribbean will continue to take varying degrees of interest in the modus operandi of political rule in the region and the political and economic quality of life there. The interest taken by these agencies and countries is not always guided by noble democratic ideals, and hence their conduct must also be monitored, even though they may be well intentioned: Good intentions are often not enough.

Tangible external support is necessary for the consolidation, and in some cases the construction, of democracy, especially of its social and economic dimensions. But several donor countries are experiencing donor fatigue and/or are reevaluating their foreign aid policies. The result is that many of them are reducing foreign aid outlays, a trend that is expected to continue for some time in most cases. This in itself serves to compromise the pursuit of democracy in the region.

International level action should in no way, however, be viewed as a substitute for domestic level actions and initiatives. In this respect an observation by Richard Millett is worthy of full replication:

Prime responsibility for the success of any democratic system rests with national elected authorities. They must deal with problems of corruption, partisan division, inefficiency, lack of accountability, impunity, and rampant insecurity. International assistance for strengthening democratic institutions needs to be enhanced, but political will can never be imported. The role of external actors is, and will remain, a necessary but by no means sufficient component of the continued development of more democratic structures in the Americas.[8]

Although most of the international level actions pertaining to democracy reflect implicit, if not explicit, concern about human rights, reference should also be made to the need for Caribbean states to be active participants in the regional and international regimes that are explicitly concerned with human rights questions. Most Caribbean countries are party to some of the hemispheric and international agreements that create human rights regimes considered essential by the international community (see Table 14.2). Yet there are some countries in the region that have not ratified or acceded to a single human rights instrument. It is perhaps understandable that Cuba, given the nature and outlook of its regime, would be party to only one such instrument.

TABLE 14.2   International Human Rights Covenants: A Caribbean Profile

Country	ICCPR	ICESCR	ACHR	CTCIDTP	CSR
Antigua-Barbuda			X	X	
Bahamas					X
Barbados	X	X	X		
Belize				X	X
Cuba				X	
Dominica	X	X	X		X
Dominican Republic	X	X	X	S	X
Grenada	X	X	X		
Guyana	X	X		X	
Haiti	X		X		
Jamaica	X	X	X		X
St. Kitts-Nevis					
St. Lucia					
St. Vincent and Grenadines	X	X			X
Suriname	X	X	X		X
Trinidad and Tobago	X	X	X		

S = signed but not yet ratified
X = party either through ratification, accession, or succession
ICCPR = International Covenant on Civil and Political Rights (1966)
ICESCR = International Covenant on Economic, Social, and Cultural Rights (1966)
CTCIDTP = Convention Against Torture and Other Cruel, Inhuman, or Degrading Treatment or Punishment (1975)
ACHR = American Convention on Human Rights (1969)
CSR = Convention Relating to the Status of Refugees (1951)
Source: Amnesty International Report 1996 (New York: Amnesty International, 1996).

However, strangely enough, St. Kitts-Nevis and St. Lucia are party to none; happily, though, these countries have no major human rights deficiencies.

It is also noteworthy that Antigua-Barbuda, the Bahamas, and Belize are party to neither the American Convention on Human Rights nor the two most important UN human rights covenants: the International Covenant on Civil and Political Rights and the International Covenant on Economic, Social, and Cultural Rights. Countries that are part of regimes do not necessarily have better human rights records, though, for Haiti is party to the International Covenant on Civil and Political Rights and the American Convention on Human Rights. However, regime participation is not only testimony to the country's commitment to uphold the rules, norms, and decisions of the regime, but it also permits individuals and groups to seek redress in institutions created by regimes, as the chapters by Alexis and by Padilla and Houppert demonstrate. Moreover, regime participation can be beneficial in helping countries to acquire and strengthen their human rights capabilities, through provision of training, technical assistance, and equipment.

In sum, this volume shows that although the Caribbean has several critical democracy and human rights challenges, a strong democracy profile and a fairly decent human rights profile characterize the region. But as one scholar correctly observed, the advent of democracy—or its maintenance, for that matter—does not automatically bring freedom and equality, growth and equity, security and opportunity, and autonomy and accountability.[9] Democracy and human rights are about much more than mere electoral formalism and power contestation; there are crucial economic and social elements that cannot be overlooked—and the economic crisis in the region constrains efforts in the socioeconomic areas. Democracy in the Caribbean is also affected by emigration, especially of people with skills and capital, and by the internationalization of crime, notably drug-related crime. It is largely because of this combination of factors that in many places in the region, when it comes to breathing full life into democracy and human rights the spirit might be willing but the body is weak.

Notes

1. Zehra R. Arat, *Democracy and Human Rights in Developing Countries* (Boulder: Lynne Rienner, 1991), p. 4.

2. Douglas W. Payne, "Caribbean Democracy," *Freedom Review*, May-June 1993, p. 9.

3. For more discussion on this subject, see Samuel Huntington, *Political Order in Changing Societies* (New Haven: Yale University Press, 1968); and Charles Andrain, *Political Change in the Third World* (Boston: Unwin Hyman, 1988).

4. See Edward M. Dew, *The Trouble in Suriname, 1975–1993* (Westport, CT: Praeger, 1994), p. 208; and Arend Lijphart, *Democracy in Plural Societies: A Comparative Exploration* (New Haven: Yale University Press, 1977), p. 209.

5. Richard L. Millett, "Beyond Sovereignty: International Efforts to Support Latin American Democracy," *Journal of Interamerican Studies and World Affairs*, vol. 36, no. 3 (Fall 1994):9.

6. Delroy Chuck, "The Right to a Fair Trial Under Caribbean Constitutional Law," in *International Human Rights Law in the Commonwealth Caribbean*, ed. Angela D. Byre and Beverly Y. Byfield (Dordrecht, Neth.: Martinus Nijhoff, 1991), p. 68.

7. U.S. Department of State, *International Narcotics Control Strategy Report*, March 1995, p. 170.

8. Millett, "Beyond Sovereignty," p. 20.

9. Philippe C. Schmitter, "Dangers and Dilemmas of Democracy," *Journal of Democracy*, vol. 5, no. 2 (1994):61–62.

About the Book

The Caribbean, like regions elsewhere, is caught in what has been called democracy's global "Third Wave." In this volume, contributors examine the nature of democratization in the region together with its affiliate, human rights. The aim is to extend the analysis and debates beyond political democracy and civil and political rights to consider also economic democracy and economic and social rights. Early chapters address issues and dilemmas common to the democracy and human rights landscape throughout the region. In particular, economic crisis, drug trafficking, and political instability continue to threaten the region's very healthy democracy human rights profiles. Next, contributors consider how the form of Caribbean democracy and the status of human rights have been influenced by foreign actors and external developments. Particular attention is paid to the role of the Organization of American States, the United Nations, nongovernmental organizations, and international law. Because the democracy and human rights challenges and dynamics vary across countries, the work also offers extensive single-country assessments.

About the Editors and Contributors

Francis Alexis, a former attorney general and minister of legal affairs of Grenada, received his doctorate as a Commonwealth Scholar from the University of Cambridge in England. Previously a law professor at the University of the West Indies, he was also deputy dean of the law school. Dr. Alexis is author of *Changing Caribbean Constitutions* and of numerous monographs and journal articles on human rights and on constitutional and administrative law.

Damian J. Fernandez is chairman of the department of international relations at Florida International University and a former director of the graduate program in international studies there. He is a widely published Cuba specialist whose works include *Cuban Studies Since the Revolution*. Dr. Fernandez is a contributor to *Transition in Cuba* and has also published in *Cuban Studies*, *Latin American Research Review*, and *Howard International Review*. He also is contributing editor (international relations) of *Handbook of Latin American Studies*.

Anselm A. Francis is a former Caribbean diplomat who now teaches international law and conflict resolution at the Institute of International Relations, University of the West Indies, where he was acting director during the 1996/97 academic year. He has contributed to several volumes, including *Peace, Development, and Security in the Caribbean*, and has published in *Caribbean Affairs*, *Journal of Interamerican Studies and World Affairs*, *International Journal of Estuaries and Coastal Law*, and elsewhere.

Dorith Grant-Wisdom, of the University of Maryland at College Park, specializes in international political economy. She has published in *Twenty-First Century Policy Review*, is a contributor to *Globalization, Communication, and Caribbean Identity*, and is author of *The Law of the Sea and Developing Countries* (forthcoming). Once a consultant to Caribbean University Services Overseas, Dr. Grant-Wisdom is a member of the Transafrica Scholars Council.

Clifford E. Griffin, of North Carolina State University, is a contributor to *Strategy and Security in the Caribbean* and has published in *Caribbean Affairs*, *Third World Quarterly*, *North-South*, *Journal of Commonwealth and Comparative Politics*, *Journal of Democracy*, and elsewhere. A 1991–1992 National Fellow at the Hoover Institution on War, Revolution, and Peace at Stanford University, he is currently writing *Democracy in the Caribbean*.

Ivelaw L. Griffith, of Florida International University, has written *The Quest for Security in the Caribbean*, *Caribbean Security on the Eve of the Twenty-First Century*, and *Drugs and Security in the Caribbean: Sovereignty Under Siege*. He edited *Strategy and Security in the Caribbean* and has published in *Caribbean Affairs*, *Caribbean Studies*, *Conflict Quarterly*, *Latin American Research Review*, *International Journal*, *Journal of Interamerican Studies and World Affairs*, *Journal of Commonwealth and Comparative Politics*, *Third World Quarterly*, and elsewhere. Griffith, who is book review editor of *Hemisphere*, is also currently editing *The Political Economy of Drugs in the Caribbean*.

259

Elizabeth A. Houppert is an attorney and a human rights specialist with the Inter-American Commission on Human Rights at the Organization of American States, where she specializes in petitions and claims analysis. A graduate of the University of Maryland at College Park and Washington College of Law at American University, she is currently a candidate for the LL.M. in international and comparative law at Georgetown University. She has published in *Emory International Law Review*, *The Americas*, and elsewhere.

Robert E. Maguire, of the Inter-American Foundation, is a Haiti expert who has traveled there some seventy times and speaks Creole. Dr. Maguire has written extensively on Haitian politics, development, and grassroots movements, and he chairs the Advanced Area Studies Seminar on Haiti at the National Foreign Affairs Training Center of the U.S. Department of State. During 1994–1995, he was a visiting scholar at the Institute for Global Studies in Culture, Power, and History at Johns Hopkins University and Coordinator of the Johns Hopkins–Georgetown Universities Haiti Study Project.

Trevor Munroe, of the University of the West Indies, is Reader in government and politics at the Mona campus in Jamaica. His doctorate in political science is from Oxford University, which he attended as a Jamaica Rhodes Scholar. Dr. Munroe is a long-standing activist-scholar and leader in Jamaica's labor movement. Among his recent books are *Jamaican Politics: A Marxist Perspective in Transition*, and *The Cold War and the Jamaican Left*. In addition to being an expert on Caribbean politics, he is a specialist on political change in developing countries.

David J. Padilla is assistant executive secretary of the Inter-American Commission on Human Rights at the Organization of American States. A former deputy general counsel of the OAS, he holds an M.A. degree from the University of Pennsylvania, an LL.M. from George Washington University, and an M.P.A. from Harvard University. He coedited *Municipal Development in Latin America* and has published in several journals, including *Lawyer in the Americas* and *Human Rights Quarterly*.

Betty N. Sedoc-Dahlberg is affiliated with the Center for Latin American Studies at the University of Florida. She is editor of *The Dutch Caribbean: Prospects for Democracy* and author of *Democracy in Suriname 1987–1993* (forthcoming). Dr. Sedoc-Dahlberg has contributed to several volumes dealing with authoritarian regimes, including *Militarization in the Non-Hispanic Caribbean*, and she has published in a variety of journals.

W. Marvin Will, of the University of Tulsa, is coeditor of *The Restless Caribbean*, collaborative author of *The Caribbean in the Pacific Century*, and contributor to several volumes, including *Biographical Dictionary of Latin American and Caribbean Leaders*. He has published in *Latin American Research Review*, *Journal of Commonwealth and Comparative Politics*, *Studies in Comparative International Development*, and other journals. Dr. Will is a founder-member of the Caribbean Studies Association and a past president of the Midwest Association of Latin American Studies. A 1991–1992 Fulbright Fellow, he has monitored elections in the Caribbean, Central America, and Southeast Asia. Dr. Will is currently writing *From Rebellion to Independence and Democracy in the Caribbean*.

Larman C. Wilson, of the School of International Service at American University, is coauthor of *Latin American Foreign Policies* and *The United States and the Trujillo*

Regime. Dr. Wilson also has published widely in various journals and has contributed to several volumes, including *Latin America: Its Problems and Its Promise, The Haitian Challenge: U.S. Foreign Policy Considerations, U.S. Latin American Policymaking*, and *UN Peacekeeping in the 1990s*. A longtime specialist on the Dominican Republic, he is currently writing a book on the travails of democracy there.

Index

For Product Safety Concerns and Information please contact our EU
representative GPSR@taylorandfrancis.com
Taylor & Francis Verlag GmbH, Kaufingerstraße 24, 80331 München, Germany

www.ingramcontent.com/pod-product-compliance
Lightning Source LLC
Chambersburg PA
CBHW070609270326
41926CB00013B/2480

9 780813 321356